Rhetoric & Society
Edited by Wayne A. Rebhorn

The Performance of Conviction

Plainness and Rhetoric in the Early English Renaissance

Kenneth J. E. Graham

CORNELL UNIVERSITY PRESS

ITHACA AND LONDON

First published 1994 by Cornell University Press.

Printed in the United States of America

⊗The paper in this book meets the minimum requirements of the American
National Standard for Information Sciences—Permanence of Paper for Printed
Library Materials, ANSI Z39.48-1984.

Library of Congress Cataloging-in-Publication Data
Graham, Kenneth J. E. (Kenneth John Emerson), 1960–
    The performance of conviction : plainness and rhetoric in the early English
Renaissance / Kenneth J. E. Graham.
        p.   cm.—(Rhetoric & society)
    Based on the author's thesis (Ph.D., University of California at Berkeley).
    Includes bibliographical references and index.
    ISBN 0-8014-2871-8 (alk. paper)
    1. English literature—Early modern, 1500–1700—History and
criticism.   2. Literature and society—England—History—16th
century.   3. Rhetoric—Social aspects—England—History.   4. Renaissance—
England.   5. Rhetoric—1500–1800.   I. Title.   II. Series.
PR418.S64G73   1994
820.9'003—dc20   93-33720

To Beth

who brings brightness to my plainness

Contents

Foreword

Stated simply, the purpose of this series is to study rhetoric in all the varied forms it has taken in human civilizations by situating it in the social and political contexts to which it is inextricably bound. Rhetoric and Society rests on the assumption that rhetoric is both an important intellectual discipline and a necessary cultural practice and that it is profoundly implicated in a large array of other disciplines and practices, from politics to literature to religion. Interdisciplinary by definition and unrestricted in range either historically or geographically, the series will investigate a wide variety of questions—among them, how rhetoric constitutes a response to historical developments in a given society, how it crystallizes cultural tensions and conflicts and defines key concepts, and how it affects and shapes the social order in its turn. Rhetoric and Society will include books that approach rhetoric as a form of signification, as a discipline that makes meaning out of other cultural practices, and as a central and defining intellectual and social activity deeply rooted in its milieu. In essence, all the books in the series will seek to demonstrate just how important rhetoric really is to human beings in society.

Ranging widely through rhetoric and literature, educational writing and theological debate, Kenneth Graham's *The Performance of Conviction: Plainness and Rhetoric in the Early En-*

glish Renaissance revises significantly our notion of what the
plain style meant for the English Renaissance. It does so by an-
alyzing the concept of plainness as a style of knowing and being
as well as a style of writing. Antirhetorical insofar as it refused
the tentativeness and need for consensus of rhetoric, plainness
constituted a response to the institutional and epistemological
crisis of the Renaissance. Countering the skepticism brought
about by humanism and the Reformation, it provided a means to
express a deep, personal conviction of truth while making personal identity immune to doubt. However, although plainness was
antirhetorical, opposed to the dialogue and debate central to humanist rhetoric, it was also deeply rhetorical as well, for the conviction it bespoke had to be acted out in the public realm, had to
persuade others of its validity. The performance of conviction
could thus undermine as well as establish the authority of conviction, a paradox Graham goes on to explore in a fresh series of
readings of important, primarily literary texts from Wyatt to
Shakespeare. As he shows how rhetorical practices are related to
philosophical, theological, and political positions, Graham reveals in these chapters how the interplay of plain conviction with
rhetorical performance subtly shapes the authority of a variety of
claims to truth. A kind of end point is reached in the works of the
satirists and writers of revenge tragedies, as well as in *Coriolanus*
and *Timon of Athens*, works that reveal how the angry truth they
offer as their version of antirhetorical plainness can find no ade-
quate communal response and ultimately turns into an amoral
performance merely designed to effect the performer's own self-
realization. The book concludes with a valuable discussion of
King Lear, showing how the play resists its own skepticism about
the notion of a plainness identified with anger and stoic withdrawal by endorsing instead a new concept of plainness as the
performance of love.

WAYNE A. REBHORN

Preface

Although my subject has usually been understood as a stylistic phenomenon, this is not a work on style. I begin with this statement not only because the temptation to identify plainness with plain style is so strong in itself, but also because my occasional discussions of style (including the plain style) will only increase that temptation. But while this book considers stylistic questions and is informed partly by research on the plain style, it remains a rhetorical, not a stylistic, study. The difference? A rhetorical study, as Joel Altman has written, "is by definition occasional, formal, psychological, and cognizant of agency."[1] Hence it includes style—the third part of rhetoric in classical treatments—along its formal axis, but also comprises questions about audience, context, motive, feeling, and person. A rhetorical study is thus arguably an attempt to address human experience in all its complex relations and is, if logocentric in bias, necessarily interdisciplinary in character.

My investigation of plainness will concentrate particularly on the political, epistemological, psychological, and theological dimensions of the subject, but I will also have occasion to consider its legal, economic, and even its sexual and physical implications.

[1] Joel B. Altman, " 'Vile Participation': The Amplification of Violence in the Theater of *Henry V*," *Shakespeare Quarterly* 42 (1991), 3–4.

I will attempt to resolve the apparent contradiction that sees plainspeakers rant (for example); to explain why the claim to speak plainly appears so often and in such different circumstances; and to show how plainness and rhetoric function as interdependent cultural alternatives. My goal is to understand plainness as a way of seeing and responding to—of being in—the world of early Renaissance England.

It is a pleasure to acknowledge the many forms of assistance I have received while writing this book. My greatest intellectual debt is to Joel Altman. Besides providing a model of scholarship in his ground-breaking studies of rhetorical anthropology, Altman exemplifies the rigorous and fair-minded criticism of the rhetorical tradition at its best. His wisdom and his eloquence, his teaching and his friendship have been equally valuable. Second in importance has been Thomas Sloane, who also witnessed the early stages of my work on plainness, and whose rhetorical brilliance I have sought to imitate. I owe an enormous debt to Christopher Drummond, who introduced me to the plain style years ago and remains a valued colleague; his unique teaching embodies the interrogative spirit. Richard Strier greatly assisted the research that led to the addition of much of the Reformation material. John Anson read an early version and responded helpfully. Janel Mueller gave several painstaking and challenging readings to the Greville chapter, forcing me to undertake revisions that have improved it immeasurably. Roy Battenhouse, John Baxter, Thom Gunn, Elizabeth Hanson, Jean MacIntyre, Conrad Olson, and Ronald A. Rebholz gave helpful responses to individual sections. John R. Knott, Jr., not only read several chapters but also allowed me to see portions of his unpublished work. Wayne Rebhorn and two anonymous reviewers read the manuscript for Cornell University Press and offered careful criticism.

I have presented portions of the book at various stages to a variety of audiences. A version of the Shakespeare material was distributed as "Literary Thin Men: Lear, Timon, Coriolanus" to a 1991 Shakespeare Association of America seminar, "Reconstructing Shakespearean Character." I am particularly grateful to the seminar leaders, Christy Desmet and Richard Finkelstein, and to

Arthur Kinney, the respondent to my paper on that occasion. The first version of Chapter 2 was written for presentation to a National Endowment for the Humanities seminar, "Renaissance and Reformation in Tudor-Stuart England," directed by Richard Strier in 1991. I thank the other participants in those memorable seven weeks, particularly Patrick Delana, Walter Lim, and Samuel Smith. The *Admonition* portion of this chapter was presented to the Canadian Society for Renaissance Studies at its 1992 meeting, where it was followed by a lively discussion. I have also presented parts of the book to audiences at McMaster University, Queen's University, the University of Alberta, the University of Wyoming, Carleton College, the University of Saskatchewan, and the University of Western Ontario. I am grateful to all these audiences for their attentiveness.

Chapter 1 first appeared in a Renaissance number of *Style* guest-edited by Marion Trousdale ("The Performance of Conviction: Wyatt's Antirhetorical Plainness," *Style* 23 [Fall 1989], 374–94), and Chapter 6 was published as "'Without the form of justice': Plainness and the Performance of Love in *King Lear*," *Shakespeare Quarterly* 42 (Winter 1991), 438–61; both appear here by permission. I also thank the publishers of the following works for permission to quote from them: *The Poems of John Marston*, ed. Arnold Davenport (Liverpool: Liverpool University Press, 1961); Fulke Greville, *The Remains*, ed. G. A. Wilkes (Oxford: Oxford University Press, 1965), reprinted by permission of Oxford University Press; Sir Thomas Wyatt, *The Complete Poems*, ed. R. A. Rebholz (Harmondsworth, Eng.: Penguin, 1978; rpt. New Haven: Yale University Press, 1981), Introduction and notes copyright © 1978 by R. A. Rebholz, reproduced by permission of Penguin Books Ltd.

Mary Marshall Durrell cheerfully granted every request for keys to the computer room. Flora Pavich handled my laser printing without fear of the viruses contracted during my often promiscuous computering. Bernhard Kendler and the staff at Cornell University Press made the entire publishing experience a pleasurable one.

I am indebted to the University of California at Berkeley for a dissertation fellowship in 1988–89; to the National Endowment for the Humanities for a fellowship to the "Renaissance and Reformation" seminar; and to the University of Alberta for a J. Gordin Kaplan Postdoctoral Fellowship in 1991–93, which allowed me to finish the book.

I extend a special thank-you to the many other people who have encouraged me during the course of a long job search. These include Connie Dickey, Don McQuade, Mark Booth, Duncan Harris, Janice Harris, Jeanne Holland, Clifford Marks, Bruce Richardson, Chris Bullock, Jonathan Hart, Tiree Macgregor, Greg Randall, Morton Ross, Bruce Stovel, and Garry Watson. Most important, however, has been the support of my family, especially my parents, William and Sydna Graham, whose conviction has never wavered, and my wife, Elizabeth Crawford Graham, whose love is both mysterious and true.

When using original-spelling texts, I have modernized the use of *i*'s and *j*'s and of *u*'s and *v*'s. I have also changed extended passages of italic type to roman in English-language source material. All references to Shakespeare's plays are to *William Shakespeare: The Complete Works*, general editor Alfred Harbage (New York: Penguin, 1969).

K. J. E. GRAHAM

Halifax, Nova Scotia

The Performance
of Conviction

Introduction.
Captive to Truth:
Rethinking Renaissance
Plainness

I'm plain Thomas; by th' rood
I'll speak the truth.
—*Thomas of Woodstock* 1.3.384–85

Fear not my truth; the moral of my wit
Is "plain and true"; there's all the reach of it.
—*Troilus and Cressida* 4.4.106–7

The very essence of Truth is plainnesse, and brightnes.
—John Milton, *Of Reformation* (1641)

What woord can be more plaine then this word plaine?
—George Pettie (1581)

If twentieth-century interpreters have disagreed about the
meaning of Renaissance plainness, it is perhaps because the period itself failed to reach a consensus. The meaning of "this word
plaine" is as plain as the meaning of "true," which is in fact its
closest synonym in the sixteenth and seventeenth centuries. To
investigate plainness is to plunge headfirst into debates—or,
more often, battles—about truth, and thus to encounter the con-
glomeration of early modern "crises" so well known to historians
of the period. It is also to encounter a distressing proliferation of
plain styles: native plain style, classical plain style, Puritan plain
style, Anglican plain style, Bacon's plain style, Herbert's plain

style, Restoration plain style—the list compiled by modern critics seems to stretch on almost endlessly, an ironic illustration of a
copiousness at odds with the brevity of most plain styles.[1] Even
such Shakespearean wordsmiths as Hotspur and Othello appear
to believe that their language is plain.

Faced with a situation in which every claim to truth is likely to
call itself plain at some point and in which, moreover, various
claims overlap and crisscross, critics must carefully define the
part of the web they choose to study. My focus falls on what R. F.
Jones has called "the moral sense of simplicity."[2] In an article of
this name, Jones thoroughly documents the pervasiveness in
sixteenth-century nonfiction texts of the claim to speak a truth
that, as Bishop John Jewel writes in his *Oratio Contra Rhetoricam*, "is clear and simple."[3] But despite John M. Wallace's assertion that this "simplicity of spirit and word . . . was in the long

[1] See, for example, Morris Croll, *"Attic" and Baroque Prose Style* (Princeton:
Princeton University Press, 1969); Perry Miller's chapter on Puritan preaching,
"The Plain Style," in *The New England Mind: The Seventeenth Century* (New
York: Macmillan, 1939); Arnold Stein, *George Herbert's Lyrics* (Baltimore: Johns
Hopkins University Press, 1968); James Stephens, *Francis Bacon and the Style of
Science* (Chicago: University of Chicago Press, 1975); John R. Knott, Jr., *The
Sword of the Spirit: Puritan Responses to the Bible* (Chicago: University of Chicago Press, 1980); and Frank Manley, "Toward a Definition of Plain Style in the
Poetry of George Herbert," in *Poetic Traditions of the English Renaissance*, ed.
Maynard Mack and George deForest Lord (New Haven: Yale University Press,
1982), pp. 203–17.
Croll's pioneering studies of a philosophical influence on seventeenth-century
prose that leads from anti-Ciceronianism toward the rationalism of modern science have been the most influential work on plain style. Later scholarship in this
general tradition includes George Williamson, *The Senecan Amble: A Study in
Prose Form from Bacon to Collier* (Chicago: University of Chicago Press, 1951);
Jonas A. Barish, *Ben Jonson and the Language of Prose Comedy* (Cambridge:
Cambridge University Press, 1960); Wesley Trimpi, *Ben Jonson's Poems: A Study
of the Plain Style* (Stanford: Stanford University Press, 1962); Robert M. Adolph,
The Rise of Modern Prose Style (Cambridge: Harvard University Press, 1968); and
Debora K. Shuger, *Sacred Rhetoric: The Christian Grand Style in the English
Renaissance* (Princeton: Princeton University Press, 1988).
[2] R. F. Jones, "The Moral Sense of Simplicity," in *Studies in Honor of Frederick
W. Shipley*, Washington University Studies n.s. 14 (St. Louis: Lancaster Press,
1942), pp. 265–87. See also Jones's *The Triumph of the English Language* (Stanford:
Stanford University Press, 1953), esp. chap. 1, "The Uneloquent Language."
[3] "Jewel's Oration against Rhetoric: A Translation," trans. Hoyt H. Hudson,
Quarterly Journal of Speech 14 (1928), 381.

run the greatest influence for plainness in England," and despite the consistent association of the plain truth with godliness throughout the period, simple plainness has received relatively little attention from students of literature and history.[4] It achieved its greatest prominence in the study of the native style of English poetry, a study led by C. S. Lewis and Yvor Winters.[5] Lewis and Winters disagreed about the value of the native (or "drab" or "moral") style, and for a while a fruitful conversation ensued; but because later critics tended either to denigrate or to apologize for native plainness, the conversation eventually came to a sterile halt. The discussion was also limited by its tendency to consider style, in new-critical fashion, in splendid isolation from other considerations. The death knell of debates about stylistic plainness was sounded by Stanley Fish in *Self-Consuming Artifacts*. Noting skeptically that "one man's plain is another man's distortion," Fish subordinated the "plain style question" in the criticism of seventeenth-century prose to the question of competing epistemologies, one of which held that truth could be known ("self-satisfying"), and another that it could not ("self-consuming"). The "true plain style," Fish proclaimed trium-

---

[4] See Wallace's foreword to Croll's "'Attic Prose' in the Seventeenth Century," in *"Attic" and Baroque Prose Style*, p. 49.

[5] Lewis's 1944 Clark lectures on the "drab" and "golden" styles of poetry are published in expanded form in *English Literature in the Sixteenth Century Excluding Drama* (Oxford: Clarendon Press, 1954). Winters's essay "The Sixteenth-Century Lyric in England," published originally in *Poetry* in 1939, is reprinted in *Elizabethan Poetry, Modern Essays in Criticism*, ed. Paul Alpers (Oxford: Oxford University Press, 1967) and appears in an enlarged form in Winters's *Forms of Discovery* (Chicago: Swallow, 1967). For important extensions of Winters's work, see Douglas L. Peterson, *The English Lyric from Wyatt to Donne: A History of the Plain and Eloquent Styles* (Princeton: Princeton University Press, 1967) and John Baxter, *Shakespeare's Poetic Styles: Verse into Drama* (London: Routledge & Kegan Paul, 1980).

The native plain style differs sharply in its ethical goals and epistemological commitments from the classically oriented plain style of the Croll tradition. The native plain style is committed to the proposition that truth is simple and known. The native style consequently strives to make us *feel* the "truth of the truism," as Winters puts it. On the other hand, the classical plain style's only commitments are, paradoxically, to avoid or at least delay commitment and to seek the truth in the context of a community of discourse. Its ideal of a flexible, conversational language that includes everything is related to the humanist epistemological ideal of *controversia*, or *argumentum in utramque partem* (see below, pp. 15–21).

phantly, "would be the one that makes plain the impossibility and presumption of making plain."[6]

Although Fish's formulation appealed to a generation of critics armed with similarly skeptical commitments, there were several problems with it. It expressed a clear bias against the belief it labeled "self-satisfying," and hence against the sense of simplicity. It also wrongly implied that epistemological sophistication and conviction are incompatible, a possibility disproved by More and Erasmus, not to mention Luther and Calvin, themselves no intellectual slouches. But a more fundamental problem with *Self-Consuming Artifacts* was that it did not sufficiently escape the exclusive new-critical emphasis on style: the study of affective stylistics as a way of determining epistemology failed to give a satisfactory account of the historical processes by which and within which the text was produced, and of which it was part. Plainness disappeared as a literary category while failing to reemerge as a historical interest and was lost in the skeptical never-never land where it still by and large remains.

I hope to help rescue this simple plainness from the dustbin of literary history by showing its vital connection to problems of conviction and performance in the early English Renaissance. I am interested in why people claim to speak the truth—what understanding of themselves and their world their claim reflects—and in what the consequences of their claim are—what actions does it require of them and what response does it call for from the world? These are questions that recent studies have increasingly returned to; but while such work approaches plainness from several directions, particularly through the lens of the Reformation, its authors have yet to acknowledge this sufficiently or to integrate the literary and historical dimensions of the subject.[7] Con-

---

[6] Stanley E. Fish, *Self-Consuming Artifacts: The Experience of Seventeenth-Century Literature* (Berkeley: University of California Press, 1972), "Epilogue: The Plain Style Question," p. 382.

[7] The most relevant recent studies of the role of conviction in Reformation writings of which I am aware are Janel M. Mueller, *The Native Tongue and the Word: Developments in English Prose Style 1380–1580* (Chicago: University of Chicago Press, 1984); Ritchie D. Kendall, *The Drama of Dissent: The Radical Poetics of Nonconformity, 1380–1590* (Chapel Hill: University of North Carolina Press, 1986); and John R. Knott, Jr., *Discourses of Martyrdom in English Litera-*

flicts about skepticism and belief, about authority and resistance to authority, about theatricality and self-presentation all bear on the question of plainness, which serves as a ground where these battles can be fought, where convictions can be performed. To see why, we need to summarize what plainness meant to those who lived with it.

The certain conviction that one knows the truth appears in the Renaissance most frequently in Reformation and Neostoic contexts. As Luther explains it, plain truth seizes people from without and holds them prisoner:

> the mind is so laid hold of by the truth itself, that, by virtue of that truth, it is able to reach certainty in any judgment. Nevertheless, the mind is unable to judge the truth as such, although it is compelled to say, when entirely confident, That is true. For example, the mind declares with infallible assurance that three and seven make ten, and yet it cannot adduce any reason why that is true, although it cannot deny its truth. The fact is that, rather than being itself the judge, the mind has been taken captive, and has accepted a verdict pronounced by the Truth herself sitting on the tribunal.[8]

By far the most important application of this sense of certain truth is in determining the "plain sense of Scripture," and Luther's anti-Erasmian tract *The Bondage of the Will* is a classic

---

ture, 1563–1694 (Cambridge: Cambridge University Press, 1993). Among work loosely classifiable as new historicist, the problems and demands of the plain truth are treated most successfully by Stephen J. Greenblatt, *Renaissance Self-Fashioning from More to Shakespeare* (Chicago: University of Chicago Press, 1980), esp. chaps. 1–3; Richard Strier, "Faithful Servants: Shakespeare's Praise of Disobedience," in *The Historical Renaissance: New Essays on Tudor and Stuart Literature and Culture*, ed. Heather Dubrow and Richard Strier (Chicago: University of Chicago Press, 1988); and Debora Kuller Shuger, *Habits of Thought in the English Renaissance: Religion, Politics, and the Dominant Culture* (Berkeley: University of California Press, 1990).

[8] Martin Luther, *The Babylonian Captivity of the Church* (1520), in *Martin Luther: Selections from His Writings*, ed. John Dillenberger (New York: Doubleday, 1961), p. 341. Luther's reply the following year to the Diet of Worms yields the most famous expression of this idea: "Unless," he says, "I am convinced by the testimony of the Scriptures or by clear reason . . . , I am bound by the Scriptures I have quoted and my conscience is captive to the Word of God" (cited by Dillenberger, intro., xxiii).

statement of the central Reformation doctrine that Scripture offers plain and certain truths on all essential matters. In Neostoic doctrine, right reason replaces Scripture as the principal source of plain truth. This doctrine is stated trenchantly by Justus Lipsius, whose place in the Neostoic movement is comparable to that of Luther in Protestantism. In his *Two Bookes of Constancie*, written in 1584 and translated into English ten years later, Lipsius distinguishes right reason from its contrary, opinion. The former is "A true sense and judgement of thinges humane and divine," while the latter is "A false and frivolous conjecture of those thinges." Right reason is "that only which is uniforme, simple, without mixture, separate from al filth or corruption: and in one word, as much as is pure & heavenlie." Opinion is "vaine, uncertaine, deceitfull, evill in counsell, evill in judgement. It depriveth the mind of Constancie and veritie. To day it desireth a thing, to morrowe it defieth the same. . . . This is unto men the mother of mischieves, the authour of a confused and troublesome life."[9]

This claim to truth has two main parts. First is the sense of the absolute difference between the certainty of conviction and the uncertain truth of mere opinion. In his *Institutes* Calvin supplies a more temperate and fully elaborated version of the doctrines set forth earlier by Luther. "As faith is not content with a doubtful and changeable opinion," Calvin writes, "so is it not content with an obscure and confused conception; but requires full and fixed certainty, such as men are wont to have from things experienced and proved."[10] The provider of this certainty is the Holy Spirit, so "if we desire to provide in the best way for our consciences—that they may not be perpetually beset by the instability of doubt or

---

[9] Justus Lipsius, *Two Bookes of Constancie*, trans. John Stradling, ed. Rudolf Kirk with notes by Clayton Morris Hall, Rutgers University Studies in English, no. 2 (New Brunswick: Rutgers University Press, 1939), pp. 79, 80, 81, and 82. Another reference appears in the text. For a recent treatment of Lipsius's stoicism, see Mark Morford, *Stoics and Neostoics: Rubens and the Circle of Lipsius* (Princeton: Princeton University Press, 1991), pp. 157–80. But for an intriguing consideration of Lipsius as first and foremost a classical philologist, see Anthony Grafton, "Portrait of Justus Lipsius," *American Scholar* 56 (1987), 382–90.

[10] John Calvin, *Institutes of the Christian Religion*, ed. John T. McNeill, trans. Ford Lewis Battles, Library of Christian Classics, vol. 20 (Philadelphia: Westminster Press, 1960), 3.2.15. Further references appear in the text.

vacillation, and that they may not also boggle at the smallest quibbles—we ought to seek our conviction in a higher place than human reasons, judgments, or conjectures, that is, in the secret testimony of the Spirit" (1.7.4). Such conviction consistently accompanies declarations of Scripture's plainness or perspicuity, which may be described as its cause. In *A Disputation on Holy Scripture* (1588), for example, William Whitaker draws on both *The Bondage of the Will* and the *Institutes* to develop an argument that "although there is much obscurity in many words and passages [of Scripture], yet all the articles of faith are plain."[11] This plainness, in Whitaker's view, is not a quality of the *words*, which are an external, intellectual manifestation of scriptural truth, but rather of the heart moved by the Spirit. We cannot, he writes, using an important word of New Testament Greek usually translated as "full assurance," "have the *plerophoria*, that is, a certain, solid, and saving knowledge, without the Holy Spirit internally illuminating our minds" (364).[12] The plainness of Scripture is finally an irresistible "internal clearness" that creates the certainty of conviction.

The second feature of the claim to truth is its authority. The central Reformed statement of this concept is Calvin's defense of Scripture as *autopistos* (*Inst.* 1.7.5), or self-authenticating.[13] Whitaker again elaborates the doctrine in an English text, arguing (always against the Catholic emphasis on the authority of the church) that "scripture is *autopistos*, that is, hath all its authority and credit from itself" (279). Whitaker also explains the relation

[11] William Whitaker, *A Disputation on Holy Scripture* (1588), ed. William Fitzgerald, Parker Society, vol. 45 (Cambridge: Cambridge University Press, 1849), p. 362. Further references appear in the text. Whitaker represented the extreme Calvinist wing of the Church of England.

[12] Luther uses the word *plerophoria* in the context of his remarks on assertions in *The Bondage of the Will*. He writes: "Let Skeptics and Academics keep well away from us Christians, but let there be among us 'assertors' twice as unyielding as the Stoics themselves. How often, I ask you, does the apostle Paul demand that *plerophoria* (as he terms it)—that most sure and unyielding assertion of conscience?" (*Bondage of the Will* [1526], trans. Philip S. Watson and Benjamin Drewery, in *Luther and Erasmus: Free Will and Salvation*, Library of Christian Classics, vol. 17 (Philadelphia: Westminster Press, 1969), p. 106.

[13] On this doctrine in Whitaker, the major Reformers, Richard Sibbes, and Milton, see Knott, *Sword of the Spirit*, pp. 34–35, 47, and 110.

of Scripture's authority to its captivating truth: "If the scripture have so great force and virtue in itself, as to draw up our souls to itself, to infuse into us an intimate persuasion of its truth, and of itself to commend itself to our belief; then it is certain that it is to us of itself *autopistos*, canonical and authentic" (335). These Reformed claims about the authority of Scripture parallel the claims made on behalf of the authority of reason in Neostoic doctrine. For Lipsius the truth of reason is the ultimate authority because "to obey [reason] is to beare rule, and to bee subject thereunto is to have the soveraintie in al humane affaires. Whoso obeyeth her is lord of al lusts in al humane affaires" (81). The similarities between Protestantism and Neostoicism are perhaps nowhere more striking than in the central paradox of the power of obedience to the truth.[14]

The question of the authority of conviction moves us toward a consideration of how plainness functions politically or historically in the Renaissance, of, that is, the nature of its performance and the relation of its truth to power. Such a consideration is my task in this book, and I examine specific examples of this performance in each chapter; but first I will distinguish two general categories into which these performances fall: private plainness and public plainness.

The first seems a clear consequence of the idea of conviction as I have elaborated it so far, especially of the doctrine of full assurance through the Holy Spirit, directed as it is against the authority of the Roman church. Whitaker, for example, notes that "it is absurd to dream of any public tribunal of the Holy Spirit" (346), whose testimony is private and secret, not public and manifest (345). But the stoic, too, is most often thought to focus on protecting private assurance in the midst of a troubled world. What I call private plainness may therefore be said to begin in resistance to public authority, in the desire for *reform*. The reforming impulse raises questions about free speech and conscience that may, from the perspective plainness offers, appear unanswerable. To Raphael Hythloday in Thomas More's *Utopia*, for example, the court of

[14] Lipsius quotes Seneca's maxim (*De Vita Beata*, 15.8) that "to obey God is libertie" (105).

the typical European prince has no room for the plain truth. Rejecting the pragmatism that speaks the truth "indirectly," Hythloday explains the problem of counsel in terms of an unsolvable either-or equation: "either I would have different ideas from the others, and that would come to the same thing as having no ideas at all, or else I would agree with them, and that . . . would merely confirm them in their madness."[15] The choice for Hythloday is between powerless disagreement or equally powerless capitulation.

Notwithstanding the pessimism of More's Hythloday or the frustration of Shakespeare's great plainspeaking counselors, John of Gaunt and Kent, plainness appears to have been a popular and even at times an effective means of expressing dissent.[16] The problem of counsel is a form of the problem of obedience, and the difficulty faced by the dissenting counselor was always to reconcile conscientious counsel with obedience. Plainness seems to have been an accepted way to strike this balance. For instance, William Hakewill, writing early in the seventeenth century, associates plainness with the essence of parliamentary government—free speech. "Every man," he writes, "ought freely boldly and plainly to speak his mind and conscience either in propounding such things as he holdeth requisite for the good of the Commonwealth, or in withstanding and denying the contrary," provided only that "he demean himself discreetly and temperately." The qualification is essential, since Hakewill's goal is to defend "this privilege or immunity of parliament for freedom of speech" in "cases where the subject's right on the one side and the King's prerogative on the other cannot possibly be severed in debate of either."[17] Speaking plainly was not only a way of asserting one's

---

[15] Thomas More, *Utopia*, ed. and trans. Robert M. Adams (New York: Norton, 1975), p. 31.

[16] On the nuances of Gaunt's plainness, see Baxter, *Shakespeare's Poetic Styles*, chap. 4. For an appraisal of Kent's plainness, see below, Chap. 6.

[17] William Hakewill, "Orders of Speaking in Parliament," pp. 46, 48, and 47. This text, British Museum, Additional MSS 36856 fols. 48–54, is published as an appendix to Elizabeth Read Foster, "Speaking in the House of Commons," *Bulletin of the Institute of Historical Research* 43 (1970), 35–55. Foster chose the latest surviving version of the text, dating from 1628 or later, but it was circulating in manuscript considerably earlier, perhaps before 1610. The emphasis Hakewill

rights, but also (at least after 1603) of impressing the king, himself a devoted plainspeaker who counseled his son to "love them best, that are plainest with you."[18] Even under James, royal prerogative and loyal privilege had to be balanced, and plainspeaking was a way simultaneously to claim and to earn the rights of a true subject.

Letters written to Queen Elizabeth by reforming clergy indicate that the political utility of private plainness did not begin with James. In 1559 Archbishop Parker headed a group who protested the presence of images in churches, writing: "We pray your majesty . . . not to be offended with this our plainness, and liberty, which all good and Christian princes have ever taken in good part at the hands of godly bishops."[19] Parker's suggestion that such plainness is loyal is more explicit in the letter Archbishop Grindal wrote to the queen in 1576 when he found he could no longer assent to the restrictions placed on preaching. "Neither do I ever intend," he writes,

> to offend your majesty in any thing, unless, in the cause of God or of his church, by necessity of office, and burden of conscience, I shall thereunto be enforced: and in those cases (which I trust in God shall never be urged upon me,) if I should use dissembling or flattering silence, I should very evil requite your Majesty's so many and so great benefits; for in so doing, both you might fall into peril towards God, and I myself into endless damnation.[20]

---

places on free speech is exemplified by the etymology he reports for "parliament": "Some men are of the opinion that the word parliament is derived from *parle la ment* for that in parliament men should speak their minds freely" (48). I am grateful to Patrick Delana for bringing this document to my attention. For a fuller discussion of parliamentary privileges, see Foster, *The House of Lords 1603–1649: Structure, Procedure, and the Nature of Its Business* (Chapel Hill: University of North Carolina Press, 1983), esp. chap. 8, "Privilege."

[18] James I of England, *Basilikon Doron*, in *The Political Works of James I*, ed. Charles Howard McIlwain, Harvard Political Classics (1918; rpt. New York: Russell & Russell, 1965), p. 33.

[19] *Correspondence of Matthew Parker, Archbishop of Canterbury*, ed. John Bruce and Thomas Thomason Perowne, Parker Society, vol. 33 (Cambridge: Cambridge University Press, 1853), p. 94. Another reference appears in the text.

[20] *The Remains of Archbishop Grindal*, ed. William Nicholson, Parker Society, vol. 19 (Cambridge: Cambridge University Press, 1843), p. 377. Another reference appears in the text. Grindal and Parker both cite St. Ambrose's letters to the

The care both letters take to explain that their apparent disobedience to the queen is in fact obedience to God supplements the care they take to explain that their dissent from the queen's authority is supported (as Parker puts it) by "those authorities of the Scriptures, reasons, and pithy persuasions" (80). To this Grindal adds only the Lutheran proof of experience:

> [Because] I am very well assured, both by reasons and arguments taken out of holy scriptures, and by experience, (the most certain seal of sure knowledge,) that the said exercises for the interpretation and exposition of the scriptures, and for exhortation and comfort drawn out of the same, are both profitable to increase knowledge among the ministers, and tendeth to the edifying of the hearers,—I am forced, with all humility, and yet plainly, to profess, that I cannot with safe conscience, and without the offence of the majesty of God, give my assent to the suppressing of the said exercises. (386)

The letters, then, show that, however strong the arguments in support of a dissenting position may have been, it was still felt to risk presumption and pride ("with all humility, and *yet* plainly") and therefore to require the special justification that the gesture of dutiful plainness provided.

Yet the letter writers' claim to speak the truth also indicates that a decisive break has occurred: despite their reasonableness, both writers appeal to a higher authority that they believe has decided the question at issue. Their plainness indicates that the limit of debate has been reached. Their minds are made up. Still, Grindal's and Parker's letters, in which plainness is a gesture of polite dissent by men who are still more or less inside the Elizabethan establishment, represent the moderate end of a spectrum of dissent in the bitter world of Reformation controversial writings. Further from the center is the "rude" species of private plainness, a blunt integrity that speaks its mind and refuses to flatter, preferring "sinceritie and playne dealing" to the "fond

---

emperors Theodosius and Valentinianus as models of obedient dissent. For a full account of the place of Grindal's letter in the dispute over "prophesyings," see Patrick Collinson, *Archbishop Grindal 1519–1583: The Struggle for a Reformed Church* (London: Jonathan Cape, 1979), chap. 13, "A Scruple of Conscience."

seeming" of public conventions.[21] To the outsider, Montaigne
notes, this "dry, plain, blunt way of speaking . . . verges a little on
the disdainful."[22] In still more polemical writings, the claim to
plain truth continues to indicate that minds are closed, but conviction becomes arguably its own most important proof, out-
weighing the supports of reason, Scripture, and learned authority.
The willingness to pay any price in order to heed Luther's call to
be "'assertors' twice as unyielding as the Stoics themselves" char-
acterizes private plainness at the extremities of debate.[23] Perhaps
the best example of this is what John Knott calls "the drama of
resistance" as it appears in the plainspeaking of Protestant martyrs, who frequently opposed their simple truth to the false theatricality of their torturers.[24] Persecution and martyrdom are the
extreme effects of the moral sense of simplicity.

Public authorities, however, lay claim to truth just as often as
do private dissenters, thereby creating our second species of plainness. Public plainness serves the state or some public group that
no more desires its policies to appear as the bald expression of
power than dissenters wish their plainspeaking to appear as the
performance of pride. It may, like private plainness, be based on a
conviction of scriptural truth. The 1547 "Homily on Obedience,"
for example, argues that "we must refer al judgement to God, to
kynges and rulers, and judges under them, which be Gods officers,
to execute justice and by plain wordes of Scripture have their
aucthoritie and use of the sword graunted from God." Repeated
claims that "Paules wordes be playn" and that "Christe taught us
plainly" are part of a texture of obviousness in which the "true
meanyng" of Scripture is presented as "manifest and evident."[25]

---

[21] Stephano Guazzo, *The Civile Conversation* (1581), trans. George Pettie and
Bartholomew Young (New York: Knopf, 1925), 1:153.

[22] Michel de Montaigne, "A Consideration upon Cicero," *The Complete Essays*, trans. Donald M. Frame (Stanford: Stanford University Press, 1958), p. 186.

[23] For the context of this remark, see note 12 above.

[24] Knott, *Discourses of Martyrdom*.

[25] "An Exhortacion concernyng Good Ordre and Obedience to Rulers and Mag-
istrates," in *Certain Sermons or Homilies (1547) and A Homily against Disobedience and Wilful Rebellion (1570)*, ed. Ronald B. Bond (Toronto: University of
Toronto Press, 1987), pp. 163, 164, 168, and 166–67. For a consideration of the
stylistic plainness of the homilies, see the introduction, pp. 26–39.

It is standard Reformation-era writing in the service of the official state church.

Royal proclamations also illustrate public plainness, beginning, as they customarily do, by stating a perception that justifies the action taken. For example, a proclamation of 3 January 1572 begins by claiming that "the unlawful retaining of multitude of unordinary servants . . . doth manifestly withdraw from her majesty's crown the due services of her officers, tenants, and subjects, and doth also plainly hinder justice and disorder the good policy of the realm." Claims of this sort tread a thin line between stating truths that will indeed appear to be self-evident and simply asserting an official position regardless of its likelihood. A proclamation of 12 October 1584 against "divers false, slanderous, wicked, seditious, and traitorous books and libels" states that the queen has "of late found, by plain and manifest means and proofs, that . . . [the authors'] purpose and chief intent [was] to bring in obloquy and hatred her majesty's principal noblemen, councilors, judges, and ministers of justice"; but it is not explained what these proofs are. A proclamation of 13 March 1562 aims to silence rumors of coin devaluation by an even more naked declaration: "Her majesty," it reads, "doth plainly and sincerely declare to all manner her subjects that these foresaid rumors and reports be untrue."[26] Rather than resting on shared standards of "reason," proclamations like this one engage in a shouting match in which "truth" is a function of the force—and not only the verbal force— with which conviction can be communicated. The claim to truth becomes a claim to authority that is made on both sides in a contest between (apparently) irreconcilable positions. It is no surprise that James's general preference for plain speech extends to his prescription of "a plaine, short, but stately stile" for proclamations: the style here matches the message.[27]

Much could be said about the style and historical importance of

---

[26] Paul L. Hughes and James F. Larkin, eds., *Tudor Royal Proclamations*, vol. 2 (New Haven: Yale University Press, 1969), pp. 350, 506–7, and 186.

[27] James I, *Basilikon Doron*, p. 47. See also pp. 27, 39, 40, 46, and 48. James concludes a speech to the House of Lords on 19 March 1603 by excusing his plainness, which he claims is proper for a king because it is unambiguous (*Political Works*, 280). I owe this reference to James Doelman.

each of these examples. A full rhetorical consideration of any royal proclamation, for example, would require study of how it attempts to impress its truth upon its audience and of what effect it actually had. We would have to consider who is speaking to whom, in what circumstances, with what motives, and with what consequences.[28] For now I am concerned only to note the presence in these texts of a certain kind of claim to truth—a claim animated by an insistent demand for certainty. Implicit in such a claim is the idea that none of the considerations I just mentioned matters, that the truth is the truth regardless of historical circumstances. I call such a claim antirhetorical to distinguish it from a very different kind of claim to truth, that made in the Renaissance most commonly in rhetorical humanism. This rhetorical truth has been the subject of a major interdisciplinary undertaking that has traced its impact through a wide range of disciplines, including moral and political philosophy, law, religion, literary studies, history, and education.[29] It is my principal foil to plainness, not because the two represent alternative styles,

---

[28] A fine example of the type of insight that a stylistic study alone cannot generate is Leah Marcus's observation that "to the extent that Anglican devotional literature can be distinguished from its Catholic and Puritan counterparts, it is often recognizable less through its style than through the use to which style is put: The plain style is employed as a persuasion to, and as evidence of, childlike obedience to the established church" ("George Herbert and the Anglican Plain Style," in *"Too Rich to Clothe the Sunne": Essays on George Herbert*, ed. Claude J. Summers and Ted-Larry Pebworth [Pittsburgh: University of Pittsburgh Press, 1980], p. 184). For a theoretical defense of rhetorical reading that focuses on the Renaissance, see William J. Kennedy, *Rhetorical Norms in Renaissance Literature* (New Haven: Yale University Press, 1978), pp. 1–19.

[29] Among the more prominent contributions to this undertaking are Hans Baron, *The Crisis of the Early Italian Renaissance: Civic Humanism and Republican Liberty in the Age of Classicism and Tyranny*, 2 vols. (Princeton: Princeton University Press, 1955); Eugenio Garin, *Italian Humanism: Philosophy and Civic Life in the Renaissance*, trans. Peter Munz (Oxford: Blackwell, 1965); William J. Bouwsma, *Venice and the Defense of Republican Liberty: Renaissance Values in the Age of the Counter-Reformation* (Berkeley: University of California Press, 1968); Nancy S. Struever, *The Language of History in the Renaissance: Rhetoric and Historical Consciousness in Florentine Humanism* (Princeton: Princeton University Press, 1970); Donald R. Kelley, *Foundations of Modern Historical Scholarship: Language, Law, and History in the French Renaissance* (New York: Columbia University Press, 1970); Quentin Skinner, *The Foundations of Modern Political Thought*, vol. 1 (Cambridge: Cambridge University Press, 1978); and the studies of rhetoric listed below (note 30).

but because they represent alternative ways of knowing and being.

Humanist rhetoric, we now understand, was much more than a
matter of style. It also involved the practice of rhetorical *controversia*, or the *argumentum in utramque partem*, arguing on both
sides of the question.[30] Truth, according to rhetorical probabil-
ism, was best approached through a collection of different and
even directly opposed perspectives. Lisa Jardine notes that early
humanist dialecticians such as Rudolph Agricola and Lorenzo
Valla found in the tradition of classical rhetorical epistemology a
philosophy that would "countenance their lack of confidence in
the attainability of certainty, and a dialectic rich enough to allow
them to explore the relative plausibility of conflicting dogmas,
while withholding assent."[31] This withholding of assent is central to the moderate skepticism of rhetorical practice. Thomas
Sloane, for example, writes that the "core of Donne's skepticism"
is "neither idealism nor doubt, but diffidence," and Joel Altman
describes the rhetorical training of humanism as "the moral cul-
tivation of ambivalence."[32] Only through the suspension of belief

---

[30] The view of rhetoric that I outline here has been influenced particularly by
Walter J. Ong, *Ramus, Method, and the Decay of Dialogue* (Cambridge: Harvard
University Press, 1958); Hanna H. Gray, "Renaissance Humanism: The Pursuit of
Eloquence," *Journal of the History of Ideas* 24 (1963), 497–514; Jerrold Seigel,
*Rhetoric and Philosophy in Renaissance Humanism: The Union of Eloquence
and Wisdom, Petrarch to Valla* (Princeton: Princeton University Press, 1968); Lisa
Jardine, *Francis Bacon: Discovery and the Art of Discourse* (Cambridge: Cam-
bridge University Press, 1974), and "Lorenzo Valla and the Intellectual Origins of
Humanist Dialectic," *Journal of the History of Philosophy* 15 (1977), 143–64;
Marjorie O'Rourke Boyle, *Erasmus on Language and Method in Theology* (Toron-
to: University of Toronto Press, 1977); Joel B. Altman, *The Tudor Play of Mind:
Rhetorical Inquiry and the Development of the Elizabethan Drama* (Berkeley:
University of California Press, 1978); Thomas O. Sloane, *Donne, Milton, and the
End of Humanist Rhetoric* (Berkeley: University of California Press, 1985); and
Victoria Kahn, *Rhetoric, Prudence, and Skepticism* (Ithaca: Cornell University
Press, 1985), and "Humanism and the Resistance to Theory," in *Literary Theo-
ry/Renaissance Texts*, ed. Patricia Parker and David Quint (Baltimore: Johns Hop-
kins University Press, 1986). For a somewhat different view of rhetoric, see Marion
Trousdale, *Shakespeare and the Rhetoricians* (Chapel Hill: University of North
Carolina Press, 1982).

[31] Jardine, "Lorenzo Valla and Intellectual Origins," p. 148.

[32] Sloane, *Donne, Milton, and the End of Humanist Rhetoric*, p. 14; Altman,
Tudor Play of Mind, chap. 2.

could language—that is, rhetoric—become a means of thought, rather than a tool for expressing a truth readily available to the contemplative intellect.

Such an epistemological model was unequivocally and resolutely social in outlook. Understanding depended on a community of individuals sharing a common language and a commitment to skeptical inquiry into the shared reality that they nevertheless experienced differently. To use language was to participate in this community, as Renaissance writers never tired of repeating. "The tongue serveth us to teache, to demaunde, to conferre, to traffike, to counsaile, to correct, to dispute, to judge, and to expresse the affection of our hearte: meanes whereby men come to love one another, and to linke themselves together," says Stephen Guazzo's Doctor in *The Civile Conversation*.[33] A common language "is a great advantage," according to Juan Vives, "for it is a bond which holds society together, since if there are peculiar ways of speaking among sections of the same nation, the effect is that of using foreign tongues; men do not understand each other thoroughly."[34] Language can function as the bond of society only if people understand one another, and a speaker will be understood, writes Thomas Wilson in *The Arte of Rhetorique*, "if he utter his mind in plain words, suche as are usually received, and tell it orderly."[35]

Wilson's call for "plain words" indicates that the social foundation of rhetoric leads to a different type of plainness, one that I will call rhetorical. In its rhetorical form of a call for a common language, plainness echoes throughout the stylistic controversies of the sixteenth century. It first appears prominently in the humanist criticism of the specialized philosophical language of the scholastics. "Speech is truly common to all," proclaims More after listing some scholastic contortions of language; "they have taken their speech from the common people and misused the

[33] Guazzo, *Civile Conversation*, p. 35.

[34] Juan Luis Vives, *Vives: On Education* (a translation of *De Tradendis Disciplinis*), ed. and trans. Foster Watson (Cambridge: Cambridge University Press, 1913), p. 14.

[35] Thomas Wilson, *The Arte of Rhetorique*, ed. Thomas J. Derrick, The Renaissance Imagination, vol. 1 (New York: Garland, 1982), p. 25. Further references appear in the text.

common meanings."[36] His response reflects the typical humanist view of dialectic, a view stated briefly by Vives: "A dialectician should use words and propositions that no one can fail to understand who knows the language he speaks."[37] The same perspective informs the arguments of anti-Ciceronians. Erasmus, for instance, satirizes the strict Ciceronian who vows to speak with no one for five years in order that no vulgar speech will distract him from the perfection of Cicero's eloquence. Such a man is out of touch with the common language and therefore the common life:

> Times are changed: our instincts, needs, ideas, are not those of Cicero. Let us indeed take example from him. He was a borrower, an imitator if you will; but he copied in order to assimilate, to bring what he found into the service of his own age. Throughout Cicero's letters,—what verve, what actuality, what life! How remote they are from the compositions of the pedant working in his study.[38]

In England the cry for a common language is heard most frequently in the neologism controversy. Roger Ascham complains in the preface to *Toxophilus* about those who, by "usinge straunge wordes as latin, french and Italian, do make all thinges darke and harde," and Thomas Wilson is no less certain that the use of inkhorn or "rope rype" terms only renders meaning "dark."[39] Wilson summarizes the choice as it appeared to the humanists: "either we must make a difference of Englishe, and saie some is learned Englishe, and other some is rude Englishe, or the one is courte talke, the other is countrey speache, or els we must of necessitee, banishe al suche affected Rhetorique, and use altogether one maner of language" (329). The midcentury poetic ex-

---

[36] Thomas More, "Letter to Martin Dorp," appendix to *Juan Luis Vives against the Pseudodialecticians*, ed. Rita Guerlac (Boston: D. Reidel, 1979), p. 175.

[37] Juan Luis Vives, *In Pseudodialecticos*, in *Juan Luis Vives*, ed. Guerlac, pp. 53–55.

[38] Quoted in *Desiderius Erasmus Concerning the Aim and Method of Education*, ed. W. H. Woodward, Research and Source Works Series, no. 714 (1904; rpt. New York: Burt Franklin, 1971), p. 53. The full text of Erasmus's *Ciceronianus* is available in an English translation by Izora Scott in his *Controversies over the Imitation of Cicero* (New York: Columbia University Teacher's College, 1910).

[39] Roger Ascham, *Toxophilus*, in *English Works*, ed. William Aldis Wright (Cambridge: Cambridge University Press, 1904), preface, p. xiv.

emplar of this rhetorical plainness, George Gascoigne, likewise counsels the would-be poet to "eschew straunge words" in favor of "apte wordes."[40] Finally, humanists associate the apt, the decorous, or the comely with this kind of plainness in stylistic prescriptions that look back to Cicero's "ut Latine, ut plane, ut ornate, ut . . . apte" for a model of plain, ordinary speech that is nonetheless quintessentially rhetorical.[41]

This concern with plain words is more than cosmetic: as More's mention of "common meanings" suggests, the sense as well as the words is required to be plain and consensual. For example, Dudley Fenner hopes that "the simple playnes" of *The Artes of Logike and Rethorike* will "drawe men to no curiouse or doubtfull discourses, but onely put them in minde of that which they may easilie seeke and knowe in most familiar examples with great fruit and delight."[42] The orator's store of truth is a common one, as Shakespeare's Antony realizes. Speaking after Brutus, he calls himself "a plain, blunt man" and says to the crowd: "I tell you that which you yourselves do know" (3.2.218, 224). Rhetorical plainness is the orthodoxy of received wisdom and ordinary modes of speech. It is what everyone knows.

There is an understandable modern tendency to think of the consensual orthodoxy to which rhetorical plainness appeals as a stifling unity, but it needn't be so. The "common sense" to which rhetoric appeals is ideally a rich pluralism, a lively dialogue of controversial voices united only by a shared commitment to society and a measure of trust that everyone will act in good faith toward the common good. It is a republican ideal that seeks to find, between learned and unlearned, governor and governed, a true common denominator. However, the ease with which such an ideal of public discourse can be corrupted by the interests of the powerful—a possibility recent criticism has emphasized—can often be glimpsed in the same writings that seem to proclaim

[40] Gascoigne, "Certayne Notes of Instruction," in *The Anchor Anthology of Sixteenth-Century Verse*, ed. Richard S. Sylvester (New York: Anchor, 1974), p. 323.
[41] Cicero, *De Oratore*, trans. H. Rackham, Loeb Classical Library (Cambridge: Harvard University Press, 1942), 3.10.37. The Loeb translation for the words quoted is "correct, lucid, ornate and . . . appropriate."
[42] Dudley Fenner, *The Artes of Logike and Rethorike* (Middlebrugh: R. Schilders, 1588), fol. A2r.

the ideal. Plainness, aptness, and comeliness frequently fall in with a fourth term, "order," which is explicitly political as well as rhetorical and thus opens an avenue for a self-serving conservatism on the part of the established powers. By "an order wee are borne, by an order wee lyve, and by an order wee make our end" (315), Wilson remarks in his discussion of rhetoric, and a fear of losing this order emerges strongly from such a book as Roger Ascham's *Scholemaster*. Without proper education "disobedience doth overflowe the bankes of good order, almoste in everie place, almoste in everie degree of man"; but with an education founded on doctrinally sound books, truth and plainness are guaranteed, because "all soch Authors, as be fullest of good matter and right judgement in doctrine, be likewise always, most proper in wordes, most apte in sentence, most plaine and pure in uttering the same."[43] Common sense can easily slide into right judgment in doctrine.

The danger of such a slide was real enough that rhetoric often appeared (and is sometimes still viewed) as an instrument of official policy, used to destroy opponents rather than to discover new possibilities.[44] This ambiguous potential reflects the uncertain political status of humanism itself, which is blamed for buttressing conservative governments as well as praised for supplying a progressive impulse. Such ambiguity points out the limit that is imposed on rhetoric's skepticism by the social outlook of the controversial model of knowledge. Since truth could be known only within the context of a particular historical and linguistic community, of custom, the belief that what the community believed to be good was in fact *good* was an article of faith necessary, some felt, for political action. In other words, humanist thought about rhetoric and politics was a form of pragmatism in which

[43] Ascham, *The Scholemaster*, in *English Works*, pp. 209, 265.
[44] For a reading of Renaissance rhetoric that emphasizes its connection to political power, see Wayne A. Rebhorn, "'The Emperour of Mens Minds': The Renaissance Trickster as *Homo Rhetoricus*," in *Creative Imagination: New Essays on Renaissance Literature in Honor of Thomas M. Greene*, ed. David Quint, Margaret W. Ferguson, G. W. Pigman III, and Wayne A. Rebhorn, Medieval and Renaissance Texts & Studies, no. 95 (Binghamton: Center for Medieval and Early Renaissance Studies, State University of New York at Binghamton, 1992), pp. 31–65.

one had to have what amounted to a faith in the ability of the community to overcome the problem of knowledge.[45] The skeptical face of rhetoric consequently placed a premium on historical awareness and particularly on knowledge of audience, since context dictated the form that utterance had to take to be persuasive—or "true." So although rhetorical culture was skeptical about the availability of certainty, it had a faith of its own in the ability of communal efforts to reach at least a satisfactory provisional truth.[46]

This requires some explanation. Identifying rhetoric with faith distinguishes it from a use of language built on conviction and thus furthers my goal of contrasting rhetoric to an antirhetorical plainness. A historical precedent for the contrast lies in William Tyndale's distinction between "historical faith" and "feeling faith." Historical faith is the faith engendered by rhetorical persuasion. According to Tyndale, it "hangeth of the truth and honesty of the teller, or of the common fame and consent of many: as if one told me that the Turk had won a city, and I believed it, moved with the honesty of the man; now if there come another that seemeth more honest, or that hath better persuasions that it is not so, I think immediately that he lied, and lose my faith again." Such a faith, concludes Tyndale, "is but an opinion." In contrast, a "feeling faith . . . is none opinion; but a sure feeling"—that is, a conviction. It is "as if a man were there present when it [the city] was won, and there were wounded, and had there lost all that he had, and were taken prisoner there also: that man should so believe, that all the world could not turn him from his faith."[47] The distinction, then, is between the degrees of certainty present in conviction and opinion. Whereas conviction, while perhaps never total, believes firmly that its judgments are the truth (and

---

[45] On the pragmatic character of humanist rhetoric, see in particular Kahn, *Rhetoric, Prudence, and Skepticism.*

[46] In the technical language of skepticism, rhetorical skepticism is an Academic rather than a Pyrrhonian skepticism. See Richard H. Popkin, *The History of Skepticism from Erasmus to Spinoza,* 2d ed. (Berkeley: University of California Press, 1979).

[47] William Tyndale, *An Answer to Sir Thomas More's Dialogue,* ed. Henry Walter, Parker Society, vol. 44 (Cambridge: Cambridge University Press, 1850), pp. 50–51.

may be willing to die for them), historical or rhetorical faith has a skeptical awareness, or doubt, but somehow (it is indeed a mystery) proceeds as if its knowledge were a sufficient guide for intelligent action.[48] That a certain kind of faith arises from doubt is a paradox that makes it worthwhile to take at face value the Ciceronian definition of rhetorical persuasion, which was the common property of Renaissance rhetorical dialectic beginning with Peter of Spain—"ratio rei dubiae faciens fidem," a means of creating faith in doubtful matters—although "conviction" is the usual translation of *fides*. *Ratio* here also implies rhetoric's "skeptical faith": it refers not to any rigorous logic or foolproof Ramistic *methodus*, but to communal standards of probability centered in linguistic custom. Although "the ocular proof" may be offered—Desdemona's handkerchief, Caesar's bloody body, a false Hero on the balcony—the proof may not function outside an argumentative context established by words, whereas words may serve very well without visual evidence. But words will serve only if the audience cooperates by acting in "good faith" itself; if it refuses to act as a friend or a partner, the appeal to linguistic probability will fail, and the bubble of dialogic faith will burst.

In using rhetorical plainness as a foil for the simple plainness that is my focus, I am in effect reversing the procedure of a number of recent students of humanist rhetoric. Richard Waswo, for example, argues that humanist rhetoric straddled an unarticulated contradiction between its theory, according to which meaning was most often understood as "referential" (or, roughly, antirhetorical), and its practice, which generally proceeded as if meaning was "relational" (or rhetorical).[49] And Victoria Kahn, to take just one more example, distinguishes between a strain of

---

[48] Calvin, insisting that faith results from a certain knowledge of God's grace, argues against using the word to refer to anything less (*Institutes*, 3.2). Despite Calvin's strictures, Whitaker continues to use Tyndale's term "historical faith" (364).

[49] Richard Waswo, *Language and Meaning in the Renaissance* (Princeton: Princeton University Press, 1987). In Waswo's terms a referential theory views meaning as certain and ahistorical, and language as a transparent transmitter that can be judged according to a "hierarchy of privilege," whereas a relational theory sees meaning as uncertain and historically variable, and language as a social activity that constitutes meaning.

humanism that emphasizes consensus and one that emphasizes conflict.[50] For the most part, studies such as these sketch anti-rhetorical positions for the purpose of establishing a contrast with rhetoric, which remains their principal interest. But they also reflect a growing interest in the competition between under-standings of knowledge and language, as well as a recognition that the study of either rhetoric or plainness needs to distinguish between them, consider their entanglements, and qualify any claims made about them accordingly. In concentrating on plain-ness, I will therefore keep in mind that there is a rhetorical di-mension to it, just as there is an antirhetorical element within humanist rhetoric; and I will make use of the theoretical perspec-tive offered by studies of rhetoric to develop a complementary understanding of the public and private forms of antirhetorical plainness.

In pursuing this potentially vast subject, I have not attempted to be exhaustive or to write a consecutive history of it. I have instead chosen what seem to me significant and to some extent representative samples from a number of important contexts in which plainness appears, hoping in this way to suggest the place of plainness in Renaissance culture between roughly Luther's break with Rome in 1521 and Shakespeare's death in 1616. I have sometimes chosen writers, works, and genres known for their plainness and have frequently emphasized their explicit claims to be plain; but I have also studied writers and areas not usually considered plain and have occasionally assumed the claim to plainness rather than belabor the obvious.

I focus on two problems presented by antirhetorical plainness. The first is the nature of the relationship between public and

---

[50] Victoria Kahn, "Habermas, Machiavelli, and the Humanist Critique of Ideol-ogy," *PMLA* 105 (1990), 464–76. Also relevant to Kahn's placement of Machiavelli in a contesting strain of humanism is Wayne A. Rebhorn's identification of an antirhetorical "rhetoric of power" in Machiavelli. See *Foxes and Lions: Machia-velli's Confidence Men* (Ithaca: Cornell University Press, 1988), chaps. 2 and 5. Probably the clearest and most fully articulated attempt to read the sixteenth century in terms of a contest between rhetorical and antirhetorical (or "philosoph-ical") anthropologies is William J. Bouwsma, *John Calvin: A Sixteenth-Century Portrait* (Oxford: Oxford University Press, 1988). Bouwsma's "philosophy," how-ever, differs significantly from my conception of plainness. Most important, plain-ness is practical and passionate rather than abstract and rational.

private plainness. At any time the line between public and private is blurry, subject to some extent to historical redefinition as the shapes of political experience and personal identity shift. What does the antirhetorical dynamic of plainness do to that line? What are the similarities and differences between public and private plainness? What significance does the relationship between them hold for questions of political and religious authority? For psychological questions? In short, how does an understanding of plainness affect our perceptions of early modern society and selfhood? My second focus is the ethical problem that plainness creates in the absence of rhetorical criteria of truth. A self-authenticating truth can expect to find its credibility questioned when it touches life outside the self. Will plainness be perceived as the performance of truth or as the performance of power? Does it assert the claim *of* truth or simply a claim *to* truth?

The first three chapters concentrate on the first problem. In Chapter 1 I examine the private plainness of Thomas Wyatt's anticourtly verse, contrasting rhetorical to antirhetorical performance and tracing the elements of persuasion in Wyatt's expressions of conviction. I identify the anger and stoic withdrawal that shape Wyatt's poetic voice as mutually reinforcing aspects of plainness. The second chapter turns to public plainness as seen in selected Reformation and humanist attempts to build Reformed communities around the conviction of a plain Word. In it I focus on the conceptions of teaching in the radical Puritan *Admonition to Parliament* and in Ascham's *Scholemaster*—specifically, on how a mixture of indoctrination and discipline nods in the direction of rhetoric and historical difference while maintaining a primary allegiance to plainness and conviction. The third chapter examines the work of Fulke Greville, one of the few writers who both theorized and practiced an antirhetorical stance. In Greville, I argue, the private and public forms of plainness unite in their common rejection of rhetoric, creating a voice in which the sounds of public order and inner peace are virtually indistinguishable.

I also find in Greville's conscious desire for an ideal union of knowing and doing an adumbration of the problematic relation of truth and power that is the focus of the final three chapters.

Through the example of anger the fourth chapter investigates the ethical problems of a conviction that is plain to those who share it, but opaque to those who do not. Study of the angry genres of satire and revenge tragedy reveals how a concern for justice can give way to a moral relativism that is content with the power of performance, whether or not it is true and just. In the fifth chapter I argue that Shakespeare develops this skeptical view of plainness in *Timon of Athens* and *Coriolanus* by portraying a plainness that is a performance of pride. The truth of plainness is clearly subordinate to its power in these plays, because the plainspeakers lack the critical self-reflection necessary to ask whether their desires are virtuous or practical. In the sixth chapter, however, I argue that *King Lear* presents plainness in a more positive light. Faced with skeptical challenges to the ethics of plainness, the play's plainspeakers abandon their initial intransigence in favor of a more flexible and rhetorically aware performance. By doing so they also alter the relation of public and private that is characteristic of plainness. The play thus offers solutions to both the problems on which I focus by showing plainness as the performance of love, an ideal relation of truth to power as well as of public to private. In *Lear* plainness proves essential to maintaining truth and justice in a corrupt world.

1 Wyatt's Antirhetorical Verse: Privilege and the Performance of Conviction

Wyatt's is a voice rich in paradox. He is at once rebellious and submissive. He is an early exemplar of the anticourtly attitude, yet he is thoroughly entangled with the court, a master of its conventions and, it seems, constitutionally incapable of breaking with it entirely. He is vengeful, yet moralistic; gruff, yet tender; self-assured, yet self-doubting; stolid, yet restless. Above all, Wyatt strikes us as angry, asserting his right in the face of its violation, yet sadly removed, content to endure without complaint the sorrows of a joyless, ascetic existence with neither the comfort of success nor the sympathy of companionship. Wyatt himself appears to embrace the paradoxes, describing himself in one of his translations of Petrarch as "feeding busily" "with sorrowful anger" (13)—a translation that emphasizes the paradox more than Petrarch's "with sorrow and anger."[1] In this chapter I argue that these appar-

---

[1] The Italian is as follows: "Se sospirare e lagrimar mai sempre, / Pascendosi di duol, d'ira e d'affano" (The Collected Poems of Sir Thomas Wyatt, ed. Kenneth Muir and Patricia Thomson [Liverpool: Liverpool University Press, 1969]). I have used Ronald A. Rebholz's edition of Wyatt, Sir Thomas Wyatt: The Complete Poems (1978; rpt. New Haven: Yale University Press, 1981). The numbers are those given to the poems in this edition.

The Wyatt canon is a very uncertain one, and in approaching it I have benefited not only from the scholarship of the editors named above but also from that of H. A. Mason, Editing Wyatt (Cambridge: Cambridge Quarterly Publications, 1972), and of Richard Harrier, The Canon of Sir Thomas Wyatt's Poetry (Cambridge:

ently very different responses to the world are twin expressions of
antirhetorical conviction, and that some of Wyatt's most compelling poetry exemplifies the private species of plainness.

   To highlight the significance of this private plainness in Wyatt,
I will organize my argument around the various meanings of
"plain" in his verse. Used to refer to speech, "plain" means direct,
emphatic, lacking subtlety and artfulness, and strongly implies
the moral values of honesty and principled conviction. "Plain"
can also refer to self-sufficiency, to separation from the emotional
involvement that might bring joy, but will surely bring sorrow. It
is, further, a verb indicating the main actions of Wyatt's courtly
and anticourtly poems, which are, respectively, moaning and
complaining. If we concentrate on the role of directness and self-
sufficiency in complaining, and compare the antirhetorical plainness of Wyatt's complaints with the more rhetorical tendencies of
his courtly moans, we will find the best account of Wyatt's characteristic attitudes.

   The nature of Wyatt's anticourtly "directness" is illustrated by
"Blame Not My Lute," a poem that modestly calls itself "somewhat plain" as well as, in the context of courtly love lyrics,
"somewhat strange":

> Blame not my lute for he must sound
> Of this or that as liketh me.
> For lack of wit the lute is bound
> To give such tunes as pleaseth me.
> Though my songs be somewhat strange
> And speaks [sic] such words as touch thy change
>   Blame not my lute.

(94)

Harvard University Press, 1975). The only poem of especially doubtful authorship
about which I have written is "I Am as I Am." Because it also exists in carol form in
a manuscript older than the Wyatt manuscripts, Muir and Thomson conclude
that Wyatt's "authorship is very uncertain" (400). Harrier believes that the additional stanzas that are present in the Wyatt manuscripts and beyond which no
claim for Wyatt's authorship can reasonably extend "could be by anyone" (54).
Nevertheless, the poem reveals a great deal about the attitude of plainness and
deserves attention in studies of Wyatt: if he did not write it, he might have, and
there is every reason to believe it would have interested him enough to play
around with it.

The poem classically illustrates what could be called an ethic of revenge. The nature of this ethic is clear enough in the statements made in the poem, but in clarifying its import the poem's stylistic plainness plays a particularly important role. "Plainness" understood as a feature of style is always, of course, a relative term, and the difficulty of defining it has contributed to the proliferation of plain styles that I noted in the Introduction. That it can be discussed at all means that it is not simply a spontaneous effusion, but is to some degree a calculated effect wrought by the manipulation of linguistic conventions. Yet conventions may be able to give the effect of spontaneous or uncalculating speech, particularly when defined against identifiably artful forms. So it is with Wyatt. What is "plain" about "Blame Not My Lute" becomes clearer when we place beside it a poem such as "Resound My Voice, Ye Woods, That Hear Me Plain," from which I quote the second stanza:

> Oft ye rivers, to hear my woeful sound,
> Have stopped your course; and, plainly to express,
> Many a tear by moisture of the ground
> The earth hath wept to hear my heaviness,
> Which causeless to suffer without redress
> The hugy oaks have roared in the wind:
> Each thing me thought complaining in their kind.
>
> (79)

We are supposed to recognize that this is not at all plain expression, but rather the kind of play with conventional figures of speech—here the apostrophe—that will please the audience. The movement of the verse, too, is intended to give pleasure. The caesura in the second line is expressive of the river's stopping; the metrical and caesural variations in the third and fifth lines contribute to the mellifluousness of the remainder. The aural seductiveness of the *e*'s in line 4, the *s*'s in line 5, and the *o*'s in line 6 complements the elegance of the rhyme royal or Troilus stanza form.[2]

---

[2] The use of the adjective "hugy" by Wyatt in this poem is an early example of a "literary" word that became a mainstay of the bombastic blank verse line later in

By comparison, the metrical and linguistic effects of "Blame Not My Lute" are indeed both strange and plain. Where the pentameter lines of "Resound My Voice" frequently have only four heavy speech stresses, the tetrameter lines of "Blame Not My Lute" rarely skip a beat. This relentlessness is emphasized by the frequent use of repetition, both in the refrain line and in individual lines, such as "Spite asketh spite and changing change." The repetition of entire words in stressed syllables allows maximum emphasis of the "eye for an eye" ethic of the poem. And where assonance and the repetition of soft concluding consonants are frequent in "Resound My Voice," in "Blame Not My Lute" beginning consonants and hard concluding consonants are more likely to recur. For example, "wreak" in line 18 picks up the *wr* of "wrongfully" and the *k* of "Break" in line 17:

> Break not them then so wrongfully
> But wreak thyself some wiser way.

All these characteristics of sound and rhythm contribute to an emphatic tone that is a hallmark of plainness.

Statements are also more straightforward and emphatic in "Blame Not My Lute." All figurative language derives from the controlling figure of the lute, which, unlike the fanciful figures in "Resound My Voice," conveys rather than masks the blunt truth about things. It permits even the frank sexual suggestion of "if till then my fingers play / By thy desert their wonted way." Accompanying the lute figure are simple statements ("Spite asketh spite"), simple reasoning ("Then since that by thine own desert / My songs do tell how true thou art / Blame not my lute"), and a large number of imperatives and statements of obligation or compulsion ("must sound," "must agree," "must needs be known"). The poem has all the subtlety—and all the force—of necessity.

One final feature of the poem contributes to its direct, emphatic tone. Wyatt sets himself up as a moral exemplar by enlisting a

---

the century. Its use here is consistent with the emphasis on a pleasant and full (some might say fulsome) sound. On "hugy," see Howard Baker, *Induction to Tragedy* (Baton Rouge: Louisiana State University Press, 1939), pp. 63–67.

wide array of emotionally charged, quasi-legal terms to speak in his behalf.[3] Among these terms are "faults," "case," "desert," and "right," all of which occur in the fourth stanza:

> Spite asketh spite and changing change
> And falsed faith must needs be known.
> The faults so great, the case so strange
> Of right it must abroad be blown.
> The since that by thine own desert
> My songs do tell how true thou art
> Blame not my lute.

These words, particularly "desert" and "right," occur with great frequency throughout Wyatt's poetry; they are part of the reason why it is sometimes impossible to tell whether Wyatt's complaint is primarily political or amatory.[4] Their significance is that they help Wyatt assert his position that truth, honesty, and constancy lie on his side by allowing him to treat the case as just that, a case at law. But it is always a case in which only one side is heard, in which the plaintiff is also the judge, and therefore the legal transcript reads very emphatically. Plainness of expression in Wyatt, then, is closely allied with the wish to communicate clearly and forcefully the complaining lover's conviction that he has been wronged and his aggressive response to the treatment he has received.

In addition to his references to plain expression, Wyatt sometimes uses the word "plain" in a very specific sense not recorded in the *Oxford English Dictionary*. A good example is Satire 2, "My Mother's Maids," where, having told the story of the mice, he gives the following advice: "Make plain thine heart that it be not knotted / With hope or dread" (150). The same association of

---

[3] Wyatt's use of legal terms has been explored by Virginia Banke Major in "Love and Legalisms in the Poetry of Sir Thomas Wyatt," *Essays in Literature* 11 (1984), 177–86. She argues that Wyatt's "poetry shows that he desired a contract between equals rather than a bond between a cold, powerful mistress and a long-suffering devotee" (177).

[4] On the interplay of politics and love in Wyatt's love lyrics, see Jonathan Z. Kamholtz, "Thomas Wyatt's Poetry: The Politics of Love," *Criticism* 20 (1978), 25.

plainness with the avoidance of emotional ties occurs in a song in
which Wyatt renounces love in favor of the "plain" sex of the
carpe diem tradition:

> Me list no more to sing
> Of love nor of such thing,
> How sore that it me wring;
> For what I sung or spake
> Men did my songs mistake.
>
> My songs were too diffuse.
> They made folk to muse.
> Therefore, me to excuse,
> They shall be sung more plain,
> Neither of joy nor pain.
>
> (135)

At this time, "diffuse" as an adjective meant "confused, distracted, perplexed; indistinct, vague, obscure, doubtful, uncertain" (OED). Once again emotion is a source of complication and
even confusion, and "plain" suggests an open, level surface free
from concealed dangers and unsuspected twists and turns, including politically dangerous misunderstandings. "Plain" in both
cases is thus opposed to the most basic emotions attending upon
sympathetic involvement with the world, an involvement that is
willing to risk disappointment while exposing its need.

Such a plainness bears a close relation to the attitude epito-
mized by "Madam, Withouten Many Words" and the variation on
it that begins:

> Since that my language without eloquence
> Is plain, unpainted, and not unknown,
> Dispatch answer with ready utterance.
>
> (193)

Plainness in such poems is more than simply a feature of language. There is also an impatience with courtly rituals, and an
attempt to withdraw from them to a form of stoic self-possession

involving simplified feelings as well as language. Things outside the self can only distract one from the goal of knowing the peace and truth that lie within, and life at court is especially hazardous to this self-knowledge, as Wyatt's brilliant translation of Seneca makes very clear:

> Stand whoso list upon the slipper top
> Of court's estates, and let me here rejoice
> And use me quiet without let or stop,
> Unknown in court that hath such brackish joys.
> In hidden place so let my days forth pass
> That, when my years be done withouten noise,
> I may die aged after the common trace.
> For him death grip'th right hard by the crop
> That is much known of other, and of himself, alas,
> Doth die unknown, dazed, with dreadful face.
>
> (49)

Although the emphasis in this poem falls on retirement to the country, Wyatt's original poems make it clear that for him a "hidden place" may be either literal or figurative: physical location is less important than the goal of emotional solitude, which alone can protect the self from the dread of pain:

> Once, as methought, Fortune me kissed
> And bade me ask what I thought best
> And I should have it as me list,
> Therewith to set my heart in rest.
>
> I asked naught but my dear heart
> To have for evermore mine own.
> Then at an end were all my smart.
> Then should I need no more to moan.
>
> (108)

In the extended play upon which this poem turns, "my dear heart" can mean not only a woman but also something very close to our modern word "self," as comparison with the following lines shows:

> But though the heaven would work me woe,
> Who hath himself shall stand upright.
>
> (102)

If one has his "heart," he has "himself." The injunction to "make plain thine heart," then, is an exhortation to turn the self inward, and to sever connections with the world. If you do so successfully, Wyatt concludes, you will

> seek no more out of thyself to find
> The thing that thou hast sought so long before,
> For thou shalt feel it sitting in thy mind.
>
> (150)

Although the phrase "stoic self-possession" may suggest a certain calm, in Wyatt the release from hope and fear often seems to be achieved instead by means of an aggressive championing of one's own convictions. The keynote of such championing is that whether anyone else agrees or even understands is not important: all that matters is that one know one's own meaning. For example, after Wyatt renounces the joy and pain of love and vows to sing more plainly in "Me List No More to Sing," he writes six stanzas of thinly veiled metaphors advocating sexual hedonism before concluding thus:

> If this be under mist,
> And not well plainly wist,
> Understand me who list
> For I reck not a bean;
> I wot what I do mean.
>
> (135)

Wyatt's pledge to sing plainer songs—songs more easily understood because free from emotional complications—has led to the emphatic and extremely confident manner characteristic of Wyatt's plain expression. Yet this manner culminates in the declaration that plainness of expression as it pertains to the hearer—that is, perspicuity—is of no consequence. Wyatt has both declared his wish to be understood and limited his ability to communicate by withdrawing emotionally.

Here we return to the paradox with which I began, a paradox that can now be stated in terms of a dynamic characteristic of plainness. On the one hand, the plain heart, secure in its own virtue, appears to be unconcerned about the opinions of others; on the other, plain speech attempts to express clearly and emphatically an aggressive response to perceived injustice and so to determine the opinions of others. These opposing impulses are expressed in miniature in the difference between "thou shalt feel it *sitting* in thy mind," with its suggestions of easy-chair comfort, and "Who hath himself shall *stand* upright," which in Wyatt's use suggests a Lutheran defiance of Roman inquisitors or an aggressive stoic response to the problems of Job. In one case Wyatt expresses the wish to withdraw from the social web to the comfort of his own absoluteness; in the other, he desires to enforce his completeness on those nearby. I suggest that in these terms his problem is something like that of the Old Testament God: despite his self-sufficiency, he continually feels the needs to declare himself in an unending display of power.

The paradox and the similarity are made somewhat comically clear in "I Am as I Am and So Will I Be." The first stanza sets the tone:

> I am as I am and so will I be
> But how that I am none knoweth truly.
> Be it evil, be it well, be I bound, be I free,
> I am as I am and so will I be.
>
> (221)

Despite the explicit possibility of evil, the whole tenor of the poem is that questions of good and evil do not apply to the speaker, whose position beyond the knowledge and power of others permits him to operate in a privileged sphere outside the reach of ordinary moral judgment and tyranny alike. Stanzas 4 through 7 confirm this initial impression and deepen the contradiction by encouraging the efforts of "every man" to judge the speaker and denying their efficacy. I quote stanzas 4 and 5:

> Diverse do judge as they do trow,
> Some of pleasure and some of woe.
> Yet for all that, nothing they know.
> But I am as I am wheresoever I go.
>
> But since that judgers do thus decay
> Let every man his judgement say.
> I will it take in sport and play
> For I am as I am whosoever say nay.

He may well take their attempts in sport and play, for people who know nothing cannot judge at all.

"I Am as I Am" also introduces the linguistic dimension of the contradiction. In the Renaissance, language was sometimes believed to be a medium of self-revelation, even of self-creation. The chief biblical precedent for this belief was God's everlasting "I am," and commentators were also fond of emphasizing that God "by his woorde . . . wonderfullye made all thinges of nothynge."[5] Wyatt emphasizes the fact of his continued linguistic self-presentation, but allows it to conflict with his assertions of verbal opacity. This contradiction is most apparent in stanzas 8 and 9:

> Praying you all that this do read
> To trust it as you do your creed
> And not to think I change my weed
> For I am as I am however I speed.
>
> But how that is I leave to you.
> Judge as ye list, false or true.
> Ye know no more than afore ye knew.
> Yet I am as I am whatever ensue.

The poet first grants this poem a privileged status as "creed," as a guide to what to believe about him and thus as the truest revelation of, or testament to, his being. But he immediately denies that we know any more about him than we knew before reading the

---

[5] Thomas Cranmer, *Catechismus* (1548), cxxxii verso. Quoted in Richard Barry Yanowitz, "Tudor Attitudes towards the Power of Language," (Ph.D. diss., University of California–Berkeley, 1978), p. 25.

poem. We may think we are learning something from this piece of writing, but we aren't; we are still supposed to judge, but our judgment has no basis in the realm of truth. There is a tension here, and it is explained by the emphatic and self-sufficient meanings of "plain." The former uses language as an instrument of aggressive self-assertion; the latter uses it as a protective wall.

As different as the extremes of withdrawal and aggression are, however, they have in common the conviction that is finally the key to Wyatt and to plainness. In this one crucial respect, it makes no difference whether the emphasis falls on the defiant conviction of plain speech or on the quiet, inner conviction of the plain heart. The two extremes share the single most important characteristic of plainness as a way of knowing and a means of expression in the sixteenth century: both seek to reach unanimity, the end of dialogue, one by exercising its will to exact conformity, the other by withdrawing to create a society of one. Both could be called absolutist in the political and the philosophical senses, as well as in a third, linguistic sense: both seek to subsume all truths, all perspectives, all voices, in one Word.

Wyatt's insistence on the importance of this Word is nowhere greater than in Satire 1, "Mine Own John Poyntz." Withdrawn by the King's order to his father's estate in Kent, Wyatt claims to prize his liberty even as he depicts the court situation whereby virtue goes unrewarded. For almost sixty lines Wyatt explains that he is too honest to succeed at court, because courtly thrivers are those who pervert the Word. The emphasis is incessantly linguistic. Wyatt cannot "dye the colour black a liar," or "frame" his "tune to feign," or complain with his words without hurting nor hurt without complaining, or "turn the word" he has spoken, or "Use wiles for wit," or "call craft counsel," or "paint" for profit, or boast enough "eloquence" to make a crow sound like a swan, or "call" things by their wrong names, or "say" untruths, or "praise" and "honour" undeserving subjects: the passage is a compendium of sixteenth-century terms for speaking. In this linguistic satire, verbal distinctions are moral distinctions, and they are all black-and-white; the conception of language the poem implies is one of perfectly concrete reference, allowing no play of meaning, and no room for disagreement. "Wit" is not a faculty for exploring linguistic/conceptual possibilities, but a tool for the inversion of truth, which is, presumably, perfectly clear to those with no wit. These features of the poem witness a deep love for a fixed truth known through a particular use of language, for a conviction centered in the words that were so important a part of Wyatt's life.

It is not surprising that conviction in Wyatt should take root in an attitude toward language, because, as we now understand, language was at the center of much of what we think of as essentially *Renaissance*. Certainly the finding of scholars such as Paul Oskar Kristeller that humanism was fundamentally an educational movement centered on a program of teaching languages and rhetoric has been widely influential.[6] But although Wyatt shares the Renaissance concern for language, his love for one Word departs from the skeptical dimension of this rhetorical center so dramatically that he can be more profitably discussed in terms of anti-rhetorical sentiments. In the background of these sentiments, the figure of Seneca looms large.

Both stylistic model and philosophical inspiration, Seneca unites the two prongs of Wyatt's private plainness. Withdrawal tinged with sorrow is sometimes traced to Boethian philosophy, or more generally to Christian asceticism, but it is also traced to Seneca and stoic self-possession; angry or heroic self-assertion, specifically as the expression of a grievance, is tied to the righteous indignation of Christianity, or to the *saeva indignatio* of classical satire, but also to Seneca and the Herculean tradition. Yet while it is often noted that Seneca offers both models, that he succeeds in uniting them is much less a subject of agreement. For example, Alan Sinfield finds in the Senecan precedents "alternative mode[s] of human assertion" that Seneca "never reconciled."[7] While Sinfield does suggest that there is a relation be-

---

[6] In addition to Paul Oskar Kristeller, *Renaissance Thought and Its Sources*, ed. Michael Mooney (New York: Columbia University Press, 1979), see especially Robert R. Bolgar, *The Classical Heritage and Its Beneficiaries* (Cambridge: Cambridge University Press, 1954). On the strengths and limitations of Kristeller's understanding of humanist rhetoric, see Thomas O. Sloane, *Donne, Milton, and the End of Humanist Rhetoric* (Berkeley: University of California Press, 1985), p. 90.

[7] Alan Sinfield, *Literature in Protestant England, 1560–1660* (Totawa, N.J.: Barnes & Noble, 1983), pp. 85–86.

tween the two, it is a peculiar relation that depends on calling stoic self-possession—which is predicated on the *withdrawal* of the individual from the surrounding world—a mode of human *assertion*.

A better explanation of the two faces of Senecanism is advanced by Gordon Braden. Tracing the origins of both faces in classical ideas of the self, Braden sees Senecanism as a means not so much of asserting the self as of privileging it. Herculean anger, first of all, originates in the *thymos*, the part of the soul that spurs the Homeric warrior's competitiveness, ambition, and desire for honor. A sort of companion to political imperialism, the thymos operates by establishing arbitrary and ever-widening borders around the self by means of anger, which is its characteristic response to perceived incursions on its privileged territory. The arbitrariness of these borders troubled public-spirited philosophers in antiquity: "Plato," Braden remarks, "is greatly concerned with the educational process that will implant the city's standards deep into the thymoeides so that its aims and the city's will coincide."[8] But the thymos remains "in itself nonrational and even potentially *misologos*," happy to assert itself through any available means. Therefore, the philosophy of Herculean anger is one of self-sufficiency: internal convictions are privileged as an ultimate truth or reality that need not be justified in terms of any external standard.

Seneca's second, Stoic face initially appears to reject the ambitious, honor-seeking anger of the warrior self. But, Braden goes on to argue, clearly the Stoic and the warrior are following different means to the same end—self-sufficiency. As the warrior is ruled by the thymos, so the Stoic is ruled by the *hegemonicon*; like the thymos, the hegemonicon "*should* be rational, but all its title actually guarantees is that it rules" (21). Both are internal principles independent of external justification, and both are interested in the outside world only insofar as it helps to define the self's tender borders. The difference between the two is that Stoicism attempts to do internally what the warrior attempts through out-

[8] Gordon Braden, *Renaissance Tragedy and the Senecan Tradition: Anger's Privilege* (New Haven: Yale University Press, 1985), p. 12. Further references appear in the text.

ward imperialism: to conquer reality by a pure, inner effort of will, rather than by exercising that will upon the world outside. Hence, Braden concludes, "imperial aggression and Stoic retreat are both informed by a drive to keep the self's boundaries under its own control" (23), a control achieved in both cases by following a privileged inner principle of value and rule.

"Privilege." In English, the word originally referred to a public law that affected one individual only. Etymologically, it means *privus-lex*: private law. The notion, I think, is invaluable in understanding the antirhetorical attitude. I take law to be a means of interpretation composed of three elements: (1) a method of determining what happened, (2) an a priori code against which what happened is held for comparison, and with reference to which it is ultimately "placed," or judged, and (3) a means of pronouncing or enforcing justice. A private law grants all three elements to an individual, leaving him to determine by himself what happened, to judge it by his own private moral code, and to pronounce and enforce that judgment as he sees fit. Normally a privilege is conferred on an individual by established authority, and there is substantial public agreement about the contents of the code to be privately applied and enforced. But a person may also claim a privilege, in defiance of public authority, when he believes that his convictions are not being served by that authority. This privilege is thus a sort of vigilantism that exists to legitimate the convictions and judgments of one person. Such a privileging of individual judgment is at the heart of the antirhetorical attitude because it overthrows the skeptical faith of humanist rhetorical practice.

Wyatt's plainness, then, offers a mainly private alternative to rhetorical skepticism's use of language. It rejects the goal of communal knowing as too dependent on the good faith of others, the ideal of skeptical inquiry or diffidence as an invitation to moral chaos and individual weakness. It proposes instead a self determined to uphold its convictions by claiming and enacting a privilege that, on the one hand, protects the self's purity by withdrawing its judgment and standards from questioning and, on the other, attacks the enemies of those convictions.

The failure to recognize the nature and importance of convic-

tion and privilege in Wyatt is the weakness of Stephen Greenblatt's fine essay on the poet. He sees the tension between anger
and withdrawal in Wyatt's work, and, in a triad of manliness,
realism, and individuality, provides a good explanation of the first
half of it. But his account of inwardness is less successful in
explaining Wyatt's withdrawal as it occurs outside the psalms. If,
as Greenblatt says, inwardness is to result from saying no to the
power of the court, there must be an alternative to which one is
saying yes, and Greenblatt makes it clear in his discussion of
Wyatt's satires that he finds no such alternative. "What is left to
express in this 'unaffected self-expression?'" he asks, and has no
answer.[9] In the absence of any affirmative values, the wish to
withdraw seems like a sulky and impetuous childishness, entirely unable to balance the momentous power plays of the court.

Another excellent study, Thomas Greene's chapter on Wyatt in
The Light in Troy, gives a more satisfactory account of Wyatt's
withdrawal. At the center of Wyatt's poetry, Greene sees "trouth,"
"the Chaucerian word that organizes Wyatt's moral code."

> In a philosophical context *trouth* meant "reality"; in a social con-
> text it meant a covenant, the kind of engagement on which the
> medieval system of fealty rested; ethically, it meant "integrity," a
> recognized continuity in word and act that renders a man authen-
> tic, which is to say real; psychologically, *trouth* meant "faith" or
> "trust," a disposition to credit realities, including the supreme
> Reality; in this sense, it was one of the three theological virtues. It
> also meant, as early as 1380, "a true statement, a true doctrine, an
> established principle"(*OED*).[10]

Greene's "trouth" is undeniably one of the central terms in Wyatt, and his essay's reminder of the Chaucerian and medieval

---

[9] Stephen Greenblatt, *Renaissance Self-Fashioning from More to Shakespeare*
(Chicago: University of Chicago Press, 1980), p. 131.

[10] Thomas Greene, *The Light in Troy: Imitation and Discovery in Renaissance
Poetry* (New Haven: Yale University Press, 1982), pp. 254–55. Both Greenblatt and
Greene mention Wyatt's plainness in passing. Greenblatt observes that Wyatt's
"country simplicity" "is both a life style and a literary style" (129), and indicates
that "the 'plain speaking' of such poems as 'Madam, Withouten Many Words' and
'You Old Mule'" is part of what he means by "realism" (155). Greene notes that
"the drabness of Wyatt's language is of course essential to his moral style" (256).

heritage of the ideal of "trouth" helps us to understand how it could function as a positive ideal of great sustaining power. But although the word "trouth" brings us closer to the source of Wyatt's withdrawal by explaining the positive source of his opposition to a morally bankrupt court, it doesn't reflect the changes that the positive source undergoes in response to courtly pressures. For as Greene admits, "trouth" in Wyatt is fighting a rearguard action and is no longer the confident abstraction of the Middle Ages.

The word "trouth," with its suggestions of medieval community, can't convey the fact that truth in Wyatt has become the product of the aggressive public performance of a private conviction. In Wyatt's anticourtly verse, "trouth" is not subject to debate, judgment is as straightforward as the reasoning of "Blame Not My Lute," and the privilege he claims is in the service of his settled convictions. To this extent his attitude is antirhetorical. But Wyatt also knows that no one has *granted* him this privilege and that he must therefore earn it by persuading his audience to trust his judgment. To this extent his antirhetorical attitude adopts rhetorical means. Consequently his anticourtly poems are not simply the unpremeditated art of an authentic self, but performances—that is, acts that attempt to affect an audience through use of a form. This is not to say there are not important differences between courtly and anticourtly performance. Each honors very different commitments; and, as I will illustrate by comparing Wyatt's courtly plaints to his anticourtly complaints, the difference that results can in good measure be characterized as the difference between rhetorical performance, the performance of dialogic faith, and private plainness, the performance of individual conviction.[11]

In contrasting plaint and complaint, I rely on the modern perception of the difference between "plaining" and "complaining," the one meaning a literary lover's moan, the other a more legalistic expression of a grievance. An understanding of this distinction could be assumed as early as Sidney, who writes in the *Arcadia*

[11] On Wyatt's Petrarchan sonnets, see especially Anne Ferry, *The "Inward" Language: Sonnets of Wyatt, Sidney, Shakespeare, Donne* (Chicago: University of Chicago Press, 1983).

that "Though he plaine, he doth not complaine; for it is a harme, but no wrong, which he has received" (*OED*). Although the two words are used interchangeably in Wyatt's day, the two forms of address are still easily distinguishable.

The characteristic emotional configuration of the plaint is illustrated by ballade 89, "En Voguant la Galère." I quote the third stanza:

> By seas and hills elonged from thy sight,
> Thy wonted grace reducing to my mind,
> In stead of sleep thus I occupy the night.
> A thousand thoughts and many doubts I find
> And still I trust thou canst not be unkind,
> Or else despair my comfort, and my cheer
> Would flee forthwith *en voguant la galère*.
>
> (89)

The language of the poem might be described, in contrast to the quasi-legal language of Wyatt's emphatic plainness, as quasi-religious: the lady, who, after the address to Cytherea in the first stanza, gradually merges with the goddess and emerges as the poem's chief audience and object of affection, is the poet's "joy," "delight," and "bliss"; her "absence" breeds "despair"; in waiting for her "grace," he alternates between "hope and fear" and needs to surrender his "will," conquer his "doubts," and show "trust" and "faith." It is a poem of great longing, made more poignant by the lover's awareness that the lady's affection may well be cold and by his determination nevertheless to remain faithful. Faithful in this context actually means "full of faith," and it is the idea of faith, in the rhetorical sense as much as the religious sense, that is the key to the performance of the poem—that is to say, to the relation of the speaker and his audience.

By calling the performance of "En Voguant La Galère" rhetorical, I refer particularly to the situation in which faith depends on words rather than the Word, in which "only words do me retain." Wyatt depends, like anyone engaging in a rhetorical process, on the good faith of his partner. If they are to share understanding and learn from each other's perspective, she must keep up her part of the bargain by continuing to act as his community, the body with which he desires to remain in contact. But he must also do his part, and his words are the evidence that he intends to persevere, the words not only witnessing his faith but also helping to create it.

Such rhetorical performance involves its speaker in a paradoxical relation of weak dependency and artful mastery. In Wyatt's plaints the weakness often appears as a disavowal of all linguistic facility. The plaint, after all, is a moan or a sigh, and therefore tends, in theory, to the speechless. We hear, for example, of plaining "without tongue" (17), and we are told that "If many sighs, with little speech to plain . . . / Be sign of love, then do I love again" (28). It is as if the lover wishes to reassure his beloved that he is not seeking linguistic dominance, that he depends on her contribution. At the same time, Wyatt's expressions of verbal helplessness are eloquent indeed, as if to persuade his beloved that his faith is genuine and that he is willing to make the same effort to continue the conversation that he is asking of her. Because he is pleasant, faithful, and in need of a complementary eloquence, the plaints ask, why should she not requite him?

The fortunes of the sigh in Wyatt also show where the plaints cease to be rhetorical. In "Go, Burning Sighs," Wyatt's mistress has stepped outside the arena of faith, and Wyatt, in attempting to "break the ice" of her "frozen heart," must respond with a different type of sigh:

> I must go work, I see, by craft and art
> For truth and faith in her is laid apart.
> Alas, I cannot therefore assail her
> With pitiful plaint and scalding fire
> That out of my breast doth strainably start.
>   Go, burning sighs.
>
> (3)

The most direct approach—"pitiful plaint and scalding fire"—is not acceptable because she doesn't share his desire or his faith. He must therefore sigh in a way that will craftily and artfully return

her to the fold. Far from acting in good faith, he attempts through
his artful sighs to manipulate her with the violence suggested by
"break" (not, as it might be, "melt"). Although he may wish to
reestablish a rhetorical relationship, then, his own faith rings
hollow in view of his unwillingness to accept her choice. The
possible need for a crafty sigh thus reminds one of the limits of
rhetoric: the lady's affection may turn out to be cold after all, or
she may otherwise violate her faith, or the lover's doubts may be
too much for his faith. In any case the fragile relation that sus-
tains rhetoric would have broken down.

These possibilities are underscored in Wyatt's plaints by hints
of a more unruly passion beneath the courtly rituals. This passion
is addressed explicitly and conventionally as *rage*, and Wyatt's
version of a common conceit in Italian love poetry describes the
qualities it often displays in "plaining" poetry:

> From these high hills as when a spring doth fall
> It trilleth down with still and subtle course,
> Of this and that it gathers ay and shall
> Till it have just off flowed the stream and force,
> Then at the foot it rageth over all—
> So fareth love when he hath ta'en a source:
> His rein is rage; resistance vaileth none;
> The first eschew is remedy alone.
>
> (47)

Love as rage is irresistible and uncontrollable, a source of passion
leading inexorably either to satisfaction or destruction. Like the
thymos and the hegemonicon, it is its own law. The poem itself,
however, is carefully governed; here and in Wyatt's plaints, rage is
made to *feel* like less of a threat than it is described as being or
than it does when Wyatt issues a stern Boethian warning in "If
Thou Wilt Mighty Be":

> If thou wilt mighty be, flee from the rage
> Of cruel will, and see thee keep thee free
> From the foul yoke of sensual bondage.
>
> (84)

In the plaints, rage is restrained by the lady's grace, by

> The sweet disdains, the pleasant wraths, and eke the lovely strife
> That wonted well to tune, in temper just and meet,
> The rage that oft did make me err by furor undiscreet.
>
> (76)

Yet there is still enough reality to this "fervent raging ire" (83) to make us wonder occasionally whether this lover might not be capable of more threatening emotions than desire and sorrow; whether, in fact, the rhetorical conventions of courtly plaining do not serve a useful purpose in socializing individual desires.

Wyatt's plaints, therefore, are not exclusively rhetorical performances. In addition to reassuring their audience of the author's intention to act in the manner prescribed by the good faith relationship of rhetoric, they suggest the possibility of action in proscribed areas—especially if the lady doesn't assist in the creation of the good faith relationship. They suggest, that is, that the author may be motivated partly by an antirhetorical conviction, by a commitment stronger than his rhetorical faith. As such they constitute a veiled threat: "beware my rage!" In this way they adumbrate the type of performance Wyatt offers in his complaints.

The complaints respond to a situation in which conviction overpowers faith and in which, consequently, the separation feared and the rage hinted at in the plaints have become accomplished facts, embraced by the speaker in the forms of withdrawal and anger. But Wyatt tries to do more than simply vent his anger and declare his independence in the complaints: he also tries to earn the privilege of enforcing his convictions. How he does so depends on whether his self-assertiveness or his self-sufficiency is in the ascendant. If the former, he seeks to persuade by pronouncing his convictions so forcefully that opposition seems impossible—physically and emotionally as much as intellectually. In one complaint, for instance, Wyatt spends five stanzas rehearsing his beloved's promise and her breaking of it. Each of the five begins with the phrase "Thy promise was" and repeats it twice more in the refrain line. The third stanza, for example, is as follows:

> Thy promise was, I tell thee plain,
> My faith should not be spent in vain,
> But to have more should be my gain
> Thy promise was, thy promise was.
>
> (214)

In the sixth and final stanza Wyatt varies the formula to deliver his own "promise":

> But since to change thou dost delight
> And that thy faith hath ta'en flight,
> As thou deserv'st I shall thee quit
> I promise thee, I promise thee.

The emphatic rhythm and argument here, like those of "Blame Not My Lute," attempt to compel belief by sheer force of will, almost by intimidation. How could anyone disagree? It's all so plain—*of course* his requital is just. Or so we are supposed to think. For firmly stated conviction is itself very persuasive.

If, on the other hand, Wyatt's independence outweighs his self-assertiveness, the emphatically vengeful tone of "Thy Promise Was" can give way to the sadness, restraint, and dignity expressed in one of Wyatt's best poems, "O, Cruel Heart":

> O, cruel heart, where is thy faith?
> Where is become thy steadfast vow?
> Thy sobbing sighs with fainting breath,
> Thy bitter tears, where are they now?
>
> Thy careful looks, thy piteous plaint,
> Thy woeful words, thy wonted cheer?
> Now may I see thou didst but paint
> And all thy craft doth plain appear. . . .
>
> To trust why did I condescend,
> And yield myself so earnestly

To her that did nothing intend
But thus to trap me craftily? . . .

And from thy words if thou wilt swerve
And swear thou didst them never say,
Thy tokens yet I do reserve
That shall declare the hour and day,

The hour and day, the time and where
That thou thyself didst them indite,
Wherein thou show'dst what dread and fear
Thou hadst once spied thy bills to write.

This proof I think may well suffice
To prove it true that here I speak.
No forged tales will I devise
But with thy hand I shall me wreak. . . .

And thus, farewell, most cruel heart.
Farewell thy falsed faith also.
Farewell my sighs, farewell my smart.
Farewell my love and all my woe.

                    (234; st. 1–2, 5, 9–11, 13)

The poem is as convincing as any of Wyatt's complaints. Like
many of them, the poem is a farewell, but unlike the vengeful
complaints it handles its withdrawal from emotional involvement relatively calmly and gently. The carefully additive and
sometimes repetitive structure produces a movement that is almost contemplative, as if he is remembering one last time what
she looked like, what she said, how he loved her. As the poem
proceeds, the contemplative tone merges with the expository, and
he seems to be explaining things to himself as much as to her. He
seems as well to be explaining things to a larger audience: although he reserves his conclusive proof for another day, he appears to be trying to close the case at a preliminary hearing, an
impression created partly by his third-person reference to her in
the fifth stanza, but more importantly by his careful explanation
of his position. Because he gives reasons, describes his evidence,
and even accepts his share of the blame, his statement that "Each

thing upon thy shame shall sound" seems more like a dispassion-
ate conclusion than a personal vendetta. And it is the dispassion-
ateness of the poem, its withdrawal, that is the core of its performance. "Blame Not My Lute" also claims to record the truth
accurately, to leave "No doubt" who is wrong, and to leave the
lady to reap what she has sown. Both poems share the "eye for an
eye" ethic of revenge. But in "O, Cruel Heart" we neither hear nor
see much evidence of the spite with which he will answer hers.
Instead, he cleverly makes her own hand the instrument of his
revenge. In this way he avoids the continuing emotional involvement betrayed by the speaker of "Blame Not My Lute," proving
himself strong enough to accept the sorrow of his undeserved loss.
Withdrawal has become a persuasive statement of conviction.

The conviction of Wyatt's complaints thus presents a striking
contrast to the uncertainty of his plaints. Whereas in "They Flee
from Me" Wyatt famously finishes the poem asking what the lady
deserves, in "Blame Not My Lute" and "Thy Promise Was" all
possibility of doubt has dissolved. We can see this movement
from doubt to conviction in miniature in a Wyatt poem that
changes from plaint to complaint only in the last two lines. I
quote the last stanza of "When That I Call unto My Mind":

> As I am one which by restraint
> Abides the time of my return
> In hope that fortune by my plaint
> Will slake the fire wherewith I burn
> Since no ways else may serve my turn,
> Yet for the doubt of this distress
> I ask by right for my redress.
>
> (185)

"Doubt," part of the quasi-religious language in which courtly
plaints are commonly couched, gives way to the conviction associated with questions of "right"—or if it doesn't actually give way
so late in this poem, at least the opposition is clear. So while both
plaints and complaints wish to persuade, the plaint attempts to
do so from a position (real or assumed) of dependence and shared
doubt and faith, whereas the complaint addresses its audience
with the powerful determination of independent conviction.

It may be argued that Wyatt is attempting to convince himself of his own resolve in his complaints, and no doubt this is partly right. Wyatt is, in a very real sense, part of his own audience, and the thought processes of the poems are at least partly his own.[12] My point, however, is that he requires a public profession of his belief to convince himself: only by persuading others of the justice of his own convictions can he reassure himself of their foundation in his own absolute sense of right. He needs to earn the public sanction of privilege partly to maintain his own solitary convictions. Although he has no wish for true dialogue, his attitude is not completely antirhetorical, and his independence is not complete. He needs an audience in front of whom he can perform his convictions, and so earn his privilege.

"Plainness" is a better term than "trouth" to describe Wyatt's antirhetorical poetry because it accounts for his anger as well as his withdrawal and thereby describes the performance of the poems. Truth is always threatening to slip away in Wyatt; it is always something that cannot be taken for granted as an abstraction, but that must instead be illustrated by the actions of a true person, that must be performed. Further, because "plainness" also signifies the private and inner dimension of "trouth" in Wyatt, reflecting in the plain heart the effort to retain conviction by turning inward, it records the foundation of Wyatt's truth in the action of privileging individual judgment. Plainness is the performance of conviction.

The effort to retain—or to find—conviction is the center of much of Wyatt's work. Finding his "trouth" attacked by unfaithful mistresses and unjust courtiers alike, Wyatt develops a defensive posture that counterattacks aggressively even as it shrinks from contact with the hostile forces. Consequently, his complaints display a mixture of anger and sorrow, of a righteous indignation that tries to justify itself by appealing to a quasi-legal code of ethics and a stoic resignation to the inevitability of a lonely existence in a strange world. "Plainness" is the term that best encompasses the performance of these extremes, signifying a con-

[12] See Walter Ong's suggestive essay, "Voice as Summons for Belief: Literature, Faith, and the Divided Self," *Thought* 32 (1958), 43–61.

viction that is neither genuinely confident of its communal acceptability nor yet willing to open itself to skeptical questioning. Chaucer, perhaps, wrote at the end of an age of "trouth"; Wyatt writes at the beginning of an age of plainness.

2 Educational Authority and the Plain Truth in the Admonition Controversy and *The Scholemaster*

To describe Wyatt's plainness as private and antirhetorical is not to deny that it possesses public and rhetorical qualities. Indeed, the presence of "trouth" in Wyatt's poetry guarantees a degree of responsiveness to public pressures, and his performance seeks public justification through means that are in part rhetorical. Still, his voice remains relatively isolated, his plainness relatively private. Its cornerstone remains a conviction that is his alone. But plainness need not be so solitary. In particular, reforming movements in sixteenth-century England tended to remain plain in character while enlisting considerable popular support.

Given the public nature of rhetoric and the (at least as it seems to modern eyes) ultimately individual nature of conviction, the notion of a public plainness may seem paradoxical. It may also seem to be at odds with the facts of reform. After all, for a dissenting community to flourish in Renaissance England (and beyond, since the chief reforming movements were international) it had to be able to recognize and adjust to historical differences, to the variations in class, education, and local tradition that marked its potential membership, in order that it might enlist the efforts of a significant number of people in support of its vision of truth. It thus had to some extent to be rhetorical. But while in the more Erasmian forms of reform these inclusive, rhetorical tendencies may have played a particularly important role, reforming movements were usually built upon the foundation provided by a plain source of truth.[1] Reformers believed they knew and acted in accordance with an unchanging law, and this belief entailed a high degree of antirhetorical exclusiveness. The educational task reforming movements faced of building communities out of conviction forced them to perform a difficult balancing act: they required a literary performance that could combine the public flexibility of rhetorical performance with the strength and privilege of antirhetorical conviction. They required, that is, an antirhetorical rhetoric, a performance of conviction no less determined than Wyatt's, but more public than private.

In this chapter I study the role of public plainness in institutionalizing feeling faith in the Puritan *Admonition to Parliament* of 1572 and in the Protestant humanist Roger Ascham's *Scholemaster* (1570). I also set these texts in the context of the two major reforming movements of the century, the Reformation and humanism. My point in doing so is not that these writers are necessarily representative or, indeed, that such movements are self-contained or easily defined, but rather that glancing at the background (the problems presented for education by the notions of *theodidacti* and a plain Word, and by the opposed ideals of philosophical truth and rhetorical conversation) is a helpful way to organize an approach to this aspect of these texts. My goal is to illustrate public plainness by showing how, despite their differences, the two texts pursue similar solutions to the problem of maintaining the educational authority of conviction in movements predicated to some extent on the universal accessibility of truth.

Preaching the Word

The Reformation conception of a Word of God that was both plain to the understanding of all readers and sufficient to guide

---

[1] On English Erasmianism, see Fritz Caspari, *Humanism and the Social Order in Tudor England* (Chicago: University of Chicago Press, 1954); James Kelsey McConica, *English Humanists and Reformation Politics under Henry VIII and Edward VI* (Oxford: Clarendon Press, 1965); and Margo Todd, *Christian Humanism and the Puritan Social Order* (Cambridge: Cambridge University Press, 1987).

their lives in all situations threatened at least in theory to eliminate the function of human teachers and to render believers entirely theodidacti, those taught of God.[2] Spurred by this view of
the Word, Reformers aimed to replace the authority of church
tradition and hierarchy, which could inspire no more than a historical faith, with the authority of Scripture as it was known to
the feeling faith of the believer. Such a project rested on the assumption that the Scriptures were a source of plain and incontrovertible doctrine, of a truth that only the wicked would dispute.[3] Consequently, like the humanism to which it was so
closely linked, the Reformation rejected the language of scholastic controversy in favor of the language of ordinary life and the
"plain sense of Scripture."[4] Specialized knowledge was infinitely
less valuable than faith, Erasmus wrote, in leading one to "a good
life, the path to which Christ intended to be accessible to all, not
by way of a difficult labyrinth of argument but by a sincere faith
and by an unfeigned charity which a confident hope accom-

---

[2] The term *theodidacti* derives from John 6:45 (King James version): "It is written in the prophets, And they shall be all taught of God. Every man therefore that
hath heard, and hath learned of the Father, cometh unto me." Reformation writers
commonly associated this text with having the law written in one's heart. Luther,
for example, refers to it in the last paragraph of *The Freedom of a Christian* (1520):
"Therefore there is need of the prayer that the Lord may give us and make us
theodidacti, that is, those taught by God [John 6:45], and himself, as he has
promised, write his law in our hearts." Tyndale connects the idea directly to his
concept of a feeling faith: "But of a feeling faith it is written (John vi.), 'They shall
be all taught of God.' That is, God shall write it in their hearts with his Holy
Spirit." See *Martin Luther: Selections from His Writings*, ed. John Dillenberger
(New York: Doubleday, 1961), p. 85; and *An Answer to Sir Thomas More's Dialogue* (1530), ed. Henry Walter, Parker Society, vol. 44 (Cambridge: Cambridge
University Press, 1850), p. 51.

[3] The contribution of this conception of Scripture to the acrimony of
Reformation-era controversial writings is suggested by Michael G. Baylor. This
"notion of Scripture," he writes, "must . . . be kept in mind to comprehend why
Luther could treat so harshly his opponents who appealed, as he did, to their
conscience. Given Luther's confidence in Scripture as a clear and simple revelation of divine authority, he could not accept that equally sincere individuals could
arrive at scriptural conclusions opposed to his own." See *Action and Person:
Conscience in Late Scholasticism and the Young Luther*, Studies in Medieval and
Reformation Thought, vol. 20 (Leiden: E. J. Brill, 1977), p. 268.

[4] On the popular influence on Reformation plainness, see John N. King, *English
Reformation Literature: The Tudor Origins of the Protestant Tradition* (Princeton: Princeton University Press, 1982), chap. 3, "Vox Populi, Vox Dei."

panies."[5] Luther, too, recognized the potential danger to the Reformation of an unclear Word when he ridiculed the specialized language of the doctrine of transubstantiation. The Scriptures' "plainest meanings are to be preserved; and, unless the context manifestly compels one to do otherwise, the words are not to be understood apart from their proper and literal sense, lest occasion be given to our adversaries to evade Scripture as a whole."[6] If the meaning truly was plain to all, Luther and the other Reformers had no need to fear exegetical controversies. But the force of "unless the context manifestly compels one to do otherwise" is to admit that the meaning may not be plain, that interpretation and teachers may after all be necessary—even as it insists ("manifestly") that such moments of darkness must themselves plainly mean something else. The question, then, is, If Scripture is not always to be understood in its plain sense, if, as Erasmus wrote, "the strange and frequently involved language as well as the figures of speech and oblique metaphors give such difficulty that even we ourselves must often make a great effort before we understand them,"[7] then what are the criteria by which the plainness or darkness, and hence the truth, of Scripture can be judged?

For example, probably no theological question divided the Reformers more than the meaning of the Lord's Supper. Luther, holding to the more conservative position, affirmed the "real presence" of Christ in the sacrament, while Zwingli and others argued for a spiritual presence only. One of the many contributions to this controversy was Archbishop Edmund Grindal's *Dialogue between Custom and Verity* (1559). In it Custom takes the Lutheran line, maintaining that the words "this is my body" "are evident and plain." Verity argues against the plain sense of the words: Scripture, she argues, "is not so to be taken always as the letter soundeth, but as the intent and purpose of the Holy Ghost was. . . . For if you follow the bare words, you will soon shake

[5] Desiderius Erasmus, "Letter to Paul Volz, 14 August 1518," in *Christian Humanism and the Reformation: Selected Writings of Erasmus*, ed. John C. Olin, 3d ed. (1965; rpt. New York: Fordham University Press, 1987), p. 112.

[6] Martin Luther, *The Babylonian Captivity of the Church* (1520), in *Martin Luther: Selections*, ed. Dillenberger, p. 266.

[7] Erasmus, "Letter to Paul Volz," p. 114.

down and overthrow the greatest part of the christian faith." Custom replies that Verity must have "strong and likely reasons" to overthrow the plain sense of the words, and, indeed, Verity marshalls an impressive array of arguments to determine "the meaning and purpose" for which the words were spoken. Her arguments fall into three categories: she studies the context of the disputed text, examining other Scriptures as well as the audience and occasion for Christ's remark; she sets out syllogisms; and she quotes generously from the church fathers. By these means she clarifies the text and wins the argument (Custom is silent at the end). In her own terms she makes plain a text that is obscure: "Thus by the word of God, by reason, and by the old fathers it is plain, that sinful men eat not the body of Christ"; "it is plain that Christ's body is meat for our spirit."[8]

What is striking in Grindal's dialogue is the need to return to the claim to plain truth, to end by implying the redundancy of the magisterial apparatus so carefully set up to explain why the plain sense of Scripture isn't the plain sense of Scripture. There is a conflict between epistemological ideals submerged in the text, between, briefly, the ideal of common access to truth through God's grace and the ideal of the truth of reason accessible through learning. A Reformer must always acknowledge that grace is the source of all authority. Grindal is no exception: though Verity's arguments all appeal to the intellect, her claim has been that the "obscure places in the scripture" are "not so obscure, but that a man with the grace of God may perceive" (52). Further, grace is in need of no natural assistance because, as Luther writes, if God "does not teach our hearts this wisdom hidden in mystery [1 Cor. 2:7], nature can only condemn it."[9] Even the suggestion that reason may assist interpretation when "the context manifestly compels one" to reject the plain sense fails to produce criteria than can supplement the judgments of faith. For example, Luther disagreed with those who, like Grindal, argued against the literal

[8] Edmund Grindal, *Dialogue between Custom and Verity*, in *The Remains of Archbishop Grindal*, ed. William Nicholson, Parker Society, vol. 19 (Cambridge: Cambridge University Press, 1843), pp. 40, 42, 59, 52. Another reference appears in the text.

[9] Luther, *Freedom of a Christian*, p. 85.

reading of "this is my body": "When I fail to understand how bread can be the body of Christ, I, for one, will take my understanding prisoner and bring it into obedience to Christ; and, holding fast with a simple mind to His words, I will firmly believe, not only that the body of Christ is in the bread, but that the bread is the body of Christ."[10] Faith can be used in this way to overrule any claims made on behalf of the understanding. Similarly, whatever authority the church has derives not from reason but from "the illumination of the spirit": "When doctrines come up for decision and approval," Luther writes, "the church possesses a 'sense' whose presence is certain, though it cannot be proved."[11] Both the church and the individual believer depend in this way on the Spirit to clarify dark and uncertain texts. But the role of the Reformed church as a teaching institution exposes the epistemological conflict; for if the church has no source of enlightenment other than that promised to every believer, why does the believer need a church or priests? Luther anticipates this question: "You will ask, 'If all who are in the church are priests, how do these whom we now call priests differ from laymen?'"[12] His answer, however—that Scripture speaks of a preaching ministry and that "although we are all equally priests, we cannot all publicly minister and teach" (65)—fails to resolve the fundamental question raised by the conflict of plain and learned authorities: if the Scriptures are sufficient and accessible to all, what is the purpose of preaching the Word?[13]

[10] Luther, *Babylonian Captivity*, p. 269.

[11] Luther, *Babylonian Captivity*, p. 341.

[12] Luther, *Freedom of a Christian*, p. 65.

[13] For the impact of the Reformation on educational practices, see Norman Wood, *The Reformation and English Education: A Study of the Influence of Religious Uniformity on English Education in the Sixteenth Century* (London: Routledge, 1931), chaps. 5 and 8; H. C. Porter, *Reformation and Reaction in Tudor Cambridge* (Cambridge: Cambridge University Press, 1958); Joan Simon, *Education and Society in Tudor England* (Cambridge: Cambridge University Press, 1966), part 2, "The Reformation in England, 1536–1553"; Gerald Strauss, *Luther's House of Learning: Indoctrination of the Young in the German Reformation* (Baltimore: Johns Hopkins University Press, 1978); C. M. Dent, *Protestant Reformers in Elizabethan Oxford* (Oxford: Oxford University Press, 1983); and Michael Van Cleave Alexander, *The Growth of English Education 1348–1648* (University Park: Pennsylvania State University Press, 1990), chaps. 5, 8, and 9. Simon concludes that "Puritanism did not wither the humanist heritage, even though

The continuing pressure of this question leads to an odd moment of self-consciousness when Luther begins his preface to the New Testament by noting that "it would be only right and proper if this volume were published without any preface," then goes on to outline his conception of the essentials of the faith.[14] An even more awkward moment occurs in Tyndale's preface "To the Reader" in *The Obedience of a Christian Man*. Tyndale anticipates that his program of vernacular translation and private Bible reading will raise an objection, which he places in the mouth of an interlocutor: "By this means, then, thou wilt that no man teach another, but that every man take the scripture, and learn by himself." Tyndale answers that this is not what he means. "Nevertheless," he continues, "seeing that ye will not teach, if any man thirst for the truth, and read the scripture by himself, desiring God to open the door of knowledge unto him, God for his truth's sake will and must teach him." Having said this, however, Tyndale goes on to describe the function he sees teachers fulfilling:

> Howbeit, my meaning is, that as a master teacheth his apprentice to know all the points of the meteyard; first, how many inches, how many feet, and the halfyard, the quarter, and the nail, and then teacheth him to mete other things thereby: even so will I that ye teach the people God's law, and what obedience God requireth of us to father and mother, master, lord, king, and all superiors, and with what friendly love he commandeth one to love another. . . . So would it come to pass, that as we know by natural wit what followeth of a true principle of natural reason; even so, by the principles of the faith, and by the plain scriptures, and by the circumstances of the text, should we judge all men's exposition, and all men's doctrine, and should receive the best, and refuse the worst.[15]

---

schools became progressively more godly, but rather developed this tradition, fostering studies as a means to the realisation of religious and social ends" (400–401).

[14] Martin Luther, Preface to the New Testament (1522), in *Martin Luther: Selections*, ed. Dillenberger, p. 14.

[15] William Tyndale, *The Obedience of a Christian Man* (1528), in *Expositions and Notes on Sundry Portions of the Holy Scriptures, together with the Practice of Prelates*, ed. Henry Walter, Parker Society, vol. 43 (Cambridge: Cambridge University Press, 1849), p. 156.

Tyndale apparently wants to distinguish "principles" from "doctrine," so that once we are taught the one we can judge the other. But how do we know that we've been taught the right principles? Tyndale is in effect arguing that people must be taught the faith so that they'll be capable of judging whether they are being taught the faith correctly.

If the circularity of such passages and of the enterprise they announce failed to trouble Luther and Tyndale, their critics recognized that the appeal to the plain sense of Scripture might disguise an attempt to substitute the Reformers' own doctrines for those of the Catholic church. More, for example, accused Luther of just such a reversal:

> For this one poynt is the very fond foundacyon and grounde of all his greate heresyes / that a man is not bounden to byleve any thynge but yf it may be provyd evydently by scrypture. And there uppon goth he so farforth / that no scrypture can be evydent to prove any thyng that he lyst to deny. For he wyll not agre it for evydent be it never so playn. And he wyll call evydent for hym that texte / that is evydent agaynst hym. And somtyme if it be to playne agaynste hym / than wyll he call it no scrypture / as he playth with the pystle of saynt Jamys.[16]

In the absence of any shared criteria for interpreting the meaning of Scripture, claiming that one believes something because Scripture plainly says it is no different from claiming that Scripture plainly says something because one believes it.

As modern critics and historians have remarked, the hermeneutic uncertainty to which such circular claims contributed allowed new forms of authority to slip into Reformation writings. Janel Mueller, for example, argues that "the exercise of linguistic authority" in Tyndale's Pauline style "arises from the resolve to provide for individual responses to Scripture and nonetheless warrant that all of them will be like in kind"; and Robert Weimann claims that Luther replaces the hierarchical authority of the me-

---

[16] Thomas More, *A Dialogue Concerning Heresies* (1529), in *The Complete Works of St. Thomas More*, vol. 6, ed. Thomas M. C. Lawler, Germain Marc'hadour, and Richard C. Marius (New Haven: Yale University Press, 1981), pp. 148–49.

dieval church with a "new concept of authority" that "is associated . . . with the deepest intellectual grasp of biblical meaning."[17] Of these two analyses, Weimann's is the less helpful, for it
leaves unanswered the question of what constitutes "intellectual
grasp." Is it an ability to harmonize different passages from Scripture? To harmonize the Bible and classical learning? Does it include experience, to which Luther often appealed? Most crucially,
by whom, or by what standards, is it to be judged? Indeed, how
does it differ from the "reason" of the medieval church? Mueller's
suggestion that authority is created by a writer's or speaker's
ability to direct an audience to a like perception, on the other
hand, seems truer to a condition of upheaval in which the new
faith progressed largely by its ability to create tightly knit communities of like-minded believers. Weimann is right to draw attention to the importance of learned authority in the Reformation, but its role there tends to be a secondary and, possibly, a
conservative one. When we look at the more radical forms of
Protestantism, we find, I believe, that authority is more a function of the affective power of linguistic performance to turn dispa-
rate individual experiences into a common conviction of religious
truth.

The controversy surrounding the publication in 1572 of *An
Admonition to the Parliament* illustrates the problem of educational authority in a radical Protestant context. Published in response to Queen Elizabeth's ban on 22 May of that year on parliamentary consideration of religious bills, the *Admonition*, written
by the Puritan ministers John Field and Thomas Wilcox, put forward the biblical case for Presbyterianism and expressed the hope
that Parliament might become the agent of reform that Convoca-
tion had failed to become.[18] The *Admonition* is noteworthy not

[17] Janel Mueller, *The Native Tongue and the Word: Developments in English
Prose Style, 1380–1580* (Chicago: University of Chicago Press, 1984), p. 198; Robert Weimann, "History and the Issue of Authority in Representation: The Elizabethan Theater and the Reformation," *New Literary History* 17 (1986), 460.

[18] Historians generally agree with J. E. Neale that this hope is genuine, and that
while the *Admonition* was "not presented to Parliament, . . . it was certainly
intended to influence opinion in the House of Commons" (*Elizabeth I and Her
Parliaments, 1559–1581* [London: Jonathan Cape, 1953], 297). Elliot Rose observes
that "if the authors themselves did not literally expect that parliament to do their

just as the first open manifesto of Presbyterian doctrine, but also for being "more outspoken than anything that had yet been published by protestants against protestants in England."[19] It thus stirred the controversial pot, extending the influence of a style of debate based very largely on the forceful declaration of conviction, and it was followed within several years by a flurry of pamphlets and treatises on both sides of the debate.

The controversy turns on the question of whether the Bible provides a complete model for church government in the form of a depiction of a primitive church. Archbishop John Whitgift, the main combatant for the Conformist cause, argued that Scripture was sufficient in all matters directly related to salvation, but that on inessential matters (*adiaphora*) such as church government Christians were left to their own devices, to, that is, reason, learning, and tradition. If a practice wasn't expressly forbidden in Scripture, it was permitted (provided, of course, that it was judged to be in accordance with the general principles of the faith). On the other hand, the Admonitioners, or the Admonitors, as Field and Wilcox became known, and Thomas Cartwright, who championed the Puritan cause after the *Second Admonition*, insisted that a model was present in Scripture, that any practice not specifically authorized by Scripture was forbidden, and, moreover, that church government was essential to salvation.[20] In fact, it is

---

work, they intended that their readers should have that kind of expectation, of that parliament or (given the time factor) more likely some other parliament" (*Cases of Conscience: Alternatives open to Recusants and Puritans under Elizabeth I and James I* [Cambridge: Cambridge University Press, 1975], 228).

[19] Patrick Collinson, *The Elizabethan Puritan Movement* (Oxford: Clarendon Press, 1967), p. 119. Although J. E. Neale asserted that the *Admonition* "marked the definite adoption by the party, or at least of its clerical leaders, of a Presbyterian platform" (*Elizabeth I and Her Parliaments, 1559–1581*, 296), Collinson notes that the *Admonition* was considered extreme in both matter and manner by most Puritan leaders and that a "more moderate brand of puritanism" remained the norm for some time after (120).

[20] Few historians now believe that Cartwright wrote the *Second Admonition*. Arguments against his authorship are presented by A. F. Scott Pearson, *Thomas Cartwright and Elizabethan Puritanism, 1535–1603* (Cambridge: Cambridge University Press, 1925), p. 74; M. M. Knappen, *Tudor Puritanism* (Chicago: University of Chicago Press, 1939), pp. 235–36; and Collinson, *Elizabethan Puritan Movement*, p. 139. Collinson suggests Christopher Goodman as a possible author. Cartwright's authorship is accepted by Donald Joseph McGinn, *The Admonition Con-*

probably a fair comment on the Puritan position to say that it rejects the essential/inessential distinction, seeing all aspects of life—with the possible exception of civil government—as essential. Consequently, Cartwright declares that Scripture contains a perfect model not only for church government, but for all of life: "I saye that the word of God contayneth the direction of all things pertayning to the church / yea of what soever things can fall into any part of mans life."[21] What Cartwright particularly objected to in the Conformist position was the suggestion that human authorities might substitute for God's; he saw and rejected the belief that "there is some star or light off reason / or learninge or other helpe / whereby some act may be well doone / and acceptably unto God / in which the worde off God was shut out / and not called to counsaile: as that which either could not / or neede not / give any direction in that behalfe."[22] For the Puritans, then, Scripture was the sole authority in all or virtually all matters, containing, in the words of the *Admonition*, "all fulness and sufficiencie to decide controversies."[23]

Since the Puritans believed that the Scriptures were by and large plain as well as sufficient, they wanted them taught directly, with a minimum of mediation. Hence the *Admonition* sounds

---

troversy, Rutgers Studies in English, no. 5 (New Brunswick: Rutgers University Press, 1949), pp. 49–50, 547. Easily the best literary analysis of Cartwright's contribution to the Admonition controversy is Ritchie D. Kendall's chapter "Thomas Cartwright: The Drama of Disputation" in *The Drama of Dissent: The Radical Poetics of Nonconformity, 1380–1590* (Chapel Hill: University of North Carolina Press, 1986), esp. pp. 157–72. Kendall's reading focuses on the "tense balance between reasoned and inspired speech" in Cartwright's disputational writings (165).

21 T.C. [Thomas Cartwright], *A Replye to an answere made of M. Doctor Whitegifte Against the Admonition to the Parliament* (London, 1573), p. 159. Further references appear in the text.

22 Thomas Cartwright, *The second replie of Thomas Cartwright: agaynst Maister Doctor Whitgiftes second answer, touching the Church Discipline* (n.p., 1575), p. 56.

23 *An Admonition to the Parliament,* in *Puritan Manifestoes: A Study of the Origin of the Puritan Revolt,* ed. W. H. Frere and C. E. Douglas, Church Historical Society, no. 72 (London: Society for Promoting Christian Knowledge, 1907), p. 24. Further references appear in the text. I am indebted to John S. Coolidge's excellent discussion of the subtle differences between the Puritan and Conformist views of scriptural authority in *The Pauline Renaissance in England: Puritanism and the Bible* (Oxford: Clarendon Press, 1970), chap. 1.

the attack on the elaborate apparatus for teaching the Word that had been inaugurated by Henry VIII, continued under Edward VI, and consolidated under Elizabeth. "Then," Field and Wilcox write in their distinctive formula, "they preached the worde one-ly: now they read homilies, articles, injunctions, etc" (11). Such guides as the homilies, the Book of Common Prayer, and Erasmus's *Paraphrases* must be stripped away so that the Word may be preached "purely," free from the unnecessary excrescences of popish authority:

> Nowe / if a man will saye that the homilies doe explane and laye open the scriptures / I answere that the word of God also is playne and easy to be understanded / and suche as giveth understanding to idiotes and to the symple. And if there be hardnes in them / yet the promise of the assistance of Gods spirite . . . will be able to weighe wyth the hardnes / and to overcome it. (*Replye* 158)

If human writings must be allowed, "those paraphrases whych in explanyng the scrypture / go least from it / and whych kepe not only the numbre of sentences but almost the very numbre of wordes / were of all most fitte to be red in the churche" (*Replye* 197). The closer to the Word of God, the better.

So again the question arises: why teach? Here Cartwright offers a theory of spiritual preaching to support the Puritans' ecclesiastical emphasis on local authority. Sermons excel homilies because they are manufactured on the spot in response to the specific rhetorical demands of their occasion:

> where sermons are applied to the present circumstance / which by chaunge off times / budding off new vices / rising of errors / &c., vary almost every day: this kinde of interpretation [homilies] (as that which is starcke and annumbed) cannot poursue them. For where the preacher with his sermon / is able according to the manifold windinges / and turninges of sinne / to winde / and turne in with yt / to the end he may stricke it: the homilies are not able to turne / nether off the right hand / nor off the left but to what quarter soever the enemies are retyred / yt must keepe the traine wherin it was set off the maker.[24]

24 Cartwright, *Second replie*, p. 395.

The need for flexibility not only makes the reading of homilies unacceptable, it makes the reading of someone else's sermons or even one's own sermon unacceptable: Cartwright's emphasis on immediacy entails something like a doctrine of inspired preaching. He even goes so far as to declare that the "word of God is not so effectuall red as preached," explaining the apparent inconsistency by means of an elaborate string of mostly biblical metaphors: preaching is a "lifting or heaving up of our saviour Christ," like "the displaying of a banner"; it is like cutting meat for easier digestion; it is like planting and watering; it is like unclasping a book; it is like blowing coals into flame; it is like breaking a spice to make it smell sweeter. Cartwright then must backpedal and, Tyndale-like, explain that the Word of God may save even without preaching—although he is less certain of this than is Tyndale: "It may bee that God doth sometymes worke fayth by reading only / especially wher preaching cannot be . . . but the ordinary wayes whereby God regenerateth hys children / is by the word of God / which is preached" (*Replye* 159). Preaching, then, has for Cartwright a rhetorical immediacy that, for some purposes at least, makes it superior to the Scriptures.

Cartwright further explains his sense of the relation of preaching to the Word by means of the Calvinist distinction between pastors and doctors. A pastor is a bishop

> who appliethe the Scriptures to the divers occasions and necessities off the church. . . . And as time and occasion serveth / to correct / reprove / and reprehend / to raise up those that be cast downe / to break the stubburne / to use exhortacions / and dehortacions / to comfort the godly with the hope off the promises / to terrifie the wiked with the thunder off the judgement off god.[25]

---

[25] Walter Travers, *A full and plaine declaration of Ecclesiasticall Discipline*, trans. Thomas Cartwright (n.p., 1584), p. 147. Further references appear in the text. Commonly known as the *Book of Discipline*, Travers's work appeared during the Admonition controversy and soon emerged as the most important statement of the Presbyterian program. I refer to it here to clarify the pastor-doctor distinction, which is present but not fully articulated in Cartwright's *Replye to an answere*. On Travers and the *Book of Discipline* more generally, see S. J. Knox, *Walter Travers: Paragon of Elizabethan Puritanism* (London: Methuen, 1962), and Collinson, *Elizabethan Puritan Movement*, pp. 291–302.

He therefore needs "greate and profounde knowledge to knowe the chaunge off times / the diversitie off thinges / the variety off persons / and to deale thus or otherwise / according to that varietie and difference." Again the office of preaching calls forth some of Cartwright's highest flights of eloquence, as he develops an extended metaphor of the pastor as a physician, who, unlike the homilies, the reading of which "can in no wise be sufficient to cure and to remedy all the sondry necessities off the church," knows "all Eden and the whole garden off God" and so knows "what so ever is proper for the curinge off every disease / and in what sort and after what manner / and at what time yt ys to be ministred and applied" (148). In comparison, a doctor is "as yt were the schole maister and teacher off the principles of Religion," "occupied in the simple teachinge and expoundinge off the holie doctrine and trew religion." He teaches "what to think off every point off Religion without those vehement speeches werby the mindes off men are either raised up and comforted / or beaten downe and made sadd" (138). Doctors are in a sense secondary to pastors, since part of their purpose is to allow pastors "more time to employ in exhorting and dehorting / and applying of the doctrine to the times and places / and persons" (*Replye* 46).

Cartwright's intention in distinguishing doctors from pastors seems straightforward: he wishes to separate the knowledge of doctrine from the gracious desire to act upon it that preaching inspires. The doctor teaches; the pastor preaches. Teaching is intellectual; preaching is affective, assuming that we know the truth but need an infusion of grace to act upon it. Preaching moves hearts, not minds. The distinction relies on an assumption that intellectual knowledge is general in character, while emotion affects the application of general knowledge to particular situations. Hence the biblical Word functions as a reservoir of general wisdom that, when present in the believer, needs only the extra spiritual push of a good sermon to come to life in any historical situation. In this way the main effect of the doctor-pastor distinction is to insulate preaching from reason and interpretation: historical adjustments are affective only.

Such a position is far from straightforward, however. The historical adjustments of time, place, and person that Cartwright expects of preaching are recognized within the rhetorical tradition as imperfect, probabilistic human attempts to adapt to changing circumstances. But Cartwright intends these adjustments to be absolutely true, in accordance with a plain Word; sermons are not "interpretations," but inspired statements of eternal truth perfectly tailored to temporal needs. The strains of this position are tremendous: Cartwright and the Puritan authors of the *Admonition* are trying to accommodate the demands of historical faith as understood through the rhetorical influence on their culture, while remaining true to the fundamental claim of a feeling faith.[26] They feel they must do this if they are to build a true church in history without sacrificing their plain beliefs to pragmatic calculation. They must do this to honor community and conviction simultaneously.

There are good reasons to question this conception of preaching as both rhetorical and noninterpretive, and Whitgift did. If "homilies interpreting the Scriptures according to the true meaning and sense of them be the 'interpretations of men' and therefore not to be read in church," he asked, "whose interpretations shall we call sermons and other readings?"[27] But the question I want to ask is not how sound such a conception is, but rather what the practical consequences of it are. What happens when rhetoric is put in the service of antirhetorical conviction? What are the relative importance in the Admonitions of the abstract Word and affective words? What combination of teacher and preacher do we find there?

Let's consider for a moment the admonition as a genre. Admonishing is at the heart of the conception of a reformed church that Field, Wilcox, and Cartwright espouse. It is principally a branch

---

[26] Coolidge is, I believe, addressing this tension in different terms when he writes that "at the very heart of Puritanism is the subtle but radical antinomy of the scriptural sense of response to God's word and the rational sense of conformity to God's truth" (*Pauline Renaissance*, 141). Coolidge sees "a mysterious reconciliation between the universalism of Greek rationality and the precious particularism of the Jewish tradition" (15) in Paul's thought, and borrows Panofsky's terms "idiographic" and "nomothetic" to discuss it.

[27] John Whitgift, *Defence of the Answer to the Admonition, against the Reply of Thomas Cartwright* (1574), in *The Works of John Whitgift*, ed. John Ayre, Parker Society, vol. 48 (Cambridge: Cambridge University Press, 1853), pp. 343–44.

of ecclesiastical discipline, the mildest form of church censure and the first step toward excommunication.[28] As the *Admonition* announces in the three-part formula that it will repeat twice more, "the outwarde markes wherby a true christian church is knowne, are preaching of the worde purely, ministring of the sacraments sincerely, and ecclesiastical discipline which consisteth in admonition and correction of faults severelie" (9). More precisely, "ecclesiastical discipline . . . is an order left by God unto his church, wherby men learne to frame their wylles and doyngs accordyng to the law of God, by instructing and admonishing one another, yea and by correcting and punishing all wylfull persones, and contemners of the same" (16). Discipline is both private and public, and the "final end" of public discipline "is the reforming of the disordered, and to bryng them to repentance, and to bridle such as wold offend" (17). Hence the Admonitions themselves, as reforming texts, are clearly intended to contribute to church discipline.

"Discipline" is an interesting word. As the Latin root suggests, it is related to learning. It was sometimes paired with "doctrine" to suggest something like teaching and learning, as in Milton's *Doctrine and Discipline of Divorce*. The *Oxford English Dictionary* dates its use in a specifically ecclesiastical context to 1549, and the early examples cited there show how it came, largely through the influence of Cartwright, Walter Travers, and translations of Calvin, to refer specifically to the "ecclesiastical polity of the Puritan or Presbyterian party." Discipline might be thought of as the branch of education most directly concerned with action, with making sure people do what is right and not what is wrong. It is also a word with much critical currency since the appearance in English of Michel Foucault's *Discipline and Punish*, where it designates a specifically modern form of social control charac-

---

[28] The significance of the title was not lost on contemporaries. According to Thomas Fuller, some members of parliament took "distaste at the title . . . ; for, seeing admonition is the lowest of ecclesiastical censures, and a preparative (if neglected) to suspension and excommunication, such suggested, that if the parliament complied not with this admonitor's desires, his party . . . would proceed to higher and louder fulminations against the parliament" (*The Church History of Britain* [1655] [Oxford: Oxford University Press, 1845], 4: 382).

terized by the penetration of public authority into the most private recesses of personal belief.[29] Such criticism may overemphasize the repressive aspects of early modern culture, but it points usefully to the connections between two different Reformed conceptions of scriptural authority: on the one hand, authority lies in the individual believer's spiritual encounter with the Word of God and is associated with Christian freedom (*self*-discipline); on the other hand, authority lies in the discipline of a particular form of church government supposedly prescribed by Scripture, to be enforced from above by the church hierarchy.

The *Admonition to Parliament* shows one way in which these two ideas of discipline and authority were connected. It is crucial to the goals of the Admonitions that the educational power of discipline be viewed as belonging to preaching rather than to teaching, to the pastor rather than to the doctor. Again the example is Calvin, who wrote, in the words of the 1562 English translation of *The Lawes and Statutes of Geneva*, that the office of the pastor was "to declare the worde of god, to teache, to admonyshe, to exhorte, to reprove as wel publikly as privatly, to minister Sacraments, & to doe brotherly correctyon with the elders."[30] This description is echoed in the *Second Admonition*: the pastor's duty is to "have the oversight & charge of the whole parish, to instruct, to admonish, to exhort, & to correct bi doctrine al and every one in the assemblies, or in the private houses of the same parishe."[31] Because discipline's educational function is tied in this way to the methods of preaching, the educational authority

[29] Michel Foucault, *Discipline and Punish: The Birth of the Prison*, trans. Alan Sheridan (New York: Vintage, 1979).

Michael Walzer explains the role of discipline in the Calvinist state in *The Revolution of the Saints: A Study in the Origins of Radical Politics* (Cambridge: Harvard University Press, 1965), pp. 45–57. Christopher Hill explores the relation of the Puritan idea of discipline to political change in *Society and Puritanism in Pre-Revolutionary England* (London: Secker & Warburg, 1964), chap. 6. And John Coolidge connects discipline to the Puritan notion of edification in *Pauline Renaissance*, pp. 60–63. For surveys of Separatist attitudes toward church discipline, see B. R. White, *The English Separatist Tradition from the Marian Martyrs to the Pilgrim Fathers* (Oxford: Oxford University Press, 1971), and Gerald R. Cragg, *Freedom and Authority* (Philadelphia: Westminster Press, 1975), chap. 8.

[30] Cited in McGinn, *Admonition Controversy*, p. 547n11.

[31] *Second Admonition*, in *Puritan Manifestoes*, ed. Frere and Douglas, p. 98.

of discipline will come less from its intellectual appeal than from its emotional appeal. The assumption will be that the truth is already known and sinners need only be brought to repentance so that they may share the fruits of the godly community.

We would therefore expect the discipline of the Word to produce a rhetoric—partly persuasive, partly coercive—concerned less with reasoned argument than with moving us to affirm what its writers are convinced is the plain truth. And this is exactly what we do find in the Puritan contributions to the Admonition controversy. The *Admonition* declares its vision of a true Christian church and provides support in the form of marginal references to the "sole authority," Scripture. Should one check these references and disagree with their meaning or relevance, as Whitgift did at great length, one can only prove one's wickedness and, therefore, one's need for more discipline, for the *Admonition* is proposing to reinstate "that order of ecclesiastical discipline which *all godly* wish to be restored" (18, emphasis added). Beyond the scriptural references, the persuasive force of the *Admonition* is concentrated in a style that announces that applying the Word to specific historical circumstances is intellectually simple, a matter of black-and-white judgment.

This style features antitheses, catalogs, and imperatives.[32] First, the elaborate antitheses of the *Admonition* try to impel readers from a deformed to a reformed state, and in this they are relentless and inventive; the second paragraph alone is a tour de force of antithetical writing, combining antitheses in what seems like every conceivable way, even rhyme: "Then it was paineful: now gaineful. Then poor and ignominious: now rich & glorious" (11). The basic movement is simple: there was then, there is now; there is the true way, there are false ways. Two complementary actions are constantly enjoined: the destruction of the erroneous way, and the construction of the true house of God: "It shall be your partes . . . to employ your whole labour and studie; not onely in abandoning al popish remnants both in ceremonies and regiment, but also in bringing in and placing in Gods church those

---

[32] Janel Mueller has shown that antitheses and catalogues are staples of the Pauline prose style. See *Native Tongue and the Word*, esp. chap. 4.

things only, which the Lord himself in his word commandeth. Because it is not enough to take paynes in takyng away evil, but also to be occupied in placing good in the stead thereof " (8). Hence, the language of building is also a feature of the tract's style. Second, the catalogs or lists raise the emotional stakes still more, building outrage by piling weight on one half of the antithesis:

> Then, after just tryal and vocation they were admitted to their function . . . : now there is . . . required an albe, a surplesse, a vestiment, a pastoral staffe. . . . (In those dayes knowne by voice, learning and doctrine: now they must be discerned from other by popish and Antichristian apparel, as cap, gowne, tippet, etc.) Then, as God gave utterance they preached the worde onely: now they read homilies, articles, injunctions, etc. Then poore and igno-minious: now rich and glorious. And therfore titles, livings, and offices by Antichrist devised are geven to them, as Metropolitane, Archbishoppe, Lordes grace, Lorde Bishop, Suffragan, Deane, Arch-deacon, Prelate of the garter, Earle, Countie Palatine, Honor, High commissioners, Justices of peace and Quorum, etc.(10–11)

Finally, imperatives serve most importantly as the culmination of the discussions of preaching (12), ministering the sacraments (14), and discipline (16), where they not only provide the obvious ver-bal force, but also help to order the exposition. The members of Parliament are told what they "have to remove" and "to bryng in"; what they "must displace," "plucke down & utterly over-throwe"; and what to "Appoint," "Remove," and "Take away" if they wish to reform preaching. There is a kind of implicit logic in all three techniques: the antitheses suggest by their firmness and clarity that reasons have been given for the distinctions they make; the catalogs, normally descriptive of "now," suggest the multiplicity of error in contrast to the simplicity of truth; and the imperatives create the impression that a logical development has reached its conclusion, an impression best illustrated by the somewhat specious "therfore" at the end of the discussion of preaching (12). But it is a logic, for the most part, of exposition; in each case the appeal remains primarily to the affections.

In addition to the "false now" and "true then" of the *Admoni-tion*, there is also an "us" and "you," and the authors try to use the emotional power of their writing to impel "you" to join "us" in the true way:

> It hath ben thought good to proferre to your godly considerations, a true platforme of a church reformed, to the end that it beyng layd before your eyes, to beholde the great unlikenes betwixt it & this our english church: you may learne either with perfect hatred to detest the one, and with singuler love to embrace, and carefull endevoir to plant the other: or els to be without excuse before the majestie of our God, who (for the discharge of our conscience, and manifestation of his truth) hath by us revealed unto you at this present, the sinceritie and simplicitie of his Gospel.(8)

The *Admonition* invites "you" to join with "us," God's preachers, to form a unity that can reform what we have in common, "our english church," in accordance with the will of "our God." It wants to assert its view emphatically, to carry its audience along by the expressive force of its conviction, and thus to create a community of the like-minded who share a belief in the truths they hold to be self-evident. The *Admonition* aims to create a godly community where the unifying authority is the evidence of truth that conviction provides.

However, the *Admonition* doesn't escape the practical difficulty of relying on the authority of conviction alone. The tract includes some of the awkward moments of self-consciousness about authority characteristic of Protestant writing. One of these occurs in the appendix, where the writers explain that they are appending two letters from "learned and reverende men" to defend themselves against the charge that they lack "the judgement of the best learned, and that therfore . . . [they] are singular, contentious, and so unstayed, that . . . [they] seeke . . . [they] can not tel what" (40). They quickly backtrack, however, realizing that such authority is, by the strict logic of their argument, irrelevant: "Albeit we must nedes say that the truthe of this cause craveth no credit, neither of their letters nor authoritie. For the scriptures are manifest" (40). Still, they publish the letters, probably with the first copies printed. Further evidence that the writers and their supporters felt the need for support from traditional forms of learned authority comes from the later publication history of the

Admonition. Probably after the second edition was published, two small additional treatises were published, "both bearing upon the *Admonition* and often found bound up with it."[33] The *Second Admonition* was published later, but still in 1572. Along with Cartwright's later additions to the controversy, these supplements to the original *Admonition* make good on its wish to be made "playner" (36), meaning here, I think, both "clearer" and "more authoritative." Thus a document that complains bitterly about the institutional framework of learned interpretation with which the Church of England has surrounded the plain Word is itself soon surrounded by a similar framework.

Yet despite these efforts to add nonscriptural authority, one of the sources of the *Admonition*'s appeal is precisely its *lack* of such authority. The authors move immediately, in their opening address "To the Godly Readers," to establish their identity as the oppressed, persecuted by the "proude, pontificall and tyrannous" (6) hierarchy "whose authoritie is forbidden of Christ" (5). In opposing this tyranny, Field and Wilcox present themselves in part as humble, which they do most explicitly at the end of the first section of the *Admonition*:

> And here to end, we desire all to suppose that we have not attempted this enterprise for vaineglorie, gayne, preferment, or any other worldly respect: neither yet judging ourselves, so exactly to have set out the state of a church reformed, as that nothyng more coulde be added, or a more perfect forme and order drawen: for that were great presumption, to arrogate so much unto ourselves, seeing that as we are but weake and simple soules, so God hath raised up men of profound judgement & notable learning. (19)

While this may contradict the belief that the Scriptures are plain, it is true to the Admonitioners' sense of themselves as different from the tyranny of the church establishment. But their best means of establishing this difference is to present themselves as martyrs, both indirectly in the early pages and more explicitly at the end of the second article: "If this can not be obtayned, we will

---

[33] Frere and Douglas, eds., *Puritan Manifestoes*, p. xiv.

by Gods grace address ourselves to defend his truth by suffring, and willingly lay our heads to the blocke, and this shal be our peace, to have quiet consciences with our God, whome we wyl abyde for, with al pacience, untyll he worke our full deliverance" (36). This appeal to the authority of suffering and martyrdom recalls Tyndale's insistence that persecution furnishes the Christian with "an evident token" that his beliefs are true.[34] Because martyrdom is the most irrevocable action that one can take in support of one's beliefs, it has the strongest persuasive power and the ultimate authority within the realm of faith. It is thus the *Admonition*'s final proof, the utter absence of worldly authority that is the proof of spiritual authority.[35]

The *Admonition*, then, exhibits a dual sense of authority. On the one hand, it possesses the authority of God; on the other, it does not possess—though it would like to—the authority of men. The paradox is that while it bases its claim to possess the authority of God on its lack of worldly authority, it wishes to make God's authority prevail among men. It wishes to educate within a framework of plain truth that makes the education of the will through preaching paramount and the education of the wit through teaching secondary. Field and Wilcox show discipline in action by admonishing the parliament, their authority to do so deriving from having "quiet consciences with our God." They do so "for the discharge of *our* conscience, and manifestation of his truth" (8), but by so doing they offer their audience the opportunity to join with them in uniting God, conscience, and true church: if "you" help "reforme these deformities" (12), they write, "God shal be glorified, *your* consciences discharged, and the flocke of Christ (purchased with his owne blood) edified" (13).

[34] Tyndale, *Obedience of a Christian Man*, p. 131.

[35] It is proof, that is, from the authors' perspective. From the perspective of worldly authority its meaning is quite different. See Elaine Scarry's account in *The Body in Pain: The Making and Unmaking of the World* (Oxford: Oxford University Press, 1985) of the way the pain of torture is used to give an appearance of legitimacy to brutal regimes; also see Elizabeth Hanson's discussion of the early modern contest between torturer and tortured to control the significance of that pain ("Torture and Truth in Renaissance England," *Representations* 34 [1991], 53–84).

Teaching Words

Roger Ascham, ever vigilant, pauses from describing the benefits of shooting long enough to warn his readers of the hazards of "hasardry," that is, dicing or gambling. He carefully paints "the monstruousenes of it," including a description of how crafty men use their "shiftes, whan they get a playne man tha[t] can no skyll of them." Once he has been enticed to the table, "than every one of them setteth his shiftes abroche, some with false dise, some wyth settynge of dyse, some with havinge outelandishe sylver coynes guylded, to put away at a tyme for good gold. Than yf ther come a thing in controversie, muste you be judged by the table, and than farewell the honest man hys parte, for he is borne downe on everye syde."[36] The fear of being "borne downe on everye syde" in public controversy was common in the sixteenth century, and it frequently caused a tension in the ideals of humanist rhetoric. From its beginnings humanism had striven to reconcile the claims of rhetoric and philosophy. Following Lorenzo Valla's lead, humanists had most frequently effected the reconciliation by privileging the claims of rhetoric, of common speech and collaborative judgment.[37] Intelligibility was the surest indicator of sense, as persuasiveness was the surest indicator of truth, and the call for the truth of common sense was heard again and again in the stylistic controversies of the century. The fear of public controversy, then, indicates a breakdown in the equation that led from a common language, through general intelligibility and persuasiveness, to truth—a breakdown arising from the humanists' competing loyalties: if the primacy of common usage in resolving disputes about grammar and style was too strong a piety to question, so too was the humanists' belief in their own position as the modern representatives of antique wisdom and, sometimes, in the legal and moral authority of the government they served.

[36] Roger Ascham, *Toxophilus*, in *English Works*, ed. William Aldis Wright (Cambridge: Cambridge University Press, 1904), pp. 25–26.

[37] On the elevation of rhetoric over philosophy, see especially Jerrold Seigel, *Rhetoric and Philosophy in Renaissance Humanism: The Union of Eloquence and Wisdom, Petrarch to Valla* (Princeton: Princeton University Press, 1968), chap. 5, "Lorenzo Valla and the Subordination of Philosophy to Rhetoric."

For the humanist as educator, guardian of the truth, and servant of the state, the unspoken question was always, Intelligible and persuasive to whom? Since there was a philosophical as well as a rhetorical answer to this question, the temptation was clear: one could continue to bow to the common language while questioning the reliability of the common judgment and thus split language from thought.

This split is enshrined in the popular saying that attempts to honor both humanist commitments simultaneously—"speak as the many, think as the few." Ascham quotes it in the context of his remarks on neologisms in the preface to *Toxophilus* and as part of his criticism of Sallust's dark style in *The Scholemaster.* He is joined by Thomas Wilson in *The Arte of Rhetorique,* where the saying supports an injunction against using "straunge ynkehorne termes," and by Stephen Guazzo in *The Civile Conversation,* where it concludes a long discussion of style.[38] In the manner of proverbs, the phrase avoids the theoretical problems it raises: are thought and speech separable? How can the thoughts of the few be communicated in the speech of the many? It does so, I contend, in order to honor the conflicting desires of rhetoric and philosophy—the desire to participate in the common political life, on the one hand, and the desire to withdraw, on the other, to the relative certainty and safety of a knowledge and conviction felt to belong to an educated few.

This conflict is treated most directly perhaps in *The Civile Conversation,* a popular book in England after its translation by George Pettie in 1581. In the dialogue between Guazzo's brother, William, and his neighbor, Doctor Anniball Magnocavalli, William, as the frustrated humanist courtier, expresses his desire to withdraw from the society that will not hear his counsel. He argues that knowledge is man's chief good and it is better found in solitude than among the "common sorte," who call "plainnesse

---

[38] Ascham, *Toxophilus,* p. xiv; Ascham, *The Scholemaster,* in *English Works,* p. 298; Thomas Wilson, *The Arte of Rhetorique,* ed. Thomas J. Derrick, The Renaissance Imagination, vol. 1 (New York: Garland, 1982), p. 325; and Stephen Guazzo, *The Civile Conversation,* trans. George Pettie and Bartholomew Young (New York: Knopf, 1925), 1: 146. Further references to *The Scholemaster* appear in the text.

of manners and gentlenesse of minde" "foolishnesse." The Doctor responds, in keeping with the double puns of the book's title, that the truly civilized life is the life led conversing with one's fellow men. That scholar is ridiculous who "doeth not frame his learning to the common life, but sheweth him selfe altogether ignorant of the affaires of the world." The sides of the controversy seem clear, but even the Doctor's arguments reveal the tension between rhetoric and philosophy. For example, he warns William not to act in a way that would set them in opposition to "general opinions," for such opinions "have such force, that reason is of no force against them"; he also slips from recommending conversation with "the common sorte" to recommending conversation with "other learned men."[39] Like much sixteenth-century writing, *The Civile Conversation* illuminates but fails to resolve a tension between an ideal of involvement in the contingent, public world and a desire to withdraw to a realm where knowledge is the absolute monarch.[40]

The humanist conflict between learned and popular authorities parallels that between feeling and historical faiths in Protestantism. Hence, the struggle between the certainty of conviction and the consensus of community unites texts as seemingly diverse as *The Scholemaster* and the *Admonition to Parliament*. There are, of course, obvious differences between the two nearly contemporary books.[41] The occasion of Ascham's book is not as pressing as is that of the *Admonition*, for one thing. For another, Ascham's ostensible subject is the teaching of classical languages and literature, not the constitution of a true Christian church. Perhaps most important, where with few exceptions the *Admonition* ac-

[39] On this slippage in humanism more generally, see Seigel, *Rhetoric and Philosophy in Renaissance Humanism*, p. 163.

[40] Guazzo, *Civile Conversation*, pp. 37, 40, 60–61, 39. Guazzo's impact in England is studied by John L. Lievsay, *Stefano Guazzo and the English Renaissance, 1575–1675* (Chapel Hill: University of North Carolina Press, 1961), and Daniel Javitch, "Rival Arts of Conduct in Elizabethan England: Guazzo's *Civile Conversation* and Castiglione's *Courtier*," *Yearbook of Italian Studies* 1 (1971), 178–98.

[41] *The Scholemaster*, published posthumously in 1570, was probably written between 1564 and Ascham's death in 1568. The first book, with which I am primarily concerned here, was probably completed by 1566. On the dates and circumstances of composition, see Lawrence V. Ryan, *Roger Ascham* (Stanford: Stanford University Press, 1963), pp. 251–54.

knowledges only the authority of the Word and refers only to
Scripture for support, Ascham has a humanist's interest in the
authority of Plato, Socrates, and Cicero, and quotes constantly
from a full range of ancient and modern authors. Surely this
chasm between the two cannot be bridged: Ascham's humanist
sense of learned authority must lead to an educational theory and
practice quite at odds with that of the *Admonition*. If the *Admonition's* concern is to preach the Word in order to purify the heart,
surely Ascham's is to teach a variety of words in order to sharpen
the mind. Nevertheless, without denying the differences between
the two, I maintain that they are alike in at least four essential
ways, these being (1) their belief that the truth is plain and only
needs to be applied in a straightforward way to specific circumstances, (2) their consequent belief that education should be
aimed first at reforming the will through true discipline, (3) the
literary effort they both make to educate by forceful communication of their conviction, and (4) their sense that all true authority,
including their own, comes from God and is best verified by conviction or feeling faith. I will discuss in order the three types of
authority present in *The Scholemaster*: learned, moral, and religious.

The chief difference between the *Admonition* and *The Scholemaster* lies in the importance Ascham attaches to the authority
of learned wit.[42] But a careful study of Ascham's theory of wit
reveals that the difference is not as large as it seems. According to
Ascham, students are of two sorts: quick wits and hard wits. Of
the two, quick wits are, despite their initial advantage, the less
promising learners: "Quicke wittes commonlie, be apte to take,
unapte to keepe: soone hote and desirous of this and that: as colde
and sone wery of the same againe: more quick to enter spedelie,
than hable to pearse farre: even like over sharpe tooles, whose
edges be verie soone turned" (188–89). There are two main reasons why quick wits disappoint their teachers. The first is already
apparent: they are changeable, unable to stay with a study long

[42] In *Wit and Rhetoric in the Renaissance* (1937; rpt. Gloucester, Mass.: Peter
Smith, 1964), William G. Crane surveys some of the many Renaissance senses of
wit and traces the tradition, reaching back to Plato and Cicero, that associates wit
with rhetoric.

enough to master it. The second, which to Ascham may be a complete explanation of the first, is that they are easily distracted by pleasure: "Soche wittes delite them selves in easie and pleasant studies, and never passe farre forward in hie and hard sciences. And therefore the quickest wittes commonlie may prove the best Poetes, but not the wisest Orators." The poetlike capriciousness and hedonism that quick wits display in their studies extend as well to the character they show elsewhere:

> Also, for maners and life, quicke wittes commonlie, be, in desire, newfangle, in purpose, unconstant, light to promise any thing, readie to forget every thing: both benefite and injurie: and therby neither fast to frend, nor fearefull to foe: inquisitive of every trifle, not secret in greatest affaires: bolde, with any person: busie, in every matter: sothing, soch as be present: nipping any that is absent: of nature also, alwaies, flattering their betters, envying their equals, despising their inferiors: and, by quicknes of witte, verie quicke and readie, to like none so well as them selves.
>
> Moreover commonlie, men, very quicke of witte, be also, verie light of conditions: and thereby, very readie of disposition, to be caried over quicklie, by any light cumpanie, to any riot and unthriftines when they be yonge: and therefore seldome, either honest of life, or riche in living, when they be olde.

Clearly we are meant to disapprove of the quick wit's self-serving and sycophantic character; but the description contains traces of a third characteristic that, although apparently associated by Ascham with a hedonistic lack of perseverance, seems like a rather important quality in a student—or in wit. The quick wit is curious. He is interested in new things—in everything, in fact. Yet as admirable as this may seem, for Ascham such curiosity is misplaced, and the word "curious" itself is a danger sign, as when he remarks that St. Chrysostom "in a sermon *contra fatum*, and the curious serchinge of nativities, doth wiselie saie, that ignorance therein, is better than knowledge" (210), or when he speaks of men who may "be caried by som curious affection of mynde . . . to hasard the triall of over manie perilous adventures" (215). Why this should be so is not immediately clear; for a clue, we must move on to Ascham's description of those who do "passe farre forward in hie and hard sciences," the hard wits.

The hard wit is the tortoise to the quick wit's hare. He is "constant without newfanglenes" and hard-working without brilliance, "bearing heavie thinges, thoughe not lightlie, yet willinglie" (191). He learns slowly but surely. So much is to be expected, but Ascham is no less consistent in contrasting the hard wit to the puzzling curiosity of the quick wit: "Also, for maners and life, hard wittes commonlie, ar hardlie caried, either to desire everie new thing, or else to mervell at every strange thinge: and therfore they be carefull and diligent in their own matters, not curious and busey in other mens affaires: and so, they becum wise them selves, and also ar counted honest by others." Their respect for privacy is a clear superiority over quick wits, but again it isn't clear why lacking the aptitude to desire new things and to marvel at "strange" things is likely to produce wisdom. Nor is the matter clarified when Ascham goes on to describe hard wits as "grave, stedfast, silent of tong, secret of hart." What *is* clear is that hard wits are as little likely to reveal the truth about themselves as they are to attempt to find it out about others. They are, in a word, withdrawn. So why is withdrawal preferable to curiosity? The rest of Ascham's description of hard wits provides the clue. They are, he says, "Not hastie in making, but constant in keping any promise. Not rashe in uttering, but ware in considering every matter: and therby, not quicke in speaking, but deepe of judgement, whether they write or give counsell in all waightie affaires." Thought always goes before utterance for the hard wit, who must think as the few before speaking as the many; his slowness and his secrecy are desirable because they enable his deep judgment to function before he commits himself to the risks of speech. The hard wit's withdrawal, then, appears to be a way of ensuring that his words will contain the truth by bringing them under the control of prior thought.

Comments Ascham makes later in *The Scholemaster* confirm that the lack of this control is at the root of the quick wit's troubles. In the second book, he discusses the Epitome, the fourth of the "six wayes appointed by the best learned men, for the

learning of tonges, and encreace of eloquence" (242). An Epitome
is a sort of distillation or summary of the wise sayings of a book,
and so resembles a book of commonplaces. Its proper use is to
organize and to trim excess matter, and thus "to induce a man,
into an orderlie general knowledge" (259), much as a physician
purges a superfluity of the humors: "And surelie mens bodies, be
not more full of ill humors, than commonlie mens myndes (if
they be yong, lustie, proude, like and love them selves well, as
most men do) be full of fansies, opinions, errors, and faultes, not
onelie in inward invention, but also in all their utterance either
by pen or taulke" (263). With this Ascham returns to quick wits,
now "quicke inventors":

> And of all other men, even those that have the inventivest heades,
> for all purposes, and roundest tonges in all matters and places (ex-
> cept they learne and use this good lesson of *Epitome*) commit com-
> monlie greater faultes, than dull, staying silent men do. . . .
>   And therefore, readie speakers, generallie be not the best, play-
> nest, and wisest writers, nor yet the deepest judgers in weightie
> affaires, bicause they do not tarry to weye and judge all thinges, as
> they should: but having their heades over full of matter, be like
> pennes over full of incke, which will soner blotte, than make any
> faire letter at all. (263–64)

Here it all comes together. The quick wit is too busy inventing to
transmit knowledge effectively. He has forgotten a crucial step:
he has not ordered and judged the matter of his invention "as [he]
should." His curiosity is condemned, therefore, because it causes
him to overfill his head with matter and to spew it forth in disor-
ganized and unjudged form, as if speech were a heuristic instrument rather than a container of prior truth.

How Ascham thinks one "should" judge provides further insight into the significance of his preference for hard wits. One
might expect the quick wit's curiosity to be useful in the pursuit
of truth, since, if he is not pronouncing the final word on the issue
at hand, he is at least exploring its dimensions, perhaps illuminating some of its nuances. But for the Ascham of *The Scholemaster*,
truth isn't *pursued* so much as it is *applied*. As it did for Wyatt
and the authors of the *Admonition*, judgment for Ascham strong-

ly tends toward the black-and-white, and he expects the educated man to be able to apply the fixed standards of learning and virtue to any situation with draftsmanlike precision:

> I lacke not good will to wisshe, that the yougthe in England, speciallie Ientlemen, and namelie nobilitie, shold be by good bringing up, so grounded in judgement of learninge, so founded in love of honestie, as, whan they shold be called forthe to the execution of great affaires, in service of their Prince and contrie, they might be hable, to use and to order, all experiences, were they good were they bad, and that, according to the square, rule, and line, of wisdom learning and vertue. (216)

Such a formulation fails to acknowledge the possibility that the rule of one's wisdom may not measure the twists of the current situation without bending. The unique circumstances of particular historical situations may elude or challenge the concepts of knowledge and require an equitable adjustment in judgment. A sympathetic construction of the quick wit might stress his interest in collecting the kind of information necessary to make such adjustments. But it appears that Ascham dislikes him precisely because his probing curiosity dwells on the type of historical detail that challenges standards and complicates judgment, making it harder to believe one's judgment contains the truth.[43]

The likelihood that being "over full of words, sentences, & matter" (260) will destroy true judgment shows the relative values in Ascham of knowledge and wit, and of precepts and experience. It is possible, despite Ascham's emphasis on the importance of words, for a speaker to be "full of wordes without witte" (185). But there is as much danger in too much invention as in too little, since "over much witte" is "commonlie" a characteristic of an ill nature (214). Ideally, one should bring the "tonge" under the governance of the "braine," and the "taulke" under the leadership of the "reason." In other words, "good understanding must first be

---

[43] Relevant to Ascham's antirhetorical and antihistoricist theory of wit is Terence Cave's remark that "Ciceronians cannot participate in colloquies; the sterilized univocity of their model is disrupted by the unpredictability of dialogue" (*The Cornucopian Text: Problems of Writing in the French Renaissance* [Oxford: Clarendon Press, 1979], p. 139).

bred in the childe"; for "where so ever knowledge doth accompanie the witte, there best utterance doth alwaies awaite upon the tonge" (186). Knowledge and good understanding are in turn derived not from experience but from the "precepts of learning," two nouns that are virtual synonyms in Ascham. Learning must be directed by prior learning, or it is likely to get lost in unknown ways: "And surelie, he that would prove wise by experience, he maie be wittie in deede, but even like a swift runner, that runneth fast out of his waie, and upon the night, he knoweth not whither" (214). When wit relies on experience rather than on received knowledge, it goes by blind chance. In contrast, "the good precepts of learning, be the eyes of the minde, to looke wiselie before a man, which waie to go right, and whiche not." But again there is a surprising twist in Ascham's explanation: "experience of all facions in yougthe" is inferior to learning not because it leads to too little knowledge, but because it leads "to overmuch knowledge" (215).

Too much matter, too much wit, too much knowledge. All prevent words from being controlled by understanding, and understanding from being controlled by precepts. All challenge the orderly transmission of the predetermined, certain standards of judgment that Ascham seeks to protect. These triple errors thus illuminate Ascham's hierarchy of values. Before all else comes preceptive wisdom, which exists in a timeless state and descends, in order, from the Bible, the Greek classics, and the Latin classics. Precepts then pass into individuals, who apply them rigidly to experience, producing understanding. Finally, understanding is uttered in words, which are only truly "words" if they have descended in this way from the true standards of judgment. In Ascham's use, then, "words," "understanding" or "knowledge," and "precepts" all refer to the same reservoir of preceptive wisdom.[44]

---

[44] This view of "words" as preceptive wisdom explains Ascham's famous complaint against those who "care not for wordes, but for matter" (265). Ascham's vision of the unity of eloquence and wisdom applies only to a narrow spectrum of learned language, not, as Richard Waswo notes in an excellent commentary on the passage, to "the wider operation of language in common speech." Waswo continues: "It is frankly a norm, not a dialectic; it postulates no continuous interaction between its terms, but merely states their coincidence on a scale of value" (*Language and Meaning in the Renaissance* [Princeton: Princeton University Press, 1987], pp. 192–93).

Hence, although Ascham's view of the learned authority of wit distinguishes *The Scholemaster* from such a text as the *Admonition*, the difference is minimized by wit's identity with preceptive wisdom, which makes wit a plain source of truth rather than a tool for invention or rhetorical inquiry. Ascham did not always support the views he expresses in *The Scholemaster*. In *Toxophilus* (1550), for example, he displays a more fully rhetorical sense of the difficulties involved in hitting the mark of truth. But in *The Scholemaster* his outlook more closely resembles that of humanism's philosophical face.[45] From such a perspective, controversy, with its threat that the truth might be "borne down," is not only unnecessary but also the sign of a moral failure in at least one of the parties: controversy necessarily involves a table of cheats.

Consequently, learned authority in *The Scholemaster* adheres closely to moral authority, and the education of the wit is subordinate to the education of the will. As Ascham agrees with the Puritans that education of the wit is relatively "simple," requiring only the straightforward application of received or revealed wisdom, so he agrees with them—and Saint Paul—that the education of the will is both more difficult and of prior importance:

> S. Paul saith, that sectes and ill opinions, be the workes of the flesh, and frutes of sinne. . . . For, ill doinges, breed ill thinkinges. And of

---

[45] This aspect of humanism has been linked to the massive educational program that Walter Ong calls "the pedagogical juggernaut" (*Ramus, Method, and the Decay of Dialogue* [Cambridge: Harvard University Press, 1958], chap. 7). Ong's controversial argument is that this humanist program led away from the dialogic and deliberative focus of traditional rhetorical education to a "didactic" education more closely resembling indoctrination into accepted truths. Although I believe that Ong exaggerates the didactic tendencies of humanist educational practices as a whole, I find his argument helpful in accounting for the antirhetorical tendencies of texts like *The Scholemaster*. For the methods and effects of humanist education more generally, see Foster Watson, intro., *Vives on Education* (Cambridge: Cambridge University Press, 1913); W. H. Woodward, *Studies in Education during the Age of the Renaissance, 1400–1600* (Cambridge: Cambridge University Press, 1924); Robert R. Bolgar, *The Classical Heritage and Its Beneficiaries* (Cambridge: Cambridge University Press, 1954); Kenneth Charlton, *Education in Renaissance England* (Toronto: University of Toronto Press, 1965); Simon, *Education and Society in Tudor England*, part 1, "The Fifteenth-Century Background and the Humanist Innovators"; and Van Cleave Alexander, *The Growth of English Education, 1348–1648*, chap. 3.

corrupted maners, spryng perverted judgementes. And how? there
be in man two speciall thinges: Mans will, mans mynde. Where
will inclineth to goodnes, the mynde is bent to troth: Where will is
caried from goodnes to vanitie, the mynde is sone drawne from
troth to false opinion. (230)

In this way the true collapses into the good, and, as Alvin Vos
notes, the tradition of rhetorical inquiry is altered: " 'Philosophy'
for Ascham . . . no longer has reference first of all to the orator's
wide knowledge of 'the whole of the contents of the life of mankind' [as it did for Cicero], but to his sincere, religious commitment to 'right judgment in doctrine'."[46] Will and wit are thus
closely connected, and the behavior of the first determines the
behavior of the second.

The closeness of wit and will in *The Scholemaster* can be illustrated by the similarity between the terms in which Ascham
describes errors of learning and those in which he describes moral
error. Ascham's long discussion of the forms of wit is complemented by equally lengthy sections dealing with the danger that
the court will corrupt boys between the ages of seventeen and
twenty-seven and that Italy will corrupt anybody. The resemblance of those corrupted by the court or Italy to quick wits is
striking. Among the consequences when the "feare to do ill" is
lost, for example, are the desires "to be busie in every matter, to
be skilfull in every thyng, [and] to acknowledge no ignorance at
all" (207). When an Englishman is corrupted by Italy, he brings
home a harvest including "for pollicie, a factious hart, a discours-
ing head, a mynde to medle in all mens matters: for experience,
plentie of new mischieves never knowne in England before: for
maners, varietie of vanities, and chaunge of filthy lyving" (229).
English Italians also become "common discoursers of all matters:
busie searchers of most secret affaires: open flatterers of great
men: privie mislikers of good men: Faire speakers, with smiling
countenances, and much curtessie openlie to all men" (236). And,

[46] Alvin Vos, " 'Good Matter and Good Utterance': The Character of English
Ciceronianism," *SEL 1500–1900* 19 (1979), 7. On the character of philosophy in
Ascham, see also Thomas M. Greene, "Roger Ascham: The Perfect End of Shoot-
ing," *ELH* 36 (1969), 609–25.

Ascham notes with sarcasm, they think they know everything. Here we see very much the same characteristics that Ascham found in the manners and life of quick wits: the meddlesome curiosity, the tendency to sow the seeds of discord, the vain love of fashion, the inconstancy, the tendency to let the tongue go before the brain, the flattery, the envy, the backbiting, and the intellectual conceit. For Ascham, it seems, all error falls into these forms; and just as discussions of wit that begin studying epistemology and language soon lead to ethical considerations, so, in Ascham's hands, ethical considerations lead to truth.

Ascham is more consistent than Cartwright, Field, and Wilcox in pursuing the pedagogical implications of the connection of wit and will. Like them, he distinguishes between different types of education and different types of educators. Among the Greeks and the Romans, for example, "children were under the rule of three persones: *Praeceptore, Paedagogo, Parente*: the scholemaster taught him learnyng with all ientlenes: the Governour corrected his maners, with moch sharpenesse: The father, held the sterne of his whole obedience" (202). Ascham doesn't distinguish further between father and governor, so in practice there are two branches and two offices in education: where Cartwright distinguished teaching from preaching, Ascham distinguishes learning from manners; where Cartwright had doctors and pastors, Ascham has masters and governors.[47] But unlike the Puritans, Ascham doesn't create an educational realm of wit that is entirely free from the will. For him, both learning and manners require discipline; both, consequently, require admonishing. Cartwright gave different types of admonishing to the same person, so that the pastor was responsible for both "exhorting" and "dehorting." But Ascham's more careful distinction allows him to give exhorting to the master and dehorting to the governor.

Ascham's discussion of these distinctions (202–3) serves as the dividing point in book one of *The Scholemaster*: before it, his concern is with learning; after, for nearly the last two-thirds of the book, he concentrates on manners. Before the division, As-

---

[47] Ascham distinguishes on separate occasions between the father and the master (202) and between the governor and the master (211).

cham argues that "love is fitter than feare, ientlenes better than beating, to bring up a childe rightlie in learninge" (187). After the division, his concern is fear and "some more severe discipline" (203). Before, he pleads for less "compulsion" (198) and more "libertie and freedome" (199) in learning; after, he complains about "licence" (204, 205) and desires a return to an age of "obedience" (204) in manners when "a yong ientleman was never free, to go where he would, and do what he liste him self" (203). Before, he advocates "cherefull admonishinge" (185), and advises a schoolmaster to "monish" a "dull" student "gentelie" (187); after, Ascham twice defends *his own* admonishing against the expected charge that it is harsh and out of place (208, 222).

These passages of self-justification link the literary mode of *The Scholemaster* to that of the *Admonition*, suggesting that a majority of the first book of *The Scholemaster* is, like the *Admonition*, a form of educational discipline. We may surmise that the resemblance was not lost on English Protestants: while Field and Wilcox were about to earn their reputation as Admonitioners, Thomas Wilson prefaced Ascham's book in 1570 by calling him "your good admonisher."[48] But can Ascham's admonishing be seen as part of a strategy of preaching comparable to that in the *Admonition*? At first this seems unlikely, since Ascham's attempt to encourage great men to serve as examples of good manners appears to require no religious authority. His first description of his purpose, for instance, places it squarely in an ethical framework: "I write not to hurte any, but to proffit som: to accuse none, but to monish soch, who, allured by ill counsell, and folowing ill example, contrarie to their good bringyng up, and against their owne good nature, yeld overmoch to thies folies and faultes" (208). At such moments Ascham seems very much the humanist at court, concerned with true counsel and the moral education of princes. Education is viewed as handmaiden to obedience and order, to the "good or ill service, of God, our Prince, and our whole countrie" (188).[49] The emphasis on "severe discipline"

---

[48] Cited in the *OED*. The *OED* also cites two examples from *The Scholemaster* itself.

[49] One of the strongest humanist statements of the importance of education in ensuring order is Sir Richard Morison, *A Remedy for Sedition* (1536), in *Humanist*

may sound ominous, and Ascham may sound like a moral conservative bent on preserving a hierarchical order of society where the great enforce whatever "will" they wish on society, their desire determining what "order" will be.

However, Ascham never sanctions an aristocratic authority that isn't anchored in a prior religious authority. This is clear when Ascham admonishes the great most directly to use their power responsibly:

> Take hede therfore, ye great ones in the Court. . . . God doth order, that all your lawes, all your authoritie, all your commaundementes, do not halfe so moch with meane men, as doth your example and maner of livinge. And for example even in the greatest matter, if yow your selves do serve God gladlie and orderlie for conscience sake, not coldlie, and somtyme for maner sake, you carie all the Courte with yow, and the whole Realme beside, earnestlie and orderlie to do the same. If yow do otherwise, yow be the onelie authors, of all misorders in Religion, not only to the Courte, but to all England beside. (220)

The court is not free from the demands of religion, for God and conscience are omnipresent. There is no doubt that Ascham understands the Protestant implications of this presence and no possibility that he is just paying lip service to them. Great men, he writes, "have authoritie to remedie" miseries "and will do so to, whan God shall think time fitte" (209). God is the supreme authority, and if the great wish to set a responsible example of manners, they must follow the dictates of true conviction, the faith, planted in man by God, that speaks through us, not from us.

Ascham's other defenses of his purpose in the first book of *The Scholemaster* also show the close connection of ethics and religion, of the authority of the great with the authority of God.

Scholarship and Public Order: Two Tracts against the Pilgrimage of Grace, ed. David Sandler Berkowitz (Washington: Folger, 1984). Ascham knew Morison well, having served as his secretary for a time in the early 1550s. On their friendship, see Ryan, *Roger Ascham*, pp. 134–35. The political conservatism of humanist education is stressed by Lawrence Stone in his chapter "Education and Culture," *The Crisis of the Aristocracy, 1558–1640*, abridged ed. (Oxford: Oxford University Press, 1967).

During his second defense, he anticipates that some will "busie them selves in merveling" why he spends his time "writyng of trifles, as the schole of shoting, the Cockpitte, and this booke of the first Principles of Grammer, rather, than to take some weightie matter in hand, either of Religion, or Civill discipline" (217). His response is cryptic but unmistakable: like Homer, Ascham suggests, he may be writing great things "within the compasse of a smal Argument" (218). In fact by this point Ascham's concern *is* largely with religion and civil discipline, and his final self-defense goes even further toward acknowledging this:

> But perchance, som will say, I have stepte to farre, out of my schole, into the common welthe, from teaching a yong scholer, to monishe greate and noble men: yet I trust good and wise men will thinke and iudge of me, that my minde was, not so moch, to be busie and bold with them, that be great now, as to give trew advise to them, that may be great hereafter. . . . Yet, if som will needes presse me . . . I will aunswere them with *S. Paul, sive per contentionem, sive quocunque modo, modo Christus praedicetur,* &tc [Whether out of contention, or in whatever manner, nevertheless Christ is preached—Philippians 1:15–18]. (222)

Ascham is preaching, and preaching is never out of season.

That Ascham can be said to be preaching by this point in *The Scholemaster* is a consequence of the gradual but steady rise in religious fervor throughout the first book. After the transition from wit to will, Ascham moves through his condemnation of the court to a survey of the dangers of traveling that passes from the literary example of Ulysses to the contemporary danger of Italy, culminating in an evocation of the horrors of English Italians that concludes by raising the spectres of Papistry and Atheism. Along the way, *The Scholemaster* becomes at times a jeremiad, as in this passage about courtly corruption:

> All thies misorders, be Goddes juste plages, by his sufferance, brought justelie upon us, for our sinnes, which be infinite in nomber, and horrible in deede, but namelie, for the great abhominable sin of unkindnesse: but what unkindnesse? even such unkindnesse as was in the Jewes, in contemninge Goddes voice, in shrinking

from his woorde, in wishing backe againe for Aegypt, in commit-
ting aduoultrie and hordom, not with the women, but with the
doctrine of Babylon, did bring all the plages, destructions, and Cap-
tivities, that fell so ofte and horriblie, upon Israell. (209)

Ascham even refers to Jeremiah, who, "crying out of the vaine &
vicious life of the *Israelites*" (227), sounds very much like Ascham.

This sense of a prophetic voice, although admittedly less than
that found in many Reformation writings, is, I suggest, the single
most important similarity between *The Scholemaster* and the
Admonition to Parliament. Though not a minister of the Word,
Ascham evidently feels that his intimacy with words and his
lifelong commitment to reform authorize him to speak on religious matters. He most directly questions the religious establishment during his attack on the licentious books that he believes
threaten "to subvert trewe Religion" (230):

Mo Papistes be made, by your mery bookes of Italie, than by your
earnest bookes of *Lovain*. And bicause our great Phisicians, do
winke at the matter, and make no counte of this sore, I, though not
admitted one of their felowshyp, yet havyng bene many yeares a
prentice to Gods trewe Religion, and trust to continewe a poore
jorney man therein all dayes of my life, for the dewtie I owe, & love
I beare, both to trewe doctrine, and honest living, though I have no
authoritie to amend the sore my selfe, yet I will declare my good
will, to discover the sore to others. (230)

Like Field and Wilcox, Ascham disavows personal authority. But
the humble stance they all adopt enables them to speak for a
greater truth. In Ascham's case, the stance is that of a Protestant
humanist, cherishing the learned truth of classical literature yet
believing that such a truth is consistent with the plain truth of
Scripture and accessible to whoever sincerely seeks it. The final
appeal of such a truth is to everyman, the honest reader who will
join with the prophet or the martyr in encouraging virtue and
contemning vice. Like the authors of the *Admonition*, Ascham
wants his readers to join with him in affirming the authority of
his conviction, of the plain truth that acts through him.

For the Ascham of at least book one of *The Scholemaster*, then, religious authority subsumes moral authority, which in turn subsumes learned authority, leaving a complex mixture that bespeaks the tensions within humanism itself. Truth, as the source of right judgment in doctrine, still dwells in an exclusive learned language, but anyone can be led to truth by the unverifiable inner reality of conviction—even those who know no learned language. Thus Ascham's truth is the private property of ancient writers and their modern descendants and a virtually self-evident possession of many, available in the common wisdom of the language (perhaps through the mediation of the Holy Spirit) to whoever faithfully seeks it. Consequently, Ascham's reevaluation of philosophy involves a popularizing at the same time that it involves a withdrawal, reflecting humanism's twin desires of a common language and an uncommon certainty. Ascham illustrates the attitude that can appeal regularly to the authority of ancient authors and simultaneously plead, in behalf of "a common Proverbe," that it is not "the opinion of one, . . . but the judgement of all" (229). He illustrates as well the need of that attitude to make authority intelligible to all and its fear that a language intelligible to all will be tainted with the false opinions of the multitude. He thus shows how the moralistic plainness he epitomizes issues from the attempt to honor the conflicting demands for rhetorical community and antirhetorical conviction: exclusiveness of some kind is necessary, but so is the maintenance of a moral community. Depending on which demand has the upper hand, the community either grows or shrinks.

As it did in Wyatt's poetry and in the *Admonition*'s Reformed emphasis on the plain sense of Scripture, the word "plain" holds a central place in this tension between communal inquiry and specialized conviction. "Plain" is the omnipresent word that describes both the plain language spoken by the many, a slightly popularized version of the Latin *plane*, and the plain truth known to the few. As such, it is a bridge term that can be used loosely to give the appearance of unity to the double demands for special truth and general perspicuity. Perhaps as a consequence of the uneasy union of these first two meanings, "plain" takes on a third relevant meaning as well. As we have seen illustrated in the trans-

formation of a "plain English man" to a "right *Italian,*" in Guazzo's complaint against those who take "plainnesse of manners
and gentleness of minde" for "foolishnesse," and in the change in
Ascham's description of the man being cheated at cards from "the
playne man" to the "honest man," it means the moral virtue of
honesty and rectitude, of freedom from deceit and vice. As such it
captures the moralistic flavor truth takes on in writers such as
Field, Wilcox, Cartwright, and Ascham. For Ascham, learned
truth, moral goodness, and religious faith are one, and to be plain
is to support an exclusive moral standard that is meant to include
the experience, and be included in the words, of every Christian.

The style of *The Scholemaster,* like that of the *Admonition,*
shows how the book's verbal performance seeks both to foster
community and to maintain belief by impelling its readers to
share the conviction it expresses. This style has already received
much study and has rightly been seen as combining Ciceronian
and Pauline models and goals.[50] The most important characteristic it shares with the style of the *Admonition* is the insistent use
of antithesis, which is again an appropriate device for expressing
the conviction that "the olde and present maners, do differ as
farre, as blacke and white, as vertue and vice" (223)—a sentence
that might have been lifted from the *Admonition.* Since the role
of antithesis and other forms of balance and opposition has been
so carefully studied at the syntactic level, I will focus instead on
the importance of such features at the structural level. The first
book of *The Scholemaster* is built around a series of related contrasts. One pattern of contrasts begins with the hard wits/quick
wits distinction and is carried over into the later distinctions
between true grace and false grace, responsible and irresponsible
courtiers, Protestants and Papists, and Englishmen and Italians.
Another involves the contrast between kinds of discipline described above. At the level of diction, pairs of opposed adjectives
and adverbs pervade the texture of Ascham's prose in a way that

---

[50] For assessments of Ascham's style, see George Philip Krapp, *The Rise of
English Literary Prose* (1915; rpt. New York: Ungar, 1963), 292–99; Alvin Vos,
"The Formation of Roger Ascham's Prose Style," *Studies in Philology* 71 (1973),
344–70; Vos, "Form and Function in Roger Ascham's Prose," *Philological Quarterly* 55 (1976), 305–22; and Mueller, *Native Tongue and the Word,* pp. 322–46.

would be difficult to overestimate. On one side, to name a few, are evil, wrong, ill, perverse, crooked, confused, barbarous, disobedient, uncomely, unhonest, monstrous, and misordered; on the other are good, true, right, plain, obedient, comely, honest, straight, and orderly. As forcefully and even as repetitively as the stylistic devices of the *Admonition*, these recurrent oppositions present a conceptual pattern, a way to organize and respond to our common experience. If they are successful, we join with Ascham because we are convinced his way is the way of God.

The Scholemaster, then, seeks to embody the discipline of true religion, to serve as an educational model that convincingly presents God's truth. In terms of the central metaphor of book one, it seeks to guide our journey, to carry us through the seas of error "under the reule of a skilfull master" (205), to ensure that we don't "hasard the triall of over manie perilous adventures" (215), to be a small boat full of "good and costlie ware" (217). This metaphor floats lazily through the book until it is brought to harbor by the danger of the Italian journey. Here Ascham, himself "a poore jorney man" (230) in religion, presents probably the central figure of book one, that of an English traveler, Ulysses-like, facing hellish dangers:

> He shall not alwayes in his absence out of England, light upon a ientle *Alcynous*, and walke in his faire gardens full of all harmelesse pleasures: but he shall sometymes, fall, either into the handes of some cruell *Cyclops*, or into the lappe of some wanton and dalying Dame *Calypso*: and so suffer the danger of many a deadlie Denne, not so full of perils, to distroy the body, as, full of vayne pleasures, to poyson the mynde. Some *Siren* shall sing to him a song, sweete in tune, but sownding in the ende, to his utter destruction. If *Scylla* drowne him not, *Carybdis* may fortune swaloe hym. Some *Circes* shall make him, of a plain English man, a right *Italian*. And at length to hell, or to some hellish place, is he likelie to go: from whence is hard returning, although one *Ulysses*, and that by *Pallas* ayde, and good counsell of *Tiresias* once escaped that horrible Den of deadly darkenes. (225)

This passage has more literal force in Ascham than it might elsewhere; in particular, his fear of the Sirens recalls his infamous claim in *Toxophilus* that "Wittes be not sharpened, but rather dulled, and made blunte" by the "sweete softenesse" of music (13), which "is farre more fitte for the womannishnesse of it to dwell in the courte among ladies, than for any great thing in it, which shoulde helpe good and sad studie, to abide in the universitie amonges scholers" (14). It is just like a quick wit to be led by his "busie" curiosity into "the inchantmentes of *Circes*, the vanitie of licencious pleasure, the inticementes of all sinne," when he should be feeding on "the herbe *Moly* . . . which, *Hesiodus* termeth the study of vertue, hard and irksome in the beginnyng, but in the end, easie and pleasant" (227). But in Ascham's reading of Homer, Christian theology still holds the wheel: Ulysses is protected by Pallas, who is "Gods speciall grace from heaven," and Moly, which is "that love of honestie, and hatred of ill, which *David* more plainly doth call the feare of God" (226). And, Ascham points out, "that, which is most to be marveled at" in this story is "that this medicine against sinne and vanitie, is not found out by man, but given and taught by God" (227).

With this reminder of the Reformed notion of theodidacti we return to Ascham's own status as teacher: he speaks not from his own invention or his own judgment, but as a representative of God's truth, authorized by his conviction. The journey he takes us on is finally God's journey:

> And thus farre have I wandred from my first purpose of teaching a child, yet not altogether out of the way, bicause this whole taulke hath tended to the onelie advauncement of troth in Religion, and honestie of living: and hath bene wholie within the compasse of learning and good maners, the speciall pointes belonging in the right bringyng up of youth.
>
> But to my matter, as I began, plainlie and simplie with my yong Scholer, so will I not leave him, God willing, untill I have brought him a perfite Scholer out of the Schole, and placed him in the Universitie, to becum a fitte student, for Logicke and Rhetoricke: and so after to Phisicke, Law, or Divinitie, as aptness of nature, advise of frendes, and Gods disposition shall lead him. (236–37)

These last two paragraphs of the first book deny that his educational efforts could take any other form than they have so far:

Ascham will continue to guide his students plainly and simply in accordance with God's will and disposition, just as he has in admonishing us.

An Admonition to the Parliament and *The Scholemaster* are both texts about education that seek to educate plainly, to create communities out of convictions. Although the humanist Ascham cares more than the Puritan authors of the *Admonition* do about human learning, both he and the Puritans believe that human wit or invention is of limited value because a complete guide to conduct in every situation is already available. Both consequently believe that education should teach precepts but focus on the will, on motivating right action in a given situation. Both see education as discipline, hence as admonishing, hence as preaching—that is, as moving people to act according to the plain truth. Both, moreover, attempt to function as models of educational discipline by speaking authoritatively about how to cure the faults of current discipline. Where do they get this authority? Ascham as prophet and Field and Wilcox as martyrs claim the authority of a moral minority, of a voice crying out in the wilderness. They present themselves as embattled, but as determined to transmit God's will whatever the personal cost. Both texts work as writing by transferring the authority located in a plain source to their own performance, even as they partly create that authority by a persuasive performance of conviction.

3 Peace, Order, and Confusion: Fulke Greville and the Inner and Outer Forms of Reform

To this point I have distinguished and illustrated the private and public forms of plainness, but in doing so have attempted to avoid postulating a simple public-private dualism. Wyatt's private plainness, I argued, required public performance to sustain it, while the public plainness of the *Admonition* and *The Scholemaster* needed to appeal strongly to the will of the individual believers. Plainness, I now suggest, involves not so much a sharp division between public and private (although this can be a part of it) as particular forms of connection between them. Plainness tends to unite public and private forms of authority in the common bond of certainty. Because both public and private plainness feature a feeling faith, they may become virtually indistinguishable, even when they seem to be most distinct. Such is the case with the plainness of Fulke Greville.

Greville's life and work have generally been understood in terms of his dualism. Critics from Geoffrey Bullough to Jonathan Dollimore have emphasized it, and the two most important book-length studies of Greville, Ronald Rebholz's *Life* and Richard Waswo's *Fatal Mirror*, build their interpretations on the foundation it offers.[1] In a dualistic reading, Greville's life is shaped large-

---

[1] The dualistic reading of Greville began with Geoffrey Bullough's argument that in Greville "the fissure [between the ideal and the actual] ran deep and unbridged, affecting his actions as well as his philosophy" ("Fulk[e] Greville, Lord

ly by his perception, in Dollimore's words, of "the gulf between God and man, divine and secular, spiritual and material, absolute and relative" (120). Greville's pessimism results from the conflict between the temporal claims of his long service at court and the eternal claims of his Protestant belief, and his career is conveniently summed up by his remark in a letter that "I know the world and believe in God"[2] or by the declaration of his Chorus Sacerdotum that it is humanity's "wearisome Condition" to be "Borne under one Law, to another bound."[3]

This reading of Greville holds to a point. It correctly identifies Greville's Calvinist claim to have distinguished the private, spiritual kingdom of religion from the public, material realm of politics. For example, when he warns not to mix "God, and earth together" because "the wisdome of the worlde, and his, are two,"[4] Greville supports Calvin's contention that

> there is a twofold government in man: one aspect is spiritual, whereby the conscience is instructed in piety and in reverencing God; the second is political, whereby man is educated for the duties of humanity and citizenship that must be maintained among men. These are usually called the "spiritual" and the "temporal" jurisdiction. . . . The former resides in the inner mind, while the latter regulates only outward behavior. . . . Now these two . . . must always be examined separately. . . . There are in man, so to

Brooke," *Modern Language Review* 28 [1933], 1–20; quotation from p. 1). Also see Una Ellis-Fermor, intro., *Caelica* (Newtown, Montgomeryshire: Gregynog Press, 1936); Ronald A. Rebholz, *The Life of Fulke Greville, First Lord Brooke* (Oxford: Clarendon Press, 1971); Richard Waswo, *The Fatal Mirror: Themes and Techniques in the Poetry of Fulke Greville* (Charlottesville: University of Virginia Press, 1972); Gary F. Waller, "Fulke Greville's Struggle with Calvinism," *Studia Neophilologica* 44 (1972), 295–314; and Jonathan Dollimore, *Radical Tragedy: Religion, Ideology, and Power in the Drama of Shakespeare and His Contemporaries* (Brighton: Harvester Press, 1984). On Greville's life, see also Joan Rees, *Fulke Greville, Lord Brooke, 1554–1628* (Berkeley: University of California Press, 1971).

[2] Cited in Rebholz, *Life of Fulke Greville*, p. 216.

[3] Fulke Greville, *Mustapha*, Chorus Sacerdotum, ll. 1–2, in *The Poems and Dramas of Fulke Greville, Lord Brooke*, ed. Geoffrey Bullough, 2 vols. (Edinburgh: Oliver & Boyd, 1939). Further references to this work (Mus) appear in the text.

[4] Greville, *A Treatie of Humane Learning*, st. 98, in *Poems and Dramas*, ed. Bullough. Further references to this work (HL) appear in the text.

speak, two worlds, over which different kings and different laws have authority.[5]

However, the dualistic reading risks accepting uncritically the claims of Greville (and other Reformed thinkers) to have separated an inner realm of religious freedom from an outer, political realm. The difficulty of maintaining such a distinction even in the abstract is amply illustrated by the *Institutes* themselves; in a wider historical context the problems of separating religious and political authorities proved practically insurmountable. Reformation Protestants faced what David Little calls "the dilemma of earthly power—of power which is fundamentally differentiated from the new order because of its coercive characteristics and which is, at the same time, subordinated and harnessed to the achievement of the new order."[6] Consequently they viewed king and bishop as agents of both repression and reformation— repression when they served papistry or some comparable tyranny (as in Greville's Turkish plays) and reformation when their power advanced true religion. Hence, the conviction that political power operated in the service of the Word was enough to satisfy most Reformers, including the many early Puritans (bishops and laypeople alike) who were content to seek reform within the Elizabethan church. For them, as Patrick Collinson has argued, private religious freedom was a secondary consideration: "Religion was a public duty, not a private opinion or a voluntary profession. . . . When the puritans attacked the imperfections of the Elizabethan religious settlement, it was not so much to request a toleration of their own consciences as to demand the imposition of true reformation, as they understood it, on the whole Church and nation, by public authority."[7] The dualistic division between

[5] John Calvin, *Institutes of the Christian Religion*, ed. John T. McNeill, trans. Ford Lewis Battles, Library of Christian Classics, vol. 21 (Philadelphia: Westminster Press, 1960), 3.19.15.

[6] David Little, *Religion, Order, and Law: A Study in Pre-Revolutionary England* (New York: Harper Torchbooks, 1969), p. 75.

[7] Patrick Collinson, *The Elizabethan Puritan Movement* (Berkeley: University of California Press, 1967), p. 25. Writing of Elizabethan and Jacobean Conformity, Collinson describes a "secondary voluntarism," which arose when the individual

"religious idealism" (which corresponds to private plainness) and "political realism" (public plainness) is thus misleading: to early Protestants political power was too obviously an enabling condition of religious reform.

Greville's view of the relation of political power to religious reform was no exception. Reform was uppermost in his mind, and he devoted much of his life to achieving it through political means. Yet earthly power remained a dilemma for him; like other Reformers, he struggled to balance politics and religion, worrying that monarchy would become tyranny and propagate false religion instead of true. His struggle is an especially interesting one for a study of plainness because his conception of *reform* is so striking. Greville says very little about a return to Scripture; he says still less about a return to a primitive church. In fact, such topical concerns as preaching, vestments, the sacraments, church government, and liturgical practices are strangely absent from his work. Instead, a fear of *confusion* suffuses Greville's writings, surfacing both in a dominant strand of figurative language and in one of his major conceptual frameworks. Confusion signifies the biblical confusion of tongues at Babel, a condition of multivocal uncertainty that Greville links with disobedience and sees as the essence of sin. The confusion of tongues is associated with debate and deliberation, and his fear of it leads Greville to reject the communal and contingent knowledge most often associated during this time with the practices of rhetoric. Since Greville shared the Reformation belief that the knowledge essential to salvation was plain and simple, true reform leads away from confusion to the certainty and unity of the one true voice of God. Sin and reform are thus, in the first place, contrasting attitudes toward language and truth: reform must cure the linguistic and epistemological confusion that weakens both the inward man and his outward institutions.

For Greville, both religion and politics offered means of reforming confusion and so returning to God. He sometimes expresses

---

will tried to conform to a God known largely through the existing practices of church and society, and eventuated in "a stereotyped, programmed corporateness." See *The Religion of Protestants: The Church in English Society, 1559–1625* (Oxford: Oxford University Press, 1982), p. 251.

the belief that no human effort can bridge the gulf between God and man. Only faith can save, he says on such occasions;[8] the political, the temporal, and the ethical are unavailing. We can close the distance between relative and absolute only if God plants the seed of grace within us. Greville most often calls this seed "peace." Yet Greville also valued willed ethical activity highly throughout his life and held a belief (which he acknowledged infrequently) that salvation might be earned by traveling an outer, political path that he, like most of his contemporaries, termed "order." While there are differences between peace and order, it is wrong to identify peace too closely with an absolute world of the spirit and order exclusively with a relative world of material reality. Greville in fact sought to avoid just such a split. To him, both peace and order were to some extent *practical* attempts to restore eternal truth to the realm of historical action. At the same time, Greville tended to treat peace and order as sources of plain truth whose authority approached the absolute—and as the sources of his own authority. There is therefore a fundamental blurring of categories in Greville that defies the neatness of a dualistic reading. Peace, denoting a private, inward religious experience, crosses with the public, outward world of political order, and relative truth crosses with absolute truth in both religion and politics.

One of my objectives in this chapter is to clarify the implications for plainness of Greville's religious and political views. I first show the pervasive influence of the triad of peace, order, and confusion in Greville's thought, and then demonstrate the difficulty of separating peace from order, or private from public plainness. I argue that Greville's writings show not so much the tension between a politician's realism and a Protestant's idealism as the compatibility of the two forms of reform when both consistently avoid rhetorical practice. In this case the authority of private religious experience fails to offer a true alternative to public authority; the conscience fails to become an effective source of resistance; and Greville's inner life strongly resembles the certainties of public plainness. But I have another goal. If anything

[8] For example, Greville, *A Treatise of Religion*, st. 79, in *The Remains*, ed. G. A. Wilkes (Oxford: Oxford University Press, 1965). Further references to this work (R) appear in the text.

about Greville other than his supposed dualism (and possibly his epitaph) has left a strong impression on the world, it is his authoritative poetic voice, which has interested Romantic and post-Romantic readers alike.[9] I conclude by arguing that Greville's voice is best understood in the context of the problem of authority in his work and, conversely, that the exact relation at any time in Greville's work between peace and order is itself partly a function of his voice.

With Greville, as with many of his contemporaries, the desire for certainty reacts against the pragmatism of humanist rhetorical and political practice. Humanism in its rhetorical aspect sought a consensual or probable truth within a historical—and thus a societal—context. Language, as the vehicle of this search, was viewed as primarily public and deliberative. For the search to continue it was crucial to maintain a faith, or trust, in the usefulness of contingent public standards of judgment; prudential wisdom (phronesis) could then function as a historically variable basis for rhetoric and politics. But Greville had no such faith in public language and public standards of judgment. Instead, he attacked human and humanist learning from the perspective of Pyrrhonist skepticism, the radical doubt transmitted by Sextus Empiricus's Outlines of Pyrrhonism to the receptive minds of Cornelius Agrippa and Montaigne, among others.[10] From this perspective, human attempts to arrive at truth could yield only confusion in both word and deed. For Greville, as for Luther, rhetoric's emphasis on free will and deliberation caused confusion precisely by separating Word from deed: a truly obedient Christian acted out the truth he already knew and left what he didn't

[9] For a survey of critical response to Greville's poetry, see Waswo, Fatal Mirror, chap. 5.

[10] On Renaissance Pyrrhonism, see Richard H. Popkin, The History of Scepticism from Erasmus to Spinoza, 2d ed. (Berkeley: University of California Press, 1979); Lawrence Manley, Convention 1500–1700 (Cambridge: Harvard University Press, 1980); Arthur F. Kinney, Humanist Poetics: Thought, Rhetoric, and Fiction in Sixteenth-Century England (Amherst: University of Massachusetts Press, 1986); and, for the impact of Pyrrhonism on legal and historical studies, Julian H. Franklin, Jean Bodin and the Sixteenth-Century Revolution in the Methodology of Law and History (New York: Columbia University Press, 1963), chap. 6.

know to God. Greville consequently sought a union of knowledge and action that would avoid the hazards of deliberation.

From his first works to his last, Greville consistently imagines the condition of sin in terms of the Tower of Babel and the confusion of tongues with which God punished its builders.[11] The lesson Greville draws from this biblical episode is, in the first place, a political one and is illustrated by *A Letter to an Honorable Lady*, Greville's early Neostoic advice to a woman "imprisond" in an unhappy marriage.[12] He counsels obedience and patience in enduring the wrongs of lawful power. Drawing the common analogy "between a wives subjection to a husband, and a subjects obedience to his soveraigne" (L 154), Greville argues that a tyrant in either position still has an authority and a power—that is, an ability to act—that a usurper would not. Attempting to encroach upon this power would be as foolhardy as building a tower to rival God:

> When the fleshlye Babylonians went about to prevent a second deluge, and so with mans power to limite Gods, they purposed to rayse a Tower equall to the heavens; thinckinge thereby that God should either favor their dwellinges, or destroy his owne. What came upon them? Marry a confusion of tongues; to the end that they, which understood not their maker, might much lesse understand themselves. An excellent course of the wisdome, to punishe vayne ends by fruictlesse labors. (L 145)

The lesson is that overstepping the divinely determined bounds of one's power and authority, attempting to do more than one can, leads one in the end to accomplish nothing.

---

[11] June Dwyer notes that for Greville the importance of the Babel story reaches beyond poetry. All arts are subject to the biblical warning. See "Fulke Greville's Aesthetic: Another Perspective," *Studies in Philology* 78 (1981), 255–74.

[12] Greville, *A Letter to an Honorable Lady*, in *The Prose Works of Fulke Greville, Lord Brooke*, ed. John Gouws (Oxford: Clarendon Press, 1986), p. 137. Further references to this work (L) appear in the text. On the analogy in this period between the king's authority in the state and the husband's authority in the family see, for example, Susan D. Amussen, "Gender, Family, and the Social Order, 1560–1725," in *Order and Disorder in Early Modern England*, ed. Anthony Fletcher and John Stevenson (Cambridge: Cambridge University Press, 1985).

This is a poignant lesson, not only for the woman but also for a
politician who, during an extraordinarily long period of service,
appears to have avoided exceeding the limits of his authority and
had little discernible influence on the course of events. But for
Greville, the image of Babel indicated more than a gap between
what one could and could not do. It indicated as well the gap
between what one did and did not know—a crucial lack of understanding punished with still more misunderstanding. In Greville's works the confusion of tongues refers to the chaotic labyrinth of competing versions of the truth that results when we try
to learn more than we should; it signifies the subjection of language to historical fluctuations and merely social conventions
that render it incapable of grasping eternal truth and directing
virtuous action.

Greville's conviction that human attempts to know exchange
an already present eternal truth for temporal confusion provides
the basis of his skeptical attack on knowledge in *A Treatie of
Humane Learning*.[13] Greville begins by arguing that the knowledge men can achieve through their own efforts is worthless because it lacks certainty. Because man is subject to the same fluctuations as all other temporal objects, his arts prove to be "fleshly
idols" that

> Confusedly doe weave within our hearts,
>   Their owne advancement, state, and declination,
>   As things whose beings are but transmutation.
>
>   (HL 55)

Human languages and arts exhibit the falseness of pride, the sin of
denying God's eternal truth and embracing the truth desired at
the moment. "The lie hath manie tongues, truth onlie one" (R
65); those who write with the "Words of men," rather than with
"Gods Word, or Penne" (HL 145), "doe but write to blot."[14] Hu-

---

[13] Greville goes on to propose a Baconian plan for reforming learning based on
simple induction, which, if properly obedient, escapes (he believes) the problem of
hermeneutic circularity by copying God's ahistorical design.

[14] Greville, *An Inquisition upon Fame and Honour*, st. 85, in *Poems and Dramas*. Further references to this work (F) appear in the text.

man knowledge is an ink stain, the meaningless din of too many
voices, a mold hopelessly out of shape:

> For if Mans wisedomes, lawes, arts, legends, schooles,
> Be built upon the knowledge of the evill;
> And if these Trophies be the onely tooles,
> Which doe maintaine the kingdome of the Divell;
>   If all these Babels had the curse of tongues,
>   So as confusion still to them belongs:
>
> Then can these moulds never containe their Maker.
>
>   (HL 46)

In Greville's terms elsewhere, probability, the "false and treach-
erous/Enemy of truth" attacked in *Caelica* 102 and 103, is confusion.[15]

Much of the brunt of Greville's attack is borne by rhetoric, the
champion of probability. In his eyes, rhetoric is just another human epistemological project, motivated by pride, that deflects
action from absolute truth. He lodges this charge repeatedly in *A
Treatie of Humane Learning*; rhetoric, he writes,

> Is growne a Siren in the formes of pleading,
> Captiving reason, with the painted skinne
> Of many words; with empty sounds misleading
>   Us to false ends, by these false forms abuse,
>   Brings never forth that Truth, whose name they use.
>
>   (HL 107)

The connection of "many words" and "false ends" is automatic
for Greville. Human learning substitutes "uselesse Arts" for "ar-

---

[15] Greville's doctrine of confusion rejects the famous anthropocentric teaching
of Protagoras echoed in the first lines of *Humane Learning*: "The Mind of Man is
this worlds true dimension; / And Knowledge is the measure of the minde" (HL
1). Human knowledge, the mind's measure, is a temporary historical product with
no connection to God's eternal truth. See the fragments of Protagoras translated
by Michael J. O'Brien in *The Older Sophists*, ed. Rosamond Kent Sprague (Columbia: University of South Carolina Press, 1972). On Renaissance understandings
and misunderstandings of Protagoras, see Charles Trinkaus, "Humanism and
Greek Sophism: Protagoras in the Renaissance," in *The Scope of Renaissance
Humanism* (Ann Arbor: University of Michigan Press, 1983), pp. 169–91.

tlesse Use" (HL 69); men "Lose that in practise, which in Arts they gaine" (HL 36). Such is the influence of "our Schooles," he concludes sententiously, that it may now be said, as it was of the schools of Athens,

> That many came first Wise men to those Schooles;
> Then grew Philosophers, or Wisdome-mongers;
> Next Rhetoricians, and at lasta grew fooles.
>
> (HL 37)

Here philosophy joins rhetoric on Greville's junk heap. He sees no essential difference between them: each involves the substitution of imperfect, probabilistic human constructions of the truth for real truth and each thereby prevents virtuous action. Like rhetoric, "Contemplation doth the world distract, / With vaine Ideas, which it cannot act" (HL 69). Both are "But bookes of Poesie, in Prose compil'd" (HL 29)—that is, they are fictions, human constructions of the truth, and therefore lies.

The remedy Greville offers for rhetorical confusion can be summed up initially in one word: obedience. Prideful man seeks "to binde, and never to be bound, / To governe God, and not be governed." This "is the cause his life is thus confused, / In his corruption, by these Arts abused" (HL 59). The true way is illustrated by those few "pure soules" who "Have no Art, but Obedience for their test" (HL 64). The need, then, is to purify the self from its wayward desires and to obey the will of God, in whom alone lies freedom. When we act in this way, all dualisms dissolve: knowing ceases to exist as an independent activity; obedience becomes indistinguishable from faith; and action dissolves into grace, an experience of total harmony with the divine will.

Greville first describes this monistic state in a remarkable passage in *A Letter to an Honorable Lady*:

> Let no ignorance seeme to excuse mankinde; since the light of truth is still neare us; . . . the lawes that guide, so good for them that obay, and the first shape of everie sinne so uglie; as whosoever doth but what he knowes, or forbeares what he doubts, shall easilie followe nature unto grace. . . . For obedience, not curiositie, as in heavenlie, so in earthlie things is the most acceptable sacrifice of

mankinde. Because this inherent tribute of nature unto power (like a revealed light of universall grace) refines mans reason; rectifies his will, turnes his industries, and learninges inward agayne whence they came; joynes words with thinges; and reduceth both of them to their first beinges. To conclude; this is that inward fabricke, by which we doe what we thinke, and speake what we doe. (L 153)

Most of what Greville stresses here is reiterated until his death— the scorn of curiosity, the respect for power, the figurative refining of reason. While some elements of his early Neostoicism are later subdued by his Christian faith—a faith that progressively distanced itself from the idea that grace could be found "easilie"—Greville's belief that obedience unites knowing and doing remained the cornerstone of his thought throughout his lifetime. For example, in the final twenty-four stanzas of *Humane Learning*, Greville discusses the obedient elect of God, praising their lack of "idle Curiositie" (HL 144), and emphasizing that their innocence of any purpose other than "to know, and doe" (HL 131) places them in an ideal world where passion and reason (HL 130), goodness and truth (HL 137), life and wisdom are one:

> For onely that man understands indeed,
> And well remembers, which he well can doe;
> The Laws live, onely where the Law doth breed
> Obedience to the workes it bindes us to:
>   And as the life of Wisedome hath exprest,
>   If this you know, then doe it, and be blest.
>
>   (HL 140)[16]

For Greville, knowledge worthy of the name is inseparable from the action it commands.

The command to obey can function in two ways, however. When rhetorical knowing has been declared a mass of confusion, truth (to the extent that it remains knowable) must be apprehended either through private insight or through the institutional exercise of power (including a theocracy). In Greville's terms, the

[16] Cf. Greville, R 12, 62, 85.

first of these options is "peace," the second "order." The first may seem more suitable to Greville the Protestant; the second, to Greville the politician: but both provide access to the truth needed to conquer confusion in an obedient union of knowing and doing.

Peace is first presented as an outcome of obedience in *A Letter to an Honorable Lady*, where Greville writes that "in all inward wayes to peace, man needes no lawes but Gods, and his owne obeydience" (L 152). The inverse relation, in which disobedience turns peace to confusion, is illustrated by *Caelica* 102:

> In sinnes excesse there yet confusions be,
> Which spoyle his peace, and passionate his wit,
>   Making his Nature lesse, his Reason thrall
>   To tyranny of vice unnaturall.[17]

Peace is the stilling of confused voices, the escape from the endless motion of the passions, the overthrow of the tyranny of desiring more knowledge. Defining peace in *Caelica* 96 as "the seed of grace, in dead flesh sowne," Greville describes its genesis: sense, desire, and wit rebel against the rule of reason, leading initially to pleasure, but eventually to a "confused sphere" in which "Flesh, with her many moulds of Change and Will," carries the affections into the pain of error and "Vice, a restlesse infinite." From the depths of this chaotic hell man cries out for grace, which begins to move him toward an apprehension of the truth he will know after his flesh has died. In this way he achieves peace, which is the goodness to do what he knows is right, that is, obey God's truth.

The second fruit of obedience is social order, which results when political unity is enforced upon confusion. Confusion is the problem of human excess, which informs human history: although God's truth is always present, it becomes lost in the Babel caused by man's efforts to compound it with knowledge of his own. As man "declines" throughout history, he moves further and further away from God's truth, yet some semblance of the divine voice remains audible among the voices of error, and some

---

[17] Greville, *Caelica* 102, in *Poems and Dramas*. Further references to this work (C) appear in the text.

semblance of God's law and order remains legible in human laws and institutions. Consequently, after describing the confused state of learning in the first sixty stanzas of *A Treatie of Humane Learning*, Greville devotes the next sixty-three stanzas to explaining that truth in learning is "a bunch of grapes sprung up among the thornes" (HL 62) and that church and state must help to separate these grapes from the thorns of confusion by enforcing stability in public opinion. In every art, he writes, "there should / One, or two Authors be selected out, / To cast the learners in a constant mould" (HL 78). When confusions do arise, it is

> to be wished, each Kingdome would
> Within her proper Soveraignity,
> Seditions, Schismes, and strange Opinions mould
> By Synods, to a setled unity.
>
> (HL 86)

A society, in Greville's view, simply cannot afford to tolerate a multiplicity of erroneous voices. Such diversity of opinion can produce only a barren confusion, not a fruitful conversation. Unity is essential, and as King Soliman says in *Mustapha*, "Order alone holds States in Unity" (Mus I.i.126).

Greville's sharp distinction of inner peace from outer order sometimes appears to include a preference for the former. Thus he remarks that "The world doth build without, our God within; / He traffiques goodnesse, and she traffiques sinne" (R 98). He frequently asserts that even true outward forms mean nothing if "in the inward man there's nothing new" (HL 81). Again, after describing for some forty stanzas in *Humane Learning* how the arts can be changed from confusion to unity, he cautions that arts so changed may "conforme," and yet "reforme us not" (HL 125).[18] The outward conformity of order evidently does not guarantee the peaceful inward reformation that is our goal: instead, "all rests in the hart" (R 95).

But despite this occasional preference for an inward experience of grace, the overall force of Greville's writing dissolves any such

---

[18] Cf. Greville's judgment in *Fame* of the human arts, "which constraine, but not instruct the minde" (F 16); also C 97, R 85.

dualism. By itself the assertion that "all rests in the hart" sounds like the sort of affirmation of the sufficiency of faith conventionally associated with the more radical forms of Protestantism, but the phrase in context is part of a rejection of separatism and apocalyptic fantasy: "Arckes nowe wee looke for none, nor signes to part / Egypt from Israel; all rests in the hart" (R 95). As sharply as he distinguishes the seen from the unseen church, Greville is content to remain within the Church of England because, like other Conformists, he believes that a legalistic alteration may bring reformation, a truly "heavenlie change" (R 44). If we could somehow "bend the force of power and witte / To worcke upon the hart," he proclaims, "Good life would finde a good Religion out" (R 15).[19] Greville can never acknowledge that he holds such a belief—which he often revealingly phrases in contrary-to-fact conditional clauses—for it betrays a residual Catholic confidence that salvation can be merited. If pressed, he would probably have responded that obedience, law, and order did not themselves occasion grace; they simply made clear to "the best" the need to endure the "paine of Regeneration," while restraining "the rest" (R 48, HL 151). But in practice the ethical emphasis revealed in Greville's insistence on obedience and the union of knowing and doing makes it impossible for him to distinguish faith from works, or peace from order, for long.

The fusion of peace and order emerges clearly in Greville's views of conscience, episcopacy, and kingship. The Reformation conception of conscience played an important role in challenging institutional authority and in establishing the authority of individual judgment. To the Middle Ages, conscience had been a judging of specific actions by the Aristotelian practical reason. But beginning with Luther, the sphere of conscience expanded from ethics to salvation: conscience became the faculty that judged the fitness of the whole person before God, apprehending both the

---

[19] On the difference between Conformist and Puritan understandings of the relation of order to spiritual reformation, see John S. Coolidge, *The Pauline Renaissance in England: Puritanism and the Bible* (Oxford: Oxford University Press, 1970), p. 49.

judgment of the Law and the promise of salvation in the Gospel.[20] Because conscience was responsible for apprehending the truth of salvation, it became closely associated with Christian liberty, the freedom from the Law brought by the believer's faith in the promise of mercy. According to Luther, Christian freedom "is a freedom of conscience which liberates the conscience from works."[21] "Neither pope, nor bishop, nor anyone else, has the right to impose so much as a single syllable of obligation upon a Christian man without his own consent."[22] Conscience was not bound by human laws or institutions, which were fallible, but only by Scripture and evident reason. The Reformation belief in freedom of conscience was therefore the precondition for challenging traditional forms of institutional authority. Faith alone led to conscience alone. At the radical limit of the Reformation, the conscience was sovereign.

Greville sometimes expresses the radical view of conscience. In his view, conscience is a certain authority, carrying a perfect impression of God's law;[23] it offers a "sentence of record" (R 14), or

---

[20] See Michael G. Baylor, *Action and Person: Conscience in Late Scholasticism and the Young Luther*, Studies in Medieval and Reformation Thought, vol. 20 (Leiden: E. J. Brill, 1977), and Bernard Lohse, "Conscience and Authority in Luther," in *Luther and the Dawn of the Modern Era*, ed. Heiko A. Oberman, Studies in the History of Christian Thought, vol. 8 (Leiden: E. J. Brill, 1974), pp. 158–83. On conscience more generally see Elliot Rose, *Cases of Conscience: Alternatives Open to Recusants and Puritans under Elizabeth I and James I* (Cambridge: Cambridge University Press, 1975), and Margo Todd, *Christian Humanism and the Puritan Social Order* (Cambridge: Cambridge University Press, 1987), chap. 6. For a brief overview of casuistry see Camille Wells Slights, *The Casuistical Tradition in Shakespeare, Donne, Herbert, and Milton* (Princeton: Princeton University Press, 1981), chaps. 1–2.

[21] Martin Luther, *The Judgment of Martin Luther on Monastic Vows* (1521), in *Luther's Works*, American Edition, vol. 44 (Philadelphia: Fortress Press, 1966), p. 298. Calvin argues that "in certain chapters of Galatians, Paul is solely trying to show how to us Christ is obscured, or rather, extinguished, unless our consciences stand firm in their freedom" (*Inst.* 3.19.14). Calvin sets forth his idea of the conscience in *Institutes* 3.13.3–5 and 4.10.3–5.

[22] Martin Luther, *The Babylonian Captivity of the Church*, in *Martin Luther: Selections from His Writings*, ed. John Dillenberger (New York: Doubleday, 1961), p. 304.

[23] Greville, *A Treatise of Monarchy*, st. 241, in *Remains*. Further references to this work (M) appear in the text. Cf. R 12.

incontrovertible evidence of right and wrong, not merely "vayne opinion (borne of sence)" (M 37).[24] Following conscience thus seems the purest form of obedience. Further, Greville demonstrates his understanding and acceptance of a conscience active toward salvation in *Caelica* 98, a prayer for deliverance:

> Thy power and mercy never comprehended
> Rest lively imag'd in my Conscience wounded;
> Mercy to grace, and power to feare extended,
> Both infinite, and I in both confounded.

Accordingly, Greville will champion Christian liberty and the "sacred stile of conscience" (M 37), urging that his readers "Make not mens conscience, wealth, and libertie / Servile without booke to unbounded will" (M 286). The church, the arena of Christian freedom, must be kept separate from the "sword of power" (R 29): "where swords and Cannons doe unite, / The peoples bondage there proves infinite" (M 210). Catholic attempts to "instruct" conscience epitomize such bondage: the Roman Church, Greville complains in a brilliant metaphor, has "Power for a pensile, conscience for a table, / To write opinion in of any fashion" (M 216).[25] Greville also saw Catholic abuses of power perpetuated by the retention of episcopacy in the Church of England.[26] His strongly antiprelatical stance finds its counterpart, moreover, in his disapproval of the principle *cuius regio eius religio*. For example, he criticizes the French belief that "one chief branch of our princes' prerogatives . . . [is] the carrying of their

---

[24] Greville disagrees here with William Perkins, who sees the conscience as the location of critical self-reflection. According to Perkins, "there be two actions of the understanding, the one is simple, which barely conceiveth or thinketh this or that: the other is a *reflecting* or doubting of the former, whereby a man conceives or thinks with himselfe what he thinkes. And this action properly pertaines to the conscience." See *A Discourse of Conscience*, in *William Perkins, 1558–1602*, ed. Thomas F. Merrill (Nieuwkoop: B. De Graaf, 1966), p. 7.

[25] Here Greville agrees with Perkins, who argues against the Catholic position that "Civill and Ecclesiasticall jurisdiction have a coactive power in the conscience" (*Discourse of Conscience*, 22).

[26] Wilkes discusses the likelihood that Greville's antiprelatical position led to the suppression in 1633 of *Religion* in his "Textual Introduction," pp. 22–23. Greville's attacks on prelacy are concentrated in R 30–31, 68–69, and 92.

people's consciences which way they list."[27] When such princes, seeking an "Authority / More absolute then God himself requires" (M 29), raise their power "Upon the base of superstitions rites" (M 37), religion becomes the "cheif strength of tirranny" (M 207). The conscience free from external constraint, then, appears to be the safest way to escape from confusion to God.

Despite such remarks, however, Greville's advocacy of safeguards for liberty of conscience proves strictly circumscribed. Like other Reformers, he tends to say one thing when facing conservative opponents and something else when facing radicals. The radical here is the subjectivism that virtually everyone feared in appeals to conscience, particularly by the unregenerate. Greville fears the human tendency to "seeke out a God" "in our selves" (R 19), where we find only the confusion, disobedience, and faithlessness bred by wit and the affections. Confusion causes people to act against their consciences, which they thereby "wound" (HL 93, C 98).[28] Because these wounds attest a continuing need for God, they should drive the regenerate toward a fuller experience of divine peace. But Greville sometimes imagines conscience, governed by "our infirmitie" (R 16), trying to escape its wounds by seeking "God, and Religion from without" (R 14). In this way it forfeits some of its freedom and becomes subject to external influence.

Although Greville sometimes condemns this influence, he more frequently defends royal implementation of religion. Kings "Derive their earthlie power from power Divine" (R 66), and should make religion "the first foundation of their Raignes" (M 202). The proper way to do so is by "that formall unitie, / Which brookes no new, or irreligious sects" (M 222). In this way kings can "plant obeying conscience" (M 222) as the "base of their authoritie" (M 238) and thus contain the confusion that makes their power necessary (M 24). Kings here regulate conscience in much the same way that Greville elsewhere deplores in prelacy. Despite a clear-eyed recognition that tyrants may abuse both roy-

---

[27] Greville, *A Dedication to Sir Philip Sidney*, in *Prose Works*, p. 31. Further references to this work (S) appear in the text.

[28] The "wounds" of conscience are also discussed by Perkins, *A Discourse of Conscience*, pp. 3, 43, and 69.

al sovereignty and religion, Greville fully endorses the authority of kings to direct behavior and conscience by means of laws and discipline.[29]

Greville's views on discipline make his monarchist sentiments especially clear. During his lifetime the word "discipline" had become virtually synonymous with Puritanism. It expressed the Presbyterian concern that the church have its own power to punish offenders, which was at least a potential challenge to state hegemony. But while Greville must have known the Presbyterian connotations well, discipline in his usage is, if sometimes a part of church practice (e.g., HL 89), nevertheless firmly enforced by the king.[30] For example, the controversy over the exercise of church censures, especially excommunication, provides an occasion for Greville to describe how the discipline of civil law, the church, and conscience can combine to direct behavior. Laws, he writes,

> must assist Church-censure, punish Error,
> Since when, from Order, Nature would decline,
> There is no other native cure but terror;
> By Discipline, to keepe the Doctrine free,
> That Faith and Power still relatives may be.

[29] Although Greville is careful to deny that kings have power over the soul (M 209), his mature view of political resistance remains the most conservative of available options—that only passive nonobedience, not active resistance, is lawful. But on his likely familiarity with and possible early sympathy for Buchanan's *De Jure Regni* and the *Vindiciae Contra Tyrannos*, see Rebholz, *Life of Fulke Greville*, pp. 28, 148–49, and Hugh N. Maclean, "Fulke Greville: Kingship and Sovereignty," *Huntington Library Quarterly* 16 (1953), 237–71. On resistance theory more generally, see especially Quentin Skinner, *Foundations of Modern Political Thought* (Cambridge: Cambridge University Press, 1978), vol. 2, and Richard L. Greaves, "Concepts of Political Obedience in Late Tudor England: Conflicting Perspectives," *Journal of British Studies* 22 (1982), 23–34. Resistance theory and casuistry were closely related studies, and the difference between Protestant and Catholic resistance theory parallels that between Protestant and Catholic casuistry. In both cases the authority that Protestants vested in personal readings of Scripture was placed by Catholics in the decisions of the church.

[30] Greville was a member of the radical Protestant party at court in the 1580s and corresponded with Thomas Wilcox. See Rebholz, *Life of Fulke Greville*, chap. 2, and Collinson, *Elizabethan Puritan Movement*, p. 86.

> Let this faire hand-maid then the Church attend,
> And to the wounds of Conscience adde her paines,
> That private hearts may unto publike ends
> Still govern'd be, by Orders easie raines;
>   And by effect, make manifest the cause
>   Of happy States to be religious Lawes.
>
>   (HL 92–93)

This passage vividly illustrates how public authority can infringe on the putative autonomy of conscience—an interest that is central to Foucauldian criticism, including John Stachniewski's argument that the internalization of Calvinist disciplinary practices contributed to an epidemic of despair in English Puritanism.[31] Royal power here harmonizes private and public interests, religion and law, by uniting conscience and external constraints, faith and power, peace and order, in the way Stachniewski describes. From this perspective Greville concluded that a monarchy offered the best chance to silence confusion with discipline and order.

But does assigning kings authority over discipline and conscience grant them reforming power, the power to save? Or do the words "Nature" and "native" in the passage just quoted indicate that spiritual regeneration is beyond the power of laws and kings? This is a difficult question, and at times Greville's choice of locutions seems to court uncertainty on this crucial point. For instance, *A Treatise of Monarchy* explains that properly religious kings may use laws to "unite, / If not in truth, at least in outward rite" (M 206), and that a man who is "instructed well [by discipline], and kept in awe, / If not the inward, keepes the outward law" (M 230). Such statements say neither that kings can assist inward truth and obedience nor that they cannot. Theirs is the power of suggestion, and they suggest that the establishment of good order won't impair regeneration and may at least help to prepare individuals for the coming of grace. A similar inconclusiveness attaches even to some very direct statements Greville

---

[31] John Stachniewski, *The Persecutory Imagination: English Puritanism and the Literature of Religious Despair* (Oxford: Clarendon Press, 1991).

makes about the relation between kings and inner life. For example, while a tyrant expects only an outward, formal obedience,

> a true kinge in his estate affects
> Soe from within man, to worke out the right,
> As his will neede not lymitt, or allay
> The liberties of Gods immortall way.
>
>   (M 231)

Here it isn't clear to what extent, if any, the general, active force
of "worke out" survives the passive specification of "not lymitt,
or allay." Still, the cumulative effect of passages like this one is, I
believe, clear enough: kings who "Rather perswade the people,
then constraine" (M 495), who use counsels "not of feare, but
love" (M 303), and in whom, as in "cleare Mirrors," their subjects
"reade the heavenly glory of the good" (HL 135), are godly kings,
touching those beneath them not just materially but spiritually.[32]
This much would be clear even if Greville hadn't invoked his
favorite metaphor for God, the mirror, and even if he hadn't
grouped kings with the elect rather than with the merely "con-
forming" arts in *A Treatie of Humane Learning*. There is more to
Greville's conception of royal power than a harsh, external discipline; it also involves a nurturing process similar to Puritan "edification." Although he states the belief cautiously and even am-
bivalently, Greville appears to hold that monarchy may lead
people toward God.

Greville's caution also makes it difficult to say whether his
opinion on the efficacy of human efforts to reach salvation
changed late in his life. There is undeniably a major change from
the stoic self-sufficiency of the early *Letter* to the position I have
been outlining. I am unconvinced, however, by Rebholz's argument that the Greville of *A Treatise of Religion* had lost his hope
that "redeemed institutions might nurture the holiness" of an
elect who were themselves "powerless to save the world" (311).

---

[32] Greville praises Queen Elizabeth for having been "more desirous to find ways
to fashion her people than colours or causes to punish them" (S 37). On Puritan
views of kingship and government, see William M. Lamont, *Godly Rule: Politics
and Religion, 1603–1660* (London: Macmillan, 1969).

Even in his earlier works Greville limited the church to performing charitable deeds and preaching "that which seemes mans life
to mend" (M 225). He advocates similar functions in *Religion*,
declaring that holy men "should be keyes to let his will passe
out, / Binde sinne, and free repentance by his word" (R 69). The
current bishops fall far short of this ideal, of course; but, as generally in Greville's writings, the elect can apparently still approach
true religion within the existing structures "by usinge all thinges
of . . . [their] owne / To others good" (R 46). It is true that Greville's emphasis on the saving power of grace was never stronger
than in *Religion*, but we should expect to find this in the chief
doctrinal statement of a Protestant who never attributed a major
role to organized religion.

As for the institution in which Greville placed most hope, his
comments in *Religion* are brief. "Crownes" derive their power
from God, and, while tyrants remain a concern, we still wish for
Davids (R 66, 91, 106). His conclusion is characteristically incon-
clusive: "Thrones are the worldes; howe they stand well with
heaven, / Those powers can judge, to whom that grace is given"
(R 91). In *Religion* Greville may not hope for much from human
institutions and efforts, but he doesn't appear to me to have less
hope than usual. He isn't yet ready to abandon the world—his
emphasis on obedience and good deeds is as strong as ever, and he
repeatedly pairs obedience with faith (R 64, 72, 102, 105). From
looking simply at *what* Greville says, then, it remains difficult to
say whether peace or order is more important.

I am also unconvinced that Greville's views have changed in
Religion because *how* he speaks has not changed significantly. I
will now examine Greville's tone, or voice—by which I mean the
rhetorical relation between speaker and audience established in
part by his style—as a testing ground for his ideas. In reflecting
on Greville's unsuccessful attempt in the last year of his life to
establish a history lectureship at Cambridge, Rebholz remarks
that Greville's "practice was still more lenient than his doctrine"
(311). But the writings in which Greville puts his doctrine forward
themselves constitute a practice we may call literary or rhetorical. What are the characteristics of this practice, and what relation does it bear to Greville's doctrine? Given Greville's distaste

for the public forum of rhetoric, we would expect his writing to be
rhetorically troublesome.[33] His dim view of worldly judgment
should make publication awkward. He chose not to publish most
of what he wrote during his lifetime, which increases the problem of a rhetorical assessment. However, he did prepare his work
carefully for posthumous publication, so it is not necessary to
devise a rhetoric of the closet. Instead, we might consider first
Greville's own theory of writing and then the evidence his style
offers of how he intended to put his theory into practice.

Greville conceives of true utterance very much as an act of
doing good. This conception extends even to the primarily inward
motion of prayer: the members of the true church "doe in pray-
inge, and still praye in doeinge; / Faith, and obedience are theyr
Contemplation" (R 64). But Greville develops the idea of language
as action mostly in the context of more public discourse. In *A
Treatise of Monarchy*, for instance, he complains about the dull
histories written by "wranglinge mouncks" and looks back to the
golden age of men of "actyve worth," "who, what by sword they
wan, / By pen as lively registred to man." From these examples
Greville concludes that

> when tymes iron days should blast
> That manlie discipline of doing well,
> The art of writing should no longer last,
> Lyke natures twynns that must together dwell;
>   Doinge and writinge being to each other,
>   As bodies be of their owne shadowes mother.
>   (M 485–89)

Good writing is produced by active men who, by writing, are
obediently doing good, just as they are in their other activities.
Philip Sidney was such a man, whose "end was not writing even
while he wrote, nor his knowledge moulded for tables or schools,
but both his wit and understanding bent upon his heart to make

---

[33] David Norbrook suggests that Greville's ambivalence about his political
themes is related to his rhetorical uncertainty, but only glances at the significance
of Greville's own rhetorical theory and practice as a response to this uncertainty.
See *Poetry and Politics in the English Renaissance* (London: Routledge & Kegan
Paul, 1984).

himself and others, not in words or opinion, but in life and action, good and great" (S 12). This "architectonical art"[34] is the basis of Greville's well known definition of eloquence in *Humane Learning*:

> For the true Art of Eloquence indeed
> Is not this craft of words, but formes of speech,
> Such as from living wisdomes doe proceed;
> Whose ends are not to flatter, or beseech,
> Insinuate, or perswade, but to declare
> What things in Nature good, or evill are.
>
> (HL 110)

Despite Greville's contrasting list of suspect alternatives, a declaration isn't just a neutral statement about something, an abstract wisdom, a value-free representation of reality; it's a formal and emphatic public action, an attempt to extend a particular conception of good and evil, and thus to participate in reality. Writing is thus not an inquiry into the true, or part of a conversation about the good, but one more opportunity to unite truth and action by obeying God's command.[35]

The consequence of this theory in Greville's mature work is a voice that can be characterized as authoritative, or commanding. As such it contrasts with the voice of the early *Caelica* poems, which often become genuinely controversial as they explore the conventions of the Petrarchan sonnet.[36] Sometimes Greville

---

[34] Cf. Philip Sidney's *Defense of Poesie*, in *Literary Criticism: Plato to Dryden*, ed. Allan H. Gilbert (Detroit: Wayne State University Press, 1940), pp. 417–18.

[35] Studies of Greville's poetic theory include chapters in Waswo, *Fatal Mirror*, and Rees, *Fulke Greville*; Norman Farmer, Jr., "Fulke Greville and the Poetic of the Plain Style," *Texas Studies in Literature and Language* 11 (1969), 657–70; Hugh N. Maclean, "Greville's 'Poetic'," *Studies in Philology* 61 (1964), 170–91; David A. Roberts, "Fulke Greville's Aesthetic Reconsidered," *Studies in Philology* 74 (1977), 388–405; and Dwyer, "Fulke Greville's Aesthetic." Maclean most clearly makes the essential point that in Greville the poetical and the rhetorical are inseparable from the political. Also see Maclean's "Fulke Greville on War," *Huntington Library Quarterly* 21 (1958), 95–109.

[36] I do not discuss Greville's prose style because the only major prose work he wrote after about 1599, *A Dedication to Sir Philip Sidney*, is also the only major exception to the rhetorical practice I am describing. Owing to the circumstances of its composition and to Greville's immediate political ends, the *Dedication to*

praises the idealizing tradition, sometimes he criticizes it, but his address generally remains suppositional, open to debate with the community he addresses. However, once Greville rejects Cupid for good in *Caelica* 84, he settles into a more peremptory, declarative style that anticipates no conversational rejoinder from its audience.[37] This style, which is more or less shared with Greville's other surviving works, and which he evidently chose quite carefully, seems designed to move his audience to obedient action; the authoritativeness of the voice it creates is the essence of Greville's antirhetorical performance, which replaces rhetorical conversation with command. This style has been the most studied aspect of Greville's writing since Morris Croll made him the subject of his thesis, and retracing the full circuit of this critical ground is unnecessary.[38] I will concentrate instead on the three features of Greville's style that I think contribute most to his authoritative tone: its inclusiveness, its definiteness, and its imperativeness.

Inclusiveness derives, in the first place, from Greville's frequent use of lists. These can fill a line ("It feares sea, earth, skie, silence, darcknesse, light" [R 20]; "Since to be reverenc'd, lov'd, obey'd, and knowne" [F 38]), several lines ("But Superstition, Heresie,

Sidney is the only work of this period in which he displays something like the subtlety he must have shown as a politician. Indicative of the difference is his willingness to make decisions based on probable knowledge in his discussions of politics in *Dedication to Sidney*. For example, in chapter 9 he refers approvingly some half-dozen times to the standard of probability. Recent appraisals of Greville's strategy in *Dedication to Sidney* include Maureen Quilligan, "Sidney and His Queen," in *The Historical Renaissance: New Essays on Tudor and Stuart Literature and Culture*, ed. Heather Dubrow and Richard Strier (Chicago: University of Chicago Press, 1988), pp. 171–96, and Albert H. Tricomi, *Anticourt Drama in England, 1603–1642* (Charlottesville: University of Virginia Press, 1989), pp. 59–62.

[37] Although the change in style toward the end of *Caelica* is strong evidence that the poems placed there were written later, the chronology remains uncertain. Stephen W. May has recently argued against the conclusion that the poems' order in the sequence reflects their order of composition. See *The Elizabethan Courtier Poets: The Poems and Their Contexts* (Columbia: University of Missouri Press, 1991), pp. 87–94.

[38] Morris Croll, *The Works of Fulke Greville: A Thesis* (Philadelphia, 1903); also see Douglas L. Peterson, *The English Lyric from Wyatt to Donne: A History of the Plain and Eloquent Styles* (Princeton: Princeton University Press, 1967), chap. 7, and Thom Gunn, intro., *Selected Poems of Fulke Greville* (London: Faber, 1968).

Schisme, Rites, / Traditions, Legends, and Hypocrisie" [HL 88]),
or most of a stanza:

> Such are extortions, crueltie, oppression,
> Covetousnes, endlesse anger, or displeasure,
> Neglect, or scorne of person, or profession,
> Pryde, basenes, rudenes, vayne expence of treasure:
>   All which like nomber multipli'd by place,
>   Doe in the man the monarchy disgrace.
>
> (M 161)

Such lists serve a variety of purposes. In the first example above,
the list itemizes basic categories of perception as a means of
comprehensive summation. In the second example, the list suggests careful distinctions among similar terms. In the third example, the list builds emphasis, here (as frequently) for a contemptu-
ous dismissal of human pretensions. In the fourth example, the
list evokes the variousness of sin, again to heighten contempt for
it. These listings most often serve to gather, organize, and present
a large amount of material in a brief space, and hence to convey
the impression that, as the final example above declares, "all"
relevant particulars have been digested.

The specious logic of such incomplete enumeration becomes
clear when, for example, Greville "proves" that "All people are
unjust" by listing eight examples (F 46). But logic isn't the source
of the lists' appeal; nor is it what causes Greville to use the word
"all" hundreds of times, or to follow a list with a concluding "all"
again and again. Lines like "When all this All doth passe from age
to age" (C 69), "Where all to come, is one with all that was" (C
87), "With all, by usinge all things of our owne" (R 46), and "He is
all, gives all, hath all where he is" (R 59) reveal an absolutist
temperament that, when applied consistently to all aspects of
life, leaves no room for exceptions to the rule. Repeated stanza
after stanza, this insistence on completeness indicates a desire
(which a reader may of course resist) to compel the reader's conviction.

Greville's use of similes or analogies also contributes to the
inclusiveness of his style. Although lengths of one or two stanzas

are perhaps too short to qualify them as epic similes, there is a similarity in function. The similes expand Greville's frame of reference and draw separate fields of learning or experience together, implicitly claiming epic scope and importance for his work. Though their range is wide, they frequently (and particularly in *Monarchy*) address the similarities between "mans litle world" and "pow'rs great world," explaining either "by what usurp't authority" passions "disfashion" both "Order, and reasons peace" (M 194) or how both private and public judgment should work:

> For as in man this little worlde of ours,
> All objects which affect him diverslie
> With payne, or pleasure, under feelinge pow'rs
> Of common sence, are summon'd presentlie,
>   And there diminisht, judged, or approv'd,
>   A Crisis made, some changed, some remov'd:
>
> So in the kingdoms generall conventions,
> By confluence of all states doth appeare,
> Who nurseth peace, who multiplies contentions,
> What is to people, what to greate men deere;
>   Whereby soveraignitie still keepes above,
>   And from her center makes these circkles move.
>   (M 290–91)[39]

Several of these similes represent the state as an organism like the human body, subject to diseases, cures, and decay, and as knowable as a whole (e.g., M 134–35, 181); they reflect Greville's conviction that "All Governments, like Man himselfe within," are "restlesse compositions of the sinne" (F 14). At the same time, the force of this comparison casts the individual too as a collection of warring factions in desperate need of a controlling authority. More generally, the similes attempt to broaden and extend Greville's own authority. Not only does he represent himself as

---

[39] Tricomi remarks that Greville "is constantly driving the vast images of the macrocosm into the little world of man, who then mirrors the outer world's confusion" (*Anticourt Drama*, 68).

knowledgeable in all areas, but his expertise in one field appears to translate into expertise in others.

Second, Greville's is not only a definite poetry but also a poetry of definition. His striking definitions provide many of the high points of his work. Particularly memorable examples include his definitions of love (C 85), grace (R 3), the "sacred band" of true religion (R 45–48), God (R 59), public peace,[40] true learning (HL 150), and, in the final stanza of *Caelica* 96, flesh:

> Flesh [is] but the Top, which onely Whips make goe,
> The Steele whose rust is by afflictions worne,
> The Dust which good men from their feet must throw,
> A living-dead thing, till it be new borne,
> A Phenix-life, that from selfe-ruine growes,
> Or Viper rather through her parents torne,
>   A boat, to which the world it selfe is Sea,
>   Wherein the minde sayles on her fatall way.

Greville's sententiousness—his mastery of the iambic pentameter line within his preferred six- or eight-line stanzas and the epigrammatic forcefulness of his couplets—has often been noted.[41] But no attention has been given to how these talents join with Greville's penchant for definition to suffuse his writing with an aura of conclusiveness. Greville doesn't use definitions so much to specify a topic to be investigated or debated as he does to declare a topic known and closed. His definitions make him an unacknowledged master of poetic closure. But this should come as no surprise: a poetry of definition is almost by definition a poetry of closure.[42]

The insistent listing, summarizing, linking, and defining of

---

[40] Greville, *A Treatie of Warres*, st. 1–5, in *Poems and Dramas*. Further references to this work (W) appear in the text.

[41] For example, in his introduction to *Seneca His Tenne Tragedies*, reprinted as "Seneca in English Translation" in *Selected Essays*, 3d ed. (London: Faber, 1951), T. S. Eliot remarks that Greville's plays "have some magnificent passages, especially in the choruses; Greville had a true gift for sententious declamation" (78).

[42] In *Poetic Closure: A Study of How Poems End* (Chicago: University of Chicago Press, 1968), Barbara Herrnstein Smith cites Greville only to illustrate "closural failure."

Greville's style lay the syntactic and semantic groundwork for his use of imperatives. Greville characteristically concludes a train of thought with an imperative addressed directly to his reader (usually "man") and introduced by a "then" that applies the force of everything he has been saying as authority for what he now enjoins. The following will illustrate: "Then man! pray, and obtaine; beleeve, and have" (R 43); "Then man! learne by thy fall, to judge of neither" (R 50); "Reader! then make time, while you be, / But steppes to your Eternitie" (C 82); "Then Man, endure thy selfe, those clouds will vanish" (C 86); "France then! thow large extended monarchie, / Keepe to thie selfe thy change of Crowne demeasne" (M 441). The concluding imperative is also a productive feature of Greville's style, as this range of variations demonstrates: "Then let not Kinges by their neglect invyte / Aspiring states, or Princes to doe wronge" (M 530); "Let therefore humane Wisedome use both these" (HL 115); "The World should therefore her instructions draw / Back unto life, and actions, whence they came" (HL 71); "Then seeke we must" (R 8); "Then must this supreame powre, this wakefull spirit [government], / Observe proportion in her industrie" (M 390); "They must preserve his Temples, not shed blood" (W 52). The frequency with which Greville declares what "must" be done is especially telling: this is not so much the voice of counsel as the voice of authority.

The further effect of many other features of Greville's style could be mentioned: strings of aphorisms without logical connectives, which generate an oracular voice; rhetorical questions that substitute for true dialogue; antitheses that invite the reader to share plain distinctions between good and evil, appearance and reality. This style is indeed declarative. But it is also imperative. It declares and defines not only what is good or evil, but also what we must do, arrogating authority by its inclusiveness and conclusiveness. Judged on the dynamics of his style, Greville's principal purpose as a writer is to compel obedience to the divine will he is convinced he transmits.

Because he speaks with the voice of an absolute authority more than of a conversational equal, then, Greville's own rhetoric serves his antirhetorical desire to compel consent and obedience—and hence to turn words into actions. This remains the dominant intention even in much of Greville's religious poetry, where the private experience of despair or grace might be expected to soften command into supplication or prayer. Greville continues to tell us to *do* certain things to earn salvation. In *Caelica* 86, the octave's declaration that the earth and man are responsible for their own pains leads to two commands: either we must endure stoically the torments we cannot escape or we must turn to heaven's purifying fires. In the first case, salvation appears clearly to lie in our "Wisedome"; but in the second, it is uncertain how much our forsaking ourselves and turning to heaven could contribute to the redemptive power of heaven's flames. The same uncertainty inhabits *Caelica* 88. The first ten lines command us not to inquire into God's "curious mysteries," which "Are nothing to the mans renewed birth." Greville next enjoins us to "let the Law plough up" our wicked hearts. Then, however, he shifts tactics and specifies several conditions we must meet in order to experience the mystery of grace:

> When thou hast swept the house that all is cleare,
> When thou the dust has shaken from thy feete,
> When Gods All-might doth in thy flesh appeare,
> Then Seas with streames above thy skye doe meet.

While the efficacy of human actions is again left unspecified, the reiterated preparations strongly suggest that Greville envisages some form of half-way covenant.[43] Yet this and the preceding example so firmly adhere to Greville's customary declarative and imperative mode that emphasis falls decisively on human effort within a public context. Both poems ask us to obey a human authority at least as much as they ask us to obey a divine authority; hence, any inward religious experience remains inseparable from an accompanying political one.

The politicizing force of Greville's poetic style varies to some extent throughout his mature work, but only rarely is politics

---

[43] Noting Greville's continuing emphasis on the importance of willed activity, Rebholz concludes that the religious poems late in *Caelica* agree with "the essential teachings of English covenant theology" (*Life of Fulke Greville*, 219).

displaced from a pivotal role in shaping experience. When this happens, the resulting vacuum is generally filled not by the assurances of peace felt within, but by the promise of apocalyptic transformation from without. Such is the dynamic that operates variously in *Caelica* 97, 98, 99, and 109. On the plane of generalization these four poems stand at only a slight remove from Greville's usual position of command, since knowing the nature of everyone's sin is akin to knowing what everyone should do to avoid sinning. But in other respects the four poems undercut all human authority and with it the unity of knowing and doing. A major shift in focus from earth to heaven is signaled by changes in audience and mode of address: *Caelica* 97, 98, and 109 speak directly to God, and *Caelica* 99, speaking to an unspecified audience, is meditative in tone. Moreover, 98 and 99 minimize human activity while maximizing divine. In the first two stanzas of 98, Greville's only action is to sin; the third stanza raises the possibility that he might "be sorry" for his sins, "implore his mercy, who can save," and so contribute to his salvation. But unlike 86 and 88, the tone of 98 does not imply that human action is essential. The confessional couplet that serves as a refrain asks rather than commands, emphasizing God's ability to deliver us from our sin to his glories and joys:

> Lord, I have sinn'd, and mine iniquity,
> Deserves this hell; yet Lord deliver me.

Divine agency is emphasized even more in 99, where God does almost everything and Greville's only action is to "see" what is being done for him. Because human actions lose their importance, commands lose their purpose and imperatives disappear. The critical verbs are predicated of God—"come," in 97, 99, and 109, and "deliver," in 98. If anything is required of Greville in return, it is a knowledge of sin that entails suffering rather than action. Greville writes as one on a private rack in the midst of a public world racked with similar pains. His hope lies neither in inward nor in outward reformation, but only in a mysterious Christian fulfillment that will come from beyond time and completely transform both inner and outer worlds.

Interestingly, it is when Greville abandons his usual authority and cries out in pain that he sounds most human to twentieth-century ears.[44] Otherwise his voice tends to sound impersonal to us, the consequence of, in Michael Walzer's description of Calvinism, "an extraordinarily successful effort to resist the religious compulsions of the personal and the emotional" (22). Yet the peace Greville seeks *is* personal and emotional; if we fail to recognize it as such, it is because we customarily think of inwardness as vast and impressionable, questioning and questing. Greville's inward peace rests instead on the authority of certain knowledge. His is a subjectivity experienced as objective fact, an inwardness that, in its absoluteness, closely resembles the outward forms of order. This is why, when order disappears from Greville's verse, peace follows suit. He can articulate neither without an authoritative voice. Despite Greville's antirhetorical intentions, his work thus suggests that dissent lacking a basis in the communal and contingent knowledge of rhetoric offers no real alternative to a public authority that functions in a similarly absolutist way: so long as private authority is conceived of as certain and closed to debate, it will fail to offer a viable political option, and dissent will either subject itself to order or take refuge in an isolated and ineffectual stoic resistance; so long as knowledge of God remains congruent with a univocal public authority and obedience to tyrants, all authority will tend to function and sound the same.

Greville's peculiar blend of views is above all a consequence of his antirhetorical fear of confusion. Inquiry, controversy, debate— these will be tolerated neither in the private realm where peace is reached by obeying God's truth impressed on the conscience, nor in public life where to achieve order it is necessary to "sacrifise invention," a vital part of rhetoric (M 221). Confusion is the fundamental problem of existence, and we are as likely to encounter it when we "seeke God, and Religion from without" (R 14) as when we "seeke out a God" "in our selves" (R 19). By the same token, reform, which is whatever reduces confusion, can begin

---

[44] A fine example of this response is Gunn's remark that in the late religious poems "the body cries out in pain at the rejections it is being forced to make, and in the note of the cry we recognize the very humanity it is a cry against" (*Selected Poems*, 41).

wherever confusion is confronted by obedience, the crucial bridge
between human and divine. As obedient responses to confusion,
peace and order both become goods in Greville. Greville isn't torn
between Tudor politics and Protestant belief; rather, these two
forms of reform converge in his writings, cooperating to give
them their characteristically authoritative tone. Greville's memorable and complex voice wishes for peace and insists upon order.
His finest formulations, such as the concluding stanza of *A Treatise of Religion*, hold the two together in one commanding vision,
combining faith and use, love and sin, fear and joy, obedience and
desire, peace and desolation:

> Then man! Rest on this feelinge from above,
> Plant thou thy faith on this celestiall way.
> The world is made for use; God is for Love;
> Sorrowe for sinne; knowledge, but to obay;
> Feare and temptation, to refine and prove;
> The heaven, for joyes; Desire that it may
>   Finde peace in endlesse, boundlesse, heavenly things;
>   Place it else where, it desolation bringes.
>
>   (R 114)

Even during this eloquent exhortation to peace, Greville refuses
to allow himself to lose sight of a political order that at best
refines and at worst desolates, the order that always shares with
peace the attempt to bring eternal truth into the historical world.
Within this world, he knew, even his own writings would eventually act. But they would do so only after he had achieved a purer
and more permanent peace.

4 The Mysterious Plainness of Anger: The Search for Justice in Satire and Revenge Tragedy

The alliance of peace and order in Greville is possible because both claims to truth are based on the unverifiable criterion of conviction. In the first three chapters I concentrated on exploring the consequences for private identity and public life of this anti-rhetorical conviction, studying its private and public forms separately and then together. In the remaining chapters I return to the topic of anger, first raised in Chapter 1, in order to focus attention on the troublesome ethics of plainness. The legal and psychological problems that anger causes in satire and revenge tragedy are the subject of this chapter.

The connection of plainness to anger in satire and revenge tragedy is easily demonstrated. For many in the Renaissance, the satirist is a plainspeaker and vice versa, as John Earle illustrates when he says that the blunt or plain man "is as squeazy of his commendations, as his courtesie, and his good word is like an Elogie in a Satyre."[1] Similarly, plainspeaking revengers appear in such important revenge plays as *The Spanish Tragedy*, *Hamlet*, *The Revenger's Tragedy*, *The Malcontent*, and *The Maid's Tragedy*. The satirist and the revenger also tend to be malcontents, and the malcontent himself is typically a plainspeaker.[2]

---

[1] John Earle, *Micro-Cosmographie; or, a Piece of the World Discovered in Essayes and Characters* (London[?]: Golden Cockerel, 1928), p. 68.

[2] For example, Lawrence Babb describes the type of malcontent he names the

The common denominator here is injustice: the satirist, the revenger, the plainspeaker, and the malcontent share a strong sense of injustice, from which their anger derives. Because plainness represents an opposing legal claim whose epistemological status is unclear, it reveals the legal problem that anger poses. On the one hand, angry people, like Wyatt, tend to seek some degree of public support for their actions. On the other hand, when they despair of public approval and seek justification solely in their own conviction, the justice they claim seems as inexplicable to others as the justice of the tyranny they oppose. Consequently, it may be impossible to tell whether an angry person is motivated by an interest in truth and justice or by self-interest. Anger in this way imposes a limit on mutual understanding, bringing communication between opposing positions to a standstill: what appears plain from one perspective will seem opaque from all others. In one direction, then, anger approaches the openness of rhetorical justice, while in another direction it becomes as secretive and peremptory as the injustice it opposes. A fundamental ambiguity resides in its plainness.

Partly because they display the ambiguity of a mysterious plainness, angry voices remain some of the most compelling and revealing expressions left to us by Renaissance culture. Much more than is sometimes acknowledged, anger is a complicated emotion that is able to register some of the complexity of history. Angry people are often self-divided, pulled in different directions by historical forces of which they may have only a dim understanding. Perhaps as much as anyone, angry people reflect the stresses and strains of historical change, of shifting conceptions of justice, of temporary injustices, of new interests struggling to assert themselves, of old interests threatened by the new. Hence, their psychological condition serves as an index to political con-

---

melancholy cynic: "His wit and wisdom in combination with his vituperative asperity and his contempt for the world make him a telling satirist. He is, furthermore, a virtuous and honest man. He hates stupidity, affectation, and vice. He speaks his mind candidly and volubly without reference to either good manners or self-interest. Other characters place a high value on his blunt frankness. The malcontent will not flatter." See *The Elizabethan Malady: A Study of Melancholia in English Literature from 1580 to 1642* (East Lansing: Michigan State College Press, 1951), p. 92.

ditions. In studying anger in this chapter I have two goals: in the first section I use the understanding of plainness that I have so far developed to show the problems caused for politics and psychology by the ethical ambiguity of anger; in the second section I use the representation of anger to suggest how the ethical deadlock attendant upon an antirhetorical perspective can lead to skeptical conclusions.

The Problem of Anger

Anger responds to perceived injustice, but the question of its own justice consistently raises controversy. Critics of anger have always been particularly troubled by the one-sidedness of its judgment. For example, one of the main criticisms leveled against the angry person in the most influential classical work on anger, Seneca's *De Ira*, is that he leaps to a conclusion and, once there, closes himself to further questioning. Such an action, Seneca stresses, is contrary to reason, which follows the procedures of the *argumentum in utramque partem*: "Reason grants a hearing to both sides [*utrique parti tempus dat*], then seeks to postpone action, even its own, in order that it may gain time to sift out the truth; but anger is precipitate [*festinat*]. Reason wishes the decision that it gives to be just; anger wishes to have the decision which it has given seem the just decision."[3] The just person desires to punish because punishment is just, not because he is angry; but the angry person desires punishment for its own sake, because it is pleasurable. He is therefore tempted to act as both plaintiff and judge. If we wish to resist the temptations of anger, Seneca counsels, "we should plead the cause of the absent person against ourselves" (2.22.2–4), and above all we should force its rash judgment to observe the due process of reason and justice:

> The best corrective of anger lies in delay. . . . If the question of even
> a small payment should come before you to be judged, you would

[3] Lucius Annaeus Seneca, *De Ira*, in *Moral Essays*, trans. John W. Basore, Loeb Classical Library (Cambridge: Harvard University Press, 1928), 1:1.18.1–2. Further references appear in the text.

require a witness to prove the claim, the witness would have no
weight except on oath, you would grant to both parties the right of
process, you would allow them time, you would give more than
one hearing; for the oftener you come to close quarters with the
truth, the more it becomes manifest. Do you condemn a friend on
the spot? Will you be angry with him before you hear his side,
before you question him, before he has a chance to know either his
accuser or the charge? What, have you already heard what is to be
said on both sides [*utrimque*]? (22.29.1–3)

Anger, then, requires a premature belief that one is in possession
of the truth and a determination both to act upon that belief and
to protect it from further questioning. True justice, in contrast,
needs to follow rational standards of evidence and fairness, and
consequently requires the law's delay.

Seneca's charges of rash judgment and defensiveness are echoed
by Renaissance moralists. Pierre de la Primaudaye, for example,
voices the conventional belief that "choler hindereth and trou-
bleth [reason] . . . in such sort, that an angrie man can not deliberate." He also suggests the angry man's imperviousness to outside
influence when he compares him to a man burning in his own
house, his soul so full of "trouble, chaffing, and noyse, that he
neither seeth nor heareth any thing that would profit him."[4]
Pierre Charron provides a more probing examination of the connection of rashness and defensiveness:

> *Choler* first enforceth us to injustice, for it is kindled and sharpned
> by a just opposition, and by knowledge that a man hath of the little
> reason hee hath to bee angry. Hee that is moved to anger upon a
> false occasion, if a man yeeld him any good reason why hee should
> not be angry, hee is presently more incensed even against the truth
> and innocensie it selfe. . . . The iniquity of anger doth make us
> more stubborne, as if it were an argument and proofe of just anger,
> to bee grievously angry.

Charron makes an important point here. Not only is anger defensive, but it is *persuasive*, swaying others by the force of its convic-

[4] Pierre de la Primaudaye, *The French Academie*, 4th ed., trans. Thomas Bowes
(London: 1602), pp. 296, 295.

tion. Charron continues: "The injustice thereof is likewise in this, that it will be both a Judge and a party, that it will that all take part with it, and growes to defiance with as many as will seeme to contradict it."[5] As a criticism like Charron's illustrates, the need to persuade, to perform conviction, also calls into question the legitimacy of anger's privilege: so one-sided a judgment may be false. Like Seneca, de la Primaudaye and Charron recognize in anger a double desire to act as a one-person legal system and to shield that questionable private system from public questioning by persuasive assertion.

These writers oppose anger to a rhetorical justice, criticizing its antirhetorical character. But in the satires and revenge tragedies written in the quarter-century between roughly 1586 and 1611, anger is rarely portrayed as an alternative to consensual reason. Rather, the context in which anger appears is usually a world governed by a demonstrably corrupt ruling elite. Anger's privilege usually opposes some form of governing prerogative, and anger becomes enmeshed in fundamental conflicts of authority.

Some of the surest signs of these conflicts appear in English revenge tragedy, now widely viewed as, in Wendy Griswold's words, "a metaphor for the social tension between state authority and individual justice."[6] A number of revenge tragedies, including *The Tragedy of Valentinian, The Revenge of Bussy D'Ambois, The Atheist's Tragedy*, and *The Maid's Tragedy*, heighten this tension by setting revenge plots in divine right monarchies. Clermont D'Ambois, for instance, concludes flatly that "There's no disputing with the acts of kings, / Revenge is impious on their sacred persons."[7] Similarly, in *The Maid's Tragedy*, Amintor refuses to seek revenge against the King, whom he addresses thus:

---

[5] Pierre Charron, *Of Wisdome* (London: 1602), pp. 92, 93.

[6] Wendy Griswold, *Renaissance Revivals: City Comedy and Revenge Tragedy in the London Theatre, 1576–1980* (Chicago: University of Chicago Press, 1986), p. 90. See also Fredson Bowers, *Elizabethan Revenge Tragedy, 1587–1642* (1940; rpt. Gloucester, Mass.: Peter Smith, 1959); Eleanor Prosser, *Hamlet and Revenge* (Stanford: Stanford University Press, 1967); and Charles A. Hallett and Elaine S. Hallett, *The Revenger's Madness* (Lincoln: University of Nebraska Press, 1980).

[7] George Chapman, *The Revenge of Bussy D'Ambois*, in *The Plays of George Chapman: The Tragedies*, ed. Thomas Marc Parrott, vol. 1 (1910; rpt. New York: Russell & Russell, 1961), 5.5.151–52.

> as you are meere man,
> I dare as easily kill you for this deede,
> As you dare thinke to doe it, but there is
> Divinitie about you, that strikes dead
> My rising passions; as you are my King,
> I fall before you and present my sword,
> To cut mine owne flesh if it be your will.[8]

But within the same play, Melantius's anger overcomes such scruples: "I hope my cause is just, I know my blood / Tels me it is, and I will credit it" (3.2.288–89); I "stand here mine owne justice" (5.2.50). Beaumont and Fletcher conclude the play with a compromise of sorts, blessing the revenge but not the revenger:

> on lustfull Kings
> Unlookt for suddaine deaths from God are sent,
> But curst is he that is their instrument.
>
> (5.3.293–95)

   In such plays we face a choice between the antirhetorical justice of anger and the justice, itself antirhetorical, of an oppressive government. Can anger claim the moral high ground in such a situation, or is it, like Greville's peace, indistinguishable from the public order that surrounds it? This is not easily answered. One contemporary view held that there was no justification for anger, which was a form of disobedience. For example, Fletcher makes the opposition between anger and obedience extremely clear in *Valentinian*. Aecius, though a plainspeaking counselor who tells Valentinian unpleasant truths, refuses to exceed his right to give true counsel. He agrees with Maximus that Valentinian's crimes "would aske a Reformation," but reminds him that as subjects "obedience / To what is done, and griefe for what is ill done, / Is all we can call ours." We must not "Like desperate and un-

---

[8] Francis Beaumont and John Fletcher, *The Maid's Tragedy*, ed. Robert K. Turner, Jr., in *The Dramatic Works of the Beaumont and Fletcher Canon*, gen. ed. Fredson Bowers (Cambridge: Cambridge University Press, 1966–92), 2:3.1.237–43. Further references appear in the text.

season'd fooles let fly / Our killing angers, and forsake our honors."⁹ Aecius will join Maximus in "faire allegiance,"

> But not in force: For durst mine own soule urge me . . .
> To turn my hand from truth, which is obedience,
> And give the helme my vertue holds, to Anger, . . .
> That daring soule, that first taught disobedience,
> Should feele the first example.
>
> (1.3.76–86)

Aecius unconditionally supports degree and order: his life belongs to those above him, just as the soldiers under his command
grant his "great Prerogative" to kill them (2.3.21). However evil he
may know the emperor to be, he steadfastly believes that disobedience would bring disaster and that only God may justly punish
him (3.3.151–63).

But as there were various justifications for disobedience, so
were there a number of perspectives that offered more favorable
views of anger. There was, first of all, the Herculean tradition,
which considered anger a part of the aggressive, warrior spirit.
This tradition found support in classical epic, Senecan tragedy,
and, at least as far back as Seneca's *De Ira*, the belief that anger
was praised by Aristotle, whom Seneca quotes to this effect: "Anger . . . is necessary, and no battle can be won without it—unless
it fills the mind and fires the soul" (1.9.2).¹⁰ Second, many, particularly among the aristocracy, still cherished the principle of legal
revenge. As Fredson Bowers long ago pointed out, Anglo-Saxon
freemen enjoyed the *privilege* of private warfare, and until the end
of the fifteenth century it was still customary for sufferers of
private wrongs and their survivors to appeal to the king for the
right to seek the "direct revenge of judicial combat." "In spite of

⁹ John Fletcher, *Valentinian*, ed. Robert K. Turner, Jr., in *Dramatic Works*,
4:1.3.15–31. Further references appear in the text.
¹⁰ See Eugene M. Waith, *The Herculean Hero in Marlowe, Chapman, Shakespeare, and Dryden* (New York: Columbia University Press, 1962), and Gordon
Braden, *Renaissance Tragedy and the Senecan Tradition: Anger's Privilege* (New
Haven: Yale University Press, 1985). Angelo Poliziano's *De ira*, a very favorable
portrayal of anger, leans heavily on the authority of Aristotle.

the fact that justice was the sole prerogative of the Elizabethan state," Bowers continues, "with any encroachment on its newly won privilege liable to severe punishment, the spirit of revenge has scarcely declined in Elizabethan times."[11] Finally, there is the Juvenalian satirical tradition of *saeva indignatio*, legitimated for a Christian culture by the Thomistic *ira per zelum*.[12] In all of these traditions anger enjoys a special status, a suggestion of divine sanction like that we have seen attaching to conscience. The possibility that anger may be divinely inspired can never be discounted during this period: Hamlet is not alone when he is led by the consequences of his rashness to reflect that "There's a divinity that shapes our ends" (5.2.10).

But the problem of anger is more than legal: it extends as well to the question anger raises about the psyche of the angry person himself. This is most visible as a concern about sanity. Because anger threatens the ideal of stoic content or Christian peace that is also central to plainness, angry people are often assumed to be mad, their reason overwhelmed by their passion. Far from enjoying the "quintessence of passions overthrown" that Greville sees in peace, the angry person is passion's slave, a fact emphasized by anger's opponents.[13] Seneca, for example, writes that anger is

> the most hideous and frenzied of all emotions. For the other emotions have in them some element of peace and calm, while this one is wholly violent and has its being in an onrush of resentment, raging with a most inhuman lust for weapons, blood, and punishment, giving no thought to itself if only it can hurt another, hurling itself upon the very point of the dagger, and eager for revenge though it may drag down the avenger along with it. Certain wise

---

[11] Bowers, *Elizabethan Revenge Tragedy*, pp. 7, 8. On the aristocratic privilege of vengeance, see also Lily B. Campbell, *Shakespeare's Tragic Heroes: Slaves of Passion* (1930; rpt. New York: Barnes & Noble, 1963), chap. 14, and Lawrence Stone, *The Crisis of the Aristocracy, 1558–1640*, abridged ed. (Oxford: Oxford University Press, 1967).

[12] On the role of anger in satire, see Alvin Kernan, *The Cankered Muse: Satire of the English Renaissance* (New Haven: Yale University Press, 1959), and Robert C. Elliott, *Satire and Magic: Magic, Ritual, Art* (Princeton: Princeton University Press, 1960).

[13] Fulke Greville, *Caelica* 85, in *The Poems and Dramas of Fulke Greville, Lord Brooke*, ed. Geoffrey Bullough, 2 vols. (Edinburgh: Oliver & Boyd, 1939).

men, therefore, have claimed that anger is temporary madness
(*brevem insaniam*). (1.1.1)

This definition (generally with *furor* in place of *insania*) became
standard in the Renaissance.[14]

The angry person is also caught between justifications of his
passion as "noble fury" or "divine rage" and condemnations of it
as "beastly."[15] He feels both in himself, since he inevitably cher-
ishes order as well as the justice he seeks. In the case of the
revenger, his conflicting views of himself—as superhuman and
subhuman—sometimes lead to talk of *confusion*, which is a
more precise term here than madness. For example, Claudius asks
why Hamlet "puts on this confusion, / Grating so harshly all his
days of quiet / With turbulent and dangerous lunacy" (3.1.1–4).
Hamlet is "turbulent," like an unruly crowd lacking both peace
and order: as in Greville, confusion denotes the presence of conflicting voices and the absence of certainty. In *The Atheist's Tragedy* Charlemont, too, is confused when his father's ghost appears
to him and, when the imperative to avenge his death becomes
clear, is tortured "between the passion of / My blood and the
religion of my soul."[16] The revenger doesn't know whether he is a
rebel or a just scourge. Hamlet is a mystery to himself, not just to
others. His confusion signifies self-division: like Charlemont, or
like Maximus in *Valentinian*, he is divided between anger and
patience (*Val.* 3.3.90–101), the imperatives of private justice and
public order, and he becomes a stranger to himself (*Val.* 3.3.128–
34).

The question of madness, then, repeats the question of justice
at the individual level. Like Greville's peace and order, anger and

[14] Aristotle's definition was less influential: "Anger may be defined as an impulse, accompanied by pain, to a conspicuous revenge for a conspicuous slight
directed without justification towards what concerns oneself or towards what
concerns one's friends." See *Rhetoric*, trans. W. Rhys Roberts, in *The Basic Works
of Aristotle*, ed. Richard McKeon (New York: Random House, 1941), 1378a31.

[15] One of the classic disagreements over the quality of fury occurs in *Timon of
Athens*. In a dispute with the senators, Alcibiades defends a friend's anger as a
"noble fury," whereas the senators condemn it as a "beastly fury" (3.5.18, 71).

[16] Cyril Tourneur, *The Atheist's Tragedy*, ed. Irving Ribner, The Revels Plays
(London: Methuen, 1964), 2.6.45–62, 3.2.35–36.

patient obedience are inseparable, but they are also opposed, the opposition being that between an antirhetorical truth known privately and an antirhetorical truth known publicly. The angry person inhabits a space between incompatible roles that yet depend on each other. Complete identification with either one would lead to self-destruction, and does. His madness or confusion reflects the stalemate between public and private authorities, his doomed attempt to forge a middle ground. The psychology and politics of anger are one.

In the remainder of this section, I examine "The Lie" and *The Spanish Tragedy* as examples of satire and revenge tragedy where the angry individual struggles with the problems of justification and madness. Both Ralegh and Hieronimo straddle a line between public and private justifications: both enjoy some public authority, but both are drawn by their anger toward an authority that rests in them alone. Consequently, both occupy an awkward position with respect to the world, maintaining some degree of rhetorical involvement while mounting an opposition that at times seems almost complete.

"The Lie" departs from a tradition of communally supported satire known as Complaint. According to John Peter, Complaint (which is not to be confused with complaint as I have distinguished it from plaint) is a medieval and early Renaissance form that is conceptual or abstract in language and vague in target (aiming at the abuse rather than the abuser). Complaint is also impersonal because it depends for its appeal on a generally accepted ethical system rather than the personality of the satirist.[17] The Complaint's purpose is corrective, and its tone is sober and "rational"; in preaching to the converted, it is only necessary to remind the audience of the values they share as common sense. The writer of Complaint, then, works within the common persuasions of a rhetorical tradition and is a long way from the outlaw status of the typical representative of private plainness.

We see an Elizabethan variation of Complaint in George Gascoigne's "The Steele Glas." Born of "Playne dealyng" and "Sim-

---

[17] John Peter, *Complaint and Satire in Early English Literature* (Folcroft, Pa.: Folcroft Press, 1956), p. 10.

plycitie," Gascoigne's satire is a metal-backed mirror that, in contrast to a crystal mirror, reveals the truth. Like the writers I've been discussing, Gascoigne claims that the truths he announces are "plain," but his use of the word reveals a purer desire to speak as the many than we have seen so far:

> Therfore I like this trustie glasse of steele. . . .
> Wherein I see, a quicke capacitye,
> Berayde with blots of light Inconstancie:
> An age suspect, bycause of youthes misdeedes.
> A poets brayne, possest with layes of love:
> A *Caesars* minde, and yet a *Codrus* might,
> A Souldiours hart, supprest with feareful doomes:
> A Philosopher, foolishly fordone.
> And to be playne, I see my self so playne,
> And yet so much unlike that most I seemde,
> As were it not that Reason ruleth me,
> I should in rage, this face of mine deface
> And cast this corps, downe headlong in dispaire,
> Bycause it is, so farre unlike it self.[18]

Gascoigne writes more personally than is usual in the Complaint tradition, and indeed his satire is in the form of a letter to Lord Grey of Wilton, whom he addresses in a friendly and familiar, if somewhat supplicatory, manner. But otherwise the poem fits Peter's description: its targets are generalized, its language is conceptual, its purpose is to correct in accordance with an accepted ethical system—the "trouth" I discussed apropos of Wyatt—and, in keeping with Gascoigne's explicit rejection of rage in favor of reason, the tone is calm, mingling a mild indignation at falseness with a firm desire for moral good. Even when he varies from the impersonality of Complaint, Gascoigne in a sense surpasses it in self-effacement with the humility that locates his own appearance among the semblances to be stripped away. Gascoigne, then, does not display any of the characteristics of private plainness that I have identified: he does not address the world with biting

---

[18] George Gascoigne, "The Steele Glas," in *The Complete Works of George Gascoigne*, ed. John W. Cunliffe, vol. 2 (1907; rpt. New York: Greenwood, 1969), ll. 232–52.

anger, and he does not separate himself from either his audience
or the world at large. His performance is rather a rhetorical one,
and his plainness is a commitment to a shared communal endeav-
or to maintain common values, which are in no more danger than
usual and which need only the assistance of clear-sighted consensual reason to thrive.

At first sight, "The Lie" seems to belong to the same tradition.
Ralegh begins the poem by exhorting his soul to perform the
satirist's task of unmasking and correcting vice, here with a verbal tongue-lashing:

> Goe soule the bodies guest
>   upon a thankelesse arrant,
> Feare not to touch the best
>   the truth shall be thy warrant:
> Goe since I needs must die,
>   and give the world the lie.[19]

By invoking something very like the medieval "trouth" as a warrant, Ralegh claims a privilege belonging to the speaker of the
common moral language. He then tells his soul to address the
world in a language full of proverbs and folk wisdom. In the second stanza, for example, he instructs his soul to imply that "all
that glisters is not gold" (suggesting his opposition to a courtly or
"golden" style) and to distinguish knowing and speaking the good
from doing the good:

> Say to the Court it glowes,
>   and shines like rotten wood,
> Say to the Church it showes
>   whats good, and doth no good.
> If Church and Court reply,
>   then give them both the lie.
>
>   (7–12)

He also aims here at two traditional sources of corruption, the

---

[19] Sir Walter Ralegh, "The Lie," in *The Poems of Sir Walter Ralegh*, ed. Agnes
M. C. Lathan (Cambridge: Harvard University Press, 1951), ll. 1–6. Further references appear in the text.

court and the church, and continues to name others—potentates, "men of high condition," "them that brave it most." So far, the poem is corrective, conceptual, generalized in target, and impersonal, just like Complaint.

The similarity ends, however, when the poem's tone becomes clear. "The Lie" is anything but sober and rational. In fact, the tone of "The Lie" is astonishingly assertive and peremptory, surpassing anything we have seen in Wyatt, the *Admonition*, Ascham, or Greville in this regard. Part of this tone can be credited to the emphatic rhythm of the regularly end-stopped trimeter lines, but much of the strength of this rhythm is in turn a consequence of the remarkably sustained repetition of simple and commanding grammatical forms:

> Tell age it daily wasteth,
>   tell honour how it alters.
> Tell beauty how she blasteth
>   tell favour how it falters
> And as they shall reply,
>   give every one the lie.
>   (37–42)

Little analysis is required. Only the first and last stanzas contain any reasoning; the rest of the poem is a string of imperatives punctuated by the pugilistic refrain, which is itself a fairly explicit substitution of aggressive insult for dialogue. Ralegh has replaced the rationality of Complaint with the anger of satirical plainness.

It also becomes clear as the poem proceeds that it is not corrective —at least not in the sense Complaint is. Although Ralegh begins with conventional attacks on the court and the church, his satirical journey proceeds with such thoroughness that we eventually realize that he expects sympathy nowhere: even charity and friendship are rotten. Ralegh depicts a world entirely hostile to "trouth," so much so, in fact, that Ralegh's use of the word is either bitterly ironic or, more likely, closer to the truth of conviction than to the social and moral "trouth" of the Middle Ages. This world, with neither truth nor "trouth," is confused—that is, its essential corruption is evinced by its inability to speak the true language of the golden time before faith fled the city, before Babel, as it were. A world that confuses love and lust is a world likely to "stab" at truth-tellers (77–78) and is probably beyond reform. Consequently, Ralegh refuses conversation with the world, and with it abandons his hope for the usual sort of correction.

But like Greville, Ralegh is not entirely content to abandon the world. Evincing, in Greenblatt's words, "a discontent hovering between faith and skepticism," Ralegh enters a relation of antagonism with the world by adopting an anger that, while "unreasonable" in most senses, is still potentially persuasive.[20] Ralegh's attack on the public world may be intended to defend it from its true enemies, and his anger may still be motivated by a desire for public justice. But at the same time that Ralegh's anger appears to invite communal verification, it protects him from the "reply" that it seems can lead only to the lie and stabbing, allowing the self to remain a mystery known only through what its anger chooses to reveal of the truth (or perhaps "trouth") in which the self believes. Once the chosen self-revelation is complete, Ralegh, like the Wyatt who commands his lute to be still, like the Hieronimo who will bite out his tongue, rests in silence and, if necessary, endurance. Ralegh enters into the madness of anger in order both to perform his conviction within the world and to protect his conviction from the world.

In its plainness, then, Ralegh's vituperative attack (like most of the harsh satire of the 1590s) occupies an ambiguous ethical position. A reader must decide whether Ralegh's indignation is righteous, or whether he is simply indulging himself in a petulant display of pique (contemporaries evidently responded both ways).[21] *The Spanish Tragedy* at first presents a clearer choice. In Hieronimo, we face a reluctant revenger who initially seeks public justice for the murder of his son. Only when his efforts fail

[20] Stephen Greenblatt, *Sir Walter Ralegh: The Renaissance Man and His Roles* (New Haven: Yale University Press, 1973), p. 101.

[21] See the responses printed by Lathan, *Poems of Sir Walter Ralegh*, pp. 135–37. Interestingly, the response that most strongly condemns the poem refers to it and its author as a "Justice revenger"—another indication of the close connection between satire and revenge.

does he adopt the role of revenger, and then his revenge is presented as a mystery or confusion of which the consequences are both public and private. The result is an ending that presents essentially the same difficulties as "The Lie," leaving a high degree of uncertainty about whether justice has been done.

The political hierarchy of *The Spanish Tragedy* is not so absolute as that of many later revenge tragedies, but the importance of degree is nevertheless clear as early as the Ghost's description of his courtship:

> My name was Don Andrea; my descent,
> Though not ignoble, yet inferior far
> To gracious fortunes of my tender youth.
> For there in prime and pride of all my years,
> By duteous service and deserving love,
> In secret I possess'd a worthy dame.[22]

The theme of birth versus the deserts of inherent worth permeates much of the opening action, as the King, exercising his "privilege" or prerogative (1.2.159), adjudicates the dispute over the prisoner Balthazar, and as another secret courtship ensues.[23] Thereafter an understanding of the potential abuse of justice by the powerful is implicit in much of Lorenzo's plotting. Kyd also plants occasional reminders of the connections of degree, power, and justice, such as Lorenzo's characterization of Horatio as "ambitious-proud" (2.4.60), Lorenzo's description of Bel-Imperia as "meanly accompanied" (3.10.57) with Horatio, and Hieronimo's belief that his enemies "Will bear me down with their nobility" (3.13.38). Royal justice, Hieronimo knows, may well be biased.

[22] Thomas Kyd, *The Spanish Tragedy*, in *The First Part of Hieronimo and The Spanish Tragedy*, ed. Andrew S. Cairncross, Regents Renaissance Drama Series (Lincoln: University of Nebraska Press, 1967), 1.1.5–10. Further references appear in the text.

[23] The language of worth and desert saturates the early acts of *The Spanish Tragedy*. See 1.2.100, 126, 136, 149–51, 179, 189; 1.3.11, 23, 81, 92; 1.4.49, 103, 131; 2.1.12; 2.2.20; 2.3.35.

The unifying presence of the question of justice in the play is discussed by G. K. Hunter, "Ironies of Justice in *The Spanish Tragedy*," *Renaissance Drama* 8 (1965), 89–104, and Ejner Jensen, "Kyd's *Spanish Tragedy*: The Play Explains Itself," *Journal of English and Germanic Philology* 64 (1965), 7–16.

As a "lesser magistrate," Hieronimo occupies an intermediate position in the play's hierarchy, a position from which some resistance theorists believed tyranny might justly be overthrown.[24] But rather than seek such an overthrow (which in any event was envisaged as a last resort), Hieronimo initially shows a strong attachment to a more rhetorical justice. When he appears in the third act his response to his son's murder is still dominated by grief (or what he calls "discontents" [3.2.19]) and by his despair at what he perceives to be the failure of divine justice:

> Oh sacred heavens! if this unhallowed deed,
> If this inhuman, barbarous attempt,
> If this incomparable murder thus
> Of mine, but now no more my son,
> Shall unreveal'd and unrevenged pass,
> How should we term your dealings to be just,
> If you unjustly deal with those that in your justice trust?
>
> (5–11)

The dramatic fourteener stands out metrically as the most important line in the soliloquy. It emphasizes a conception of justice as a joint endeavor requiring trust, that is, a reliance on someone or something else to do his part. Hieronimo's conception of judicial trust thus resembles rhetorical faith in that it is satisfied to live without certain knowledge and to depend on the performance of others—and as Hieronimo makes no suggestion that he is seeking the direct intervention of God, it is fair to assume that these others include earthly ministers of God's justice. When this trust is betrayed, Hieronimo feels he must rely entirely on himself, and night, hell, and day seem to him to be calling on him to take justice into his own hands:

---

[24] The significance of Hieronimo's position as a magistrate for the question of disobedience was first noted by Howard Baker, Induction to Tragedy (Baton Rouge: Louisiana State University Press, 1939), p. 215. See also S. F. Johnson, "The Spanish Tragedy, or Babylon Revisited," in Essays on Shakespeare and Elizabethan Drama in Honor of Hardin Craig, ed. Richard Hosley (Columbia: University of Missouri Press, 1962), pp. 23–36.

> The ugly fiends do sally forth of hell,
> And frame my steps to unfrequented paths,
> And fear my heart with fierce inflamed thoughts.
>
> (16–18)

But the terms he chooses to express these promptings show that they are not welcome. They are visions that Hieronimo at this point wishes to escape.

At the time of the "Oh eyes! no eyes" soliloquy, then, Hieronimo still exists primarily within the conceptual framework that associates justice with a relationship of trust. The murder is an undesired interruption of the trust that he wishes to reestablish. Thus his discontent, lacking the conviction of plainness, has more to do with woe than with anger. Thereafter, interest centers on his transformation from a judge trained in rhetorical procedures to a revenger bordering on madness.

At the beginning of act 3, scene 7, Hieronimo has still made no attempt to revenge Horatio's death. Instead, he is plaining to the winds, the trees, the meadows, the mountains, and whatever else will hear him:

> Where shall I run to breathe abroad my woes,
> My woes, whose weight hath wearied the earth?
> Or mine exclaims, that have surcharged the air
> With ceaseless plaints for my deceased son?
>
> (3.7.1–4)

Hieronimo's plaining is not exactly the same as the plaining of the lover in Wyatt's poems: Hieronimo's woe is greater and his performance correspondingly less. But the two plaints share the hope that an object of trust (the woman, God) will perform his or her part of the bargain, thus completing the desired action (love, justice); and both attempt to persuade the object of trust by breathing their woes:

> Yet still tormented is my tortured soul
> With broken sighs and restless passions,
> That, winged, mount and, hovering in the air,

> Beat at the windows of the brightest heavens,
> Soliciting for justice and revenge.
>
> (10–14)

Although the mention of soliciting does give these lines a slight legal cast, it is only a request, and the dominant language of the speech remains strikingly that of the plaining lover:

> The blust'ring winds, conspiring with my words,
> At my lament have moved the leaveless trees,
> Disrob'd the meadows of their flower'd green,
> Made mountains marsh with spring-tides of my tears. . . .
> But they [justice and revenge] are plac'd in those empyreal heights,
> Where, countermur'd with walls of diamond,
> I find the place impregnable; and they
> Resist my woes, and give my words no way.
>
> (5–8; 15–18)

The impregnable walls of diamond that complete the speech, like the sympathetic pastoral scene in its first half, are the common property of every plaining lover in the Renaissance.[25] Hieronimo remains a long way from the conviction and anger of plainness.

When Hieronimo finally does become convinced of the authenticity of Bel-Imperia's letter, his response to Horatio's murder undergoes a change from what I have called plaint to complaint. Upon reading Pedringano's letter, he berates himself for not seeing the truth sooner, then forms his resolution:

> But wherefore waste I mine unfruitful words,
> When naught but blood will satisfy my woes?
> I will go plain me to my lord the king,
> And cry aloud for justice through the court,
> Wearing the flints with these my withered feet,

---

[25] Peter Sacks argues, however, that part of the Elizabethan revenger's predicament is the decline of the pastoral elegy, which, like the declining belief in both human and divine justice, was no longer able to contain grief. See "Where Words Prevail Not: Grief, Revenge, and Language in Kyd and Shakespeare," *ELH* 49 (1982), 576–601. See also Joost Daalder, "The Role of 'Senex' in Kyd's *The Spanish Tragedy*," *Comparative Drama* 20 (1986), 247–60.

> And either purchase justice by entreats,
> Or tire them all with my revenging threats.
>
> (67–73)

The helpless discontent of woe has given way to the determined discontent of anger, and Hieronimo is ready to abandon justice based on trust in order to give aggressive expression to a grievance adjudicated privately.

At this point, however, Hieronimo is controlled by his anger in a way described by anger's critics. Montaigne, for example, writes that while "Aristotle says that anger sometimes serves as a weapon for virtue and valor," others answer that "it is a weapon whose use is novel. For we move other weapons, this one moves us; our hand does not guide it, it guides our hand; it holds us, we do not hold it."[26] Anger is as much a measure of the world's control of the angry person as of his resistance to that control. Hieronimo's anger has prevented him from achieving stoic withdrawal from the world and has also deprived him of the ability to reason, which would allow him to speak or act effectively within the world. He does not realize that his cries for justice will be incomprehensible to the King, who sees them as an "outrage" (3.12.79) and as signs of Hieronimo's "fury" (80) and "melancholy" (99). His lack of control allows the world to label him mad and confused, the speaker of an unknown language. Because his perceptions now lie outside society's conceptual framework, and because he is so controlled by them that he is unable to act within the circumstances of society to perform his revenge, his relation to the world must change again before he can become a true revenger.

This change occurs in the "Vindicta mihi" soliloquy. His complaint having failed, Hieronimo resolves to take the law into his own hands. But he now recognizes the necessity of working within historical or rhetorical circumstances:

> Wise men will take their opportunity,
> Closely and safely fitting things to time. . . .

26 Michel de Montaigne, "Of Anger," in *The Complete Essays*, trans. Donald M. Frame (Stanford: Stanford University Press, 1958), p. 545.

No, no, Hieronimo, thou must enjoin
Thine eyes to observation . . .
Till to revenge thou know when, where, and how.

(3.13.25–44)

Because words, even violent words, can no longer prevail, Hieronimo recognizes that his conviction will remain ineffective unless it seeks remedy in pragmatic nonverbal action—that is, in a
politically feasible plan for revenge.[27]

The necessity of political performance leads Hieronimo into a
paradoxical new state:

Thus therefore will I rest me in unrest,
Dissembling quiet in unquietness,
Not seeming that I know their villainies.

(29–31)

The first two lines above are the central expression in *The Spanish Tragedy* of the psychological and political reality of anger.
They mean that Hieronimo will hide his unrest and unquietness
in an appearance of rest and quiet. This is confirmed when Revenge remarks near the end of act 3 that "in unquiet, quietness
is feign'd" (3.15.23). But the lines could easily be read as saying
that Hieronimo will disguise his quiet in an appearance of
unquietness—as many later revengers will do. It is in fact unclear
whether rest or unrest has the upper hand, and it is impossible to
separate the two: because individual and society are fundamentally opposed yet inextricably intertwined, rest for one is unrest
for the other. Just as public wrongs cause private griefs that revenge seeks to relieve, so revenge subverts public order, causing
public unrest at the same time as private rest. If he is to engage
publicly with society, the private revenger must contain this opposition within himself. Hieronimo, that is, must accept the qui-

---

[27] Hieronimo's concern for personal safety in this speech is stressed by John D.
Ratliff, "Hieronimo Explains Himself," *Studies in Philology* 54 (1957), 112–18,
and Scott McMillin, "The Book of Seneca in *The Spanish Tragedy*," *SEL* 14 (1974),
201–8.

et of public order now, even though he is suffering personal up-heaval; later he must be prepared to experience public unrest when he achieves private satisfaction. Performing his conviction thus involves him in a world of controversy and contradiction, part of which is his own continuing belief that patience and order may surpass revenge and disorder on an ethical scale (he dismisses patience early in the soliloquy [10] only to call it back near the end [42]). The relief he seeks in revenge can never satisfy him completely.

The revenger's ambiguous relation to society—opposed yet intertwined—complicates understanding between the two. Anger does communicate, but its desire to shield itself from questioning severely limits its effectiveness as communication. Kyd drama-tizes this limitation by making Hieronimo's revenge the final mystery in the play. Three mysteries are referred to before the final playlet, all of them artistic productions: the tragedy of the main action itself, as referred to by Revenge (1.1.90–91); Hiero-nimo's masque in the first act (1.4.139); and the dumb show at the end of the third act (3.15.28). Though Hieronimo's play of Soliman and Perseda is called a "confusion" rather than a "mystery," it belongs with the other three, requiring, as they do, an interpreter. Mysteries, like convictions, are unverifiable; they may speak a truth to some yet be inexplicable to others. They consequently reflect the situation of revenge, where the unverifiable conviction of anger's privilege battles the unverifiable judgments of royal prerogative, and no mutual understanding is possible. As a re-venger unable to gain public justification but mindful of public realities, Hieronimo must await the circumstances that will al-low him to join vengeful ire to the normal course of social events in one mutually uncomprehending confusion.

The final court entertainment is his opportunity. As the charac-ters recognize, it is fundamentally intended to confuse. Upon hearing that each participant will speak a different language, Bal-thazar exclaims:

> But this will be a mere confusion
> And hardly shall we all be understood.
>
> (4.1.176–77)

Hieronimo reassures him, but, when left alone, reveals that this is indeed his plan:

> Now shall I see the fall of Babylon,
> Wrought by the heavens in this confusion.
>   (190–91)

To Hieronimo (and Bel-Imperia), this is a heavenly confusion, but to the others it will be the confusion of hell. The appropriateness of mysteries to the situation of anger is that they permit such complete disagreements.

Noting the importance of confusion in the play, a number of critics have identified a patriotic political allegory in it: Spain, as the Catholic Babylon-Babel, is destroyed by God through his Anglophile minister, Hieronimo.[28] While this reading has been persuasively argued, it shouldn't be allowed to deflect the political implications of the apocalyptic conclusion away from England entirely. Some Reformers, after all, thought English Conformity was Romish; a tyrannical regime anywhere might be thought to trample, popelike, on Christian freedom and the true church. But the most important aspect of the play's conclusion is not the confusion visited upon Babylon-Spain. It is the discovery that, as in Greville, the mysteries of apocalyptic judgment shatter the private individual as well as the public world. Hieronimo's anger destroys him. He is trapped inside the ambiguities of a justice that is both perfectly plain and perfectly unknown, a justice that commands him to assault (in order to protect) the public order he

---

[28] See Johnson, "*The Spanish Tragedy*, or Babylon Revisited"; Eugene D. Hill, "Senecan and Vergilian Perspectives in *The Spanish Tragedy*," *English Literary Renaissance* 15 (1985), 143–65; and Frank Ardolino, *Thomas Kyd's Mystery Play: Myth and Ritual in 'The Spanish Tragedy'*, American University Studies (New York: Peter Lang, 1985) and "'Now Shall I See the Fall of Babylon': *The Spanish Tragedy* as a Reformation Play of Daniel," *Renaissance and Reformation* 14 (1990), 49–55. Ardolino summarizes the argument as follows: "It is my contention that Kyd conceived of *The Spanish Tragedy* as a sixteenth-century play of Daniel intended to represent to English audiences the fall of Babylon-Spain. . . . *The Spanish Tragedy* is a mystery play in which Hieronimo, the Danielic figure, the judge, the bearer of the sacred name (*hieros nym*), Anglophile representative of God's will at the court of Babylon-Spain, author, actor, and revenger, creates the Spanish tragedy and the English comedy" ("'Now Shall I See'," 51).

values as a judge. He is, he says, "Author and actor in this tragedy" (4.4.147), a combination that captures the ambiguities of his
position beautifully. As author he has a control and an authority
that stand at one remove from his creation, while as actor he is
immersed in it, instrumental in bringing it to fruition yet also
potentially trapped by its imperfections. The action demanded by
anger complicates the simplicity of conviction, uncovering conflicting allegiances within the author that might otherwise remain hidden. Performance clouds conviction. Once he becomes a
revenger, Hieronimo is at once obedient and disobedient, just and
unjust, contented and malcontented. Like most revenge tragedies,
The Spanish Tragedy is tragic because it offers no escape from
this circle, no compromise between competing interests and conflicting mysteries, no unambiguous ethical or legal position.

Given the diversity of Renaissance opinions of anger and the
representation of the full range of this diversity in revenge tragedy, it is unsurprising that critics continue to disagree about
whether the form is essentially conservative or essentially radical.[29] The same disagreement continues about *The Spanish Tragedy*, the question here being the extent to which Hieronimo's
revenge succeeds in taking on the characteristics of a publicly
justifiable action. C. L. Barber's discussion of the play represents
both sides of the question as carefully as any. Claiming that the
play offers no political alternative to conventional values, Barber
writes of Hieronimo: "As long as his protest remains charged
with the sense of outraged commitment to traditional society, it
has the heroic dignity of a desperate reinvestment of social piety.
But the final scenes are devoted largely to a nihilistic wish-

---

[29] For example, Henry E. Jacobs and Darryll Grantley both study the dislocation
of social rituals—particularly of the masque—in revenge tragedy, yet reach opposite conclusions about its meaning. For Jacobs the form reinforces orthodoxy by
showing revenge as disruptive; for Grantley it subverts official ideology by showing that state power is itself corrupt. See Jacobs, "The Banquet of Blood and the
Masque of Death: Social Ritual and Ideology in English Revenge Tragedy," in
Renaissance Papers, 1985 (Durham, N.C.: Southeastern Renaissance Conference,
1985), pp. 39–50; and Grantley, "Masques and Murderers: Dramatic Method and
Ideology in Revenge Tragedy and the Court Masque," in *Jacobean Poetry and
Prose: Rhetoric, Representation, and the Popular Imagination*, ed. Clive Bloom
(New York: St. Martin's Press, 1988), pp. 194–212.

fulfillment, the motive contracted entirely to the enjoyment of quid-pro-quo violence."[30] Although he fails to recognize that Hieronimo's suicide may itself be considered necessary to restore order, and although to describe Hieronimo's emotion as "enjoyment" seems to mistake the pain that his "confusion" causes him, Barber is correct to acknowledge both Hieronimo's concern for justice and the possibility that he violates it in the end: Kyd wants us to have both reactions. It is my contention, however, that we are not required to take sides. Rather, we are called upon to understand both the political and the psychological conflicts, and thus to recognize that they cannot be solved in their own terms. Violence by itself cannot restore justice to public life, but neither can an unjust situation be allowed to continue. The problem of anger is that it offers no escape from escalating injustice and madness.

The Transformation of Anger

Anger, as I have illustrated with Ralegh and Kyd, is part of a plainness that yearns for "trouth," even if it finds only truth. To put it another way, Hieronimo as revenger and Ralegh as satirist substitute anger's privilege for public justice reluctantly and believe, at least partly, that in the long run their actions will be supported by the community they still hope to serve. Their plainness can therefore be called moral even though it fails to find a satisfactory moral solution. But when their verbal and physical violence is considered, a case can also be made that they are no better than the corruption they oppose. For such is the ambiguity fundamental to anger's privilege: the conviction on which anger is based may be true, but the manner in which that anger is performed makes the truth as mysterious as it does plain. And there is nothing in the definition of plainness that requires it to be moral. On the contrary, the lack of a moral and rational guarantee is an essential part of the phenomenon. As Braden notes of the

---

[30] C. L. Barber, *Creating Elizabethan Tragedy: The Theater of Marlowe and Kyd*, ed. Richard P. Wheeler (Chicago: University of Chicago Press, 1988), p. 159.

stoic precedents, the thymos asserts itself, the hegemonicon rules, and that is all their names mean. The mysterious nature of angry plainness in "The Lie" and *The Spanish Tragedy*—the uncertain public status of the private conviction that supports it— finally emphasizes the uncertainty of conviction as an ethical criterion. By doing so it suggests the possibility of a skeptical response to the conflict anger signals between antirhetorical authorities. Such a response is illustrated in John Marston's mature satire and early drama, where a relatively low degree of moral concern gives rise to a sometimes whimsical anger and a skeptical emphasis on performance as an end in itself.

Marston claims plainness for *The Scourge of Villanie* in a context that suggests a rhetorical outlook something like Gascoigne's. In his prefatory letter, "To those that seeme judiciall perusers," Marston quarrels with those who prefer their satire obscure:

> Know I hate to affect too much obscuritie, & harshnes, because they profit no sence. To note vices, so that no man can understand them, is as fonde, as the French execution in picture. Yet there are some, (too many) that think nothing good, that is so curteous, as to come within their reach. Tearming all Satyres (bastard) which are not palpable darke, and so rough writ, that the hearing of them read, would set a mans teeth on edge.

Marston mildly censures Persius and Juvenal for being, respectively, "crabby" and "gloomie." Near the end of the letter he mentions plainness in the same context of obscurity and harshness: "I cannot, nay I will not delude your sight with mists; yet I dare defend my plainnes gainst the verivyce face, of the crabbed'st Satyrist that ever stuttered."[31] In this context, "plainnes" suggests the classical plain style of the ancient satirist *not* censured by Marston—Horace. To readers around the turn of the century, and especially to those who valued him as a model, most notably Ben Jonson and his circle, Horace stood for an urbane, conversa-

---

[31] John Marston, *The Scourge of Villanie*, in *The Poems of John Marston*, ed. Arnold Davenport (Liverpool: Liverpool University Press, 1961), pp. 100, 101. Further references to satire and line numbers appear in the text.

tional style notable for its familiarity and easy self-revelation. Horace thus offered an alternative to the blunt plainness of anger and stoic withdrawal. As Raman Selden observes, "Horace is the master of dialectical reasoning, preferring the interplay of dialogue and the exploration of nuances to the crudeness of blunt assertion and the absolute judgements of the Stoics."[32] In objecting to obscurity and harshness, then, Marston seems to be rejecting the anger and withdrawal of private plainness.

However, Marston's attitude in *The Scourge of Villanie* has much less in common with Horace's than with Ralegh's or, for that matter, with Juvenal's, which displays an apparently uneasy blend of passionless Stoic withdrawal and furious indignation.[33] Marston's two prefatory poems represent this attitude better than does his prefatory letter. In "To *Detraction* I present my *Poesie*," Marston assumes a hostile stance toward those who would find fault with his poetry. There is no possibility of dialogue with such detractors, for they have only "Opinion" on their side, while Marston has "True judgement" on his (17). Instead, Marston emphasizes his scorn for the opinions of critics and proclaims his superiority to them: "Spight of despight, and rancors villanie, / I am my selfe, so is my poesie" (23–24). These lines end the poem with the stoic ideal of a self known fully to itself and unaffected by the uncomprehending world around it. The poem, though, leaves us wondering why the stoical Marston chooses to "expose" the "issue of [his] braine" in the first place (4–5).

The second prefatory poem attempts to answer this question and in so doing emphasizes the importance of anger in Marston's satirical project. Marston imagines a public that includes "mechanick slave[s]"; fashion-mongers; stupid law students, who tear satire's rhymes, "quite altering the sence"; and "perfum'd *Castilio*," who cannot hope to understand "sharpe-fang'd poesie" be-

---

[32] Raman Selden, *English Verse Satire, 1590–1765* (London: Allen & Unwin, 1978), p. 28.

[33] The mixture of withdrawal and anger is an acknowledged feature of Juvenal's satires. Kernan, for instance, writes that "the pose of the Stoic conflicts with the furious indignation which is so omnipresent in Juvenal's satire" (*Cankered Muse*, 75). Of Marston's satirist, Selden remarks that he "combines the excoriating fury of Juvenal with the Stoic role of 'happy man' whose soul is above the vile spirit of the malignant detractor" (*English Verse Satire*, 71).

cause he "Nere in his life did other language use, / But, Sweete Lady, faire Mistres, kind hart, deare couse" (1–20). All these readers lack the ability to appreciate Marston's satire—it is anything but *plain* to them. So, Marston asks, will satire go among them and suffer indignity? It will, satire answers, and, after welcoming the crowd to feast on it, indirectly reveals why: "Welcome I-fayth, but may you nere depart, / Till I have made your gauled hides to smart" (35–36). Here Marston suggests that, whatever may be misunderstood by parts of his audience, they will most certainly understand his fury. Thus Marston embraces the privileged dynamic of anger and withdrawal that defines the satire of "The Lie." The satirist is separate from the world, and speaks a different language from it. The world is corrupt, but the satirist is honest and just. He exposes himself to the world to the extent that he lets it feel his anger, but the measure of his withdrawal is the uncomprehending response he expects:

> Nay then come all, I prostitute my Muse,
> For all the swarme of Idiots to abuse.
> Reade all, view all, even with my full consent,
> So you will know that which I never meant;
> So you will nere conceive, and yet dispraise,
> That which you nere conceiv'd, & laughter raise:
> Where I but strive in honest seriousnes,
> To scourge some soule-poluting beastliness.
>
> (61–68)

Marston, then, works with an understanding of the privilege, the "honest seriousnes" or "sacred parentage" ("To *Detraction*," 12), that allows both an involvement with and a separation from the audience, both a rejection of stoic content in favor of the satirist's rage (see Satyre 2) and an embracing of stoic absoluteness.

There is, however, a question about how far Marston's "honest seriousnes" extends. A host of twentieth-century detractors, including C. S. Lewis, T. S. Eliot, A. J. Axelrad, and John Peter, have accused Marston of insincerity and philosophical impurity. Others, such as Arnold Davenport, Anthony Caputi, and R. C. Horne, have defended Marston's sincere intention and ideological consistency.[34] Still others have taken a third approach that sees in Marston a rhetorical ambivalence and a willingness to explore. Caputi, for example, while defending Marston's ideas, is more interested in studying "his work as a continuous experiment in satiricomic forms," and R. A. Foakes writes that "Marston was perhaps uncertain of his own criteria, or at any rate had an ambivalent attitude toward the stances he enacted, so that his satires are neither wholly serious, nor wholly fooling, written with a harsh force that at times seems to embody an extremity of passion, yet disclaimed at the outset in his address to the reader." Foakes also suggests that "Marston's satires perhaps provide above all a sense of exploring" the malcontent type.[35] This third line moves toward the argument I wish to make: that Marston's work shows us a plainness largely free from the values of "trouth," and thus able to question all values, even its own. The result is an attitude sometimes skeptical, sometimes comic, but still governed by the anger that can perform its discontents well enough to earn its privilege.[36]

Marston himself calls into question the value of plain virtue in Satire 5. The satirist argues that virtue is not rewarded in the present age; rather, force and guile triumph:

> Sleight, Force, are mighty things,
> From which, much, (if not most) earths glory springs.

[34] C. S. Lewis, *English Literature in the Sixteenth Century Excluding Drama* (Oxford: Clarendon Press, 1954); T. S. Eliot, *Selected Essays* (London: Faber, 1934); A. J. Axelraad, *Un Malcontent Elizabéthain: John Marston* (Paris: Didier, 1955); Peter, *Complaint and Satire*; Davenport, intro., *Poems of John Marston*; Anthony Caputi, *John Marston, Satirist* (1961; rpt. New York: Octagon Books, 1976), p. viii; R. C. Horne, "Voices of Alienation: The Moral Significance of Marston's Satiric Strategy," *Modern Language Review* 81 (1986), 18–33.

[35] R. A. Foakes, *Marston and Tourneur* (London: Longman, 1978), pp. 13, 12.

[36] In a judicious essay, Scott Colley argues that Marston's skepticism of convention and Calvinist sense of the pervasiveness of "mixture" in human life led to an honest and humble confusion in his writings. I agree with his analysis, but disagree with his conclusion: I argue instead that Marston's spirited performance in his early work creates above all a sense of the individual's power to manipulate conventions for private ends. The noble individual becomes a playwright, rather than just a player. See "Marston, Calvinism, and Satire," *Medieval and Renaissance Drama in England* 1 (1984), 85–96.

> If Vertues self, were clad in humane shape,
> Vertue without these, might goe beg and scrape.
> The naked truth is, a well clothed lie,
> A nimble quick-pate mounts to dignitie.
> By force, or fraude, that matters not a jot,
> So massie wealth may fall unto thy lot.
>
> (40–47)

The satire is of course critical of this state of affairs, but Marston leaves some doubt about exactly how *he* intends to proceed in the circumstances. For example, after fifteen lines he replies to an anticipated complaint about his "Harsh lines":

> Rude limping lines fits this leud halting age,
> Sweet senting *Curus*, pardon then my rage,
> When wisards sweare plaine vertue never thrives,
> None but *Priapus* by plaine dealing wives.
>
> (18–21)

Are "Rude limping lines" the same as "plaine dealing," and is rage consistent with "plaine vertue"? If not, then Marston is saying that he has abandoned plain virtue and plain dealing in order to have some effect on the world through the force of rage and rude lines. If so, how can we reconcile the profession of plain virtue with the lewd play on the idea that "it is a precious jewel to be plain," a favorite joke of Marston's to which he returns later in the same satire?[37] Either way, Marston seems less than fully committed to plain virtue and his own "plainnes."

It is not that Marston has lost the ability to speak the language of "trouth." For example:

> Would truth did know I lyde, but truth, and I,
> Doe know that fence [i.e., a ward] is borne to miserie.
>
> (2:64–65)

---

[37] Cf. "That sole *Priapus* by plaine dealing mounts" (l. 89). Davenport compares a passage from Marston's *The Mountebank's Mask*: "plain dealing is a jewel, and there is no lady but desires her lap full of them" (318).

> What, shall law, nature, vertue, be rejected,
> Shall these world Arteries be soule infected,
> With corrupt blood?
>
> (3:159–61)

Or one might quote from the longer philosophical passages favored by Marston's apologists. It is rather that he doesn't appear to want to do so exclusively, and in fact does so far less than any writer I have discussed. Marston prefers instead to speak a language full of obscure allusions, invented vocabulary, abrupt changes of direction, and loose and contorted syntax. Marston's satirical language, far from being corrective or even directed in its rage, seems instead to be controlled only by the author's capricious wit, which in its playfulness is capable of imbuing even ostensibly serious passages with a comic feel. For example:

> Civill *Socrates*,
> Clip not the youth of *Alcebiades*
> With unchast armes. Disguised *Messaline*,
> I'le teare thy maske, and bare thee to the eyne
> Of hissing boyes, if to the Theaters
> I finde thee once more come for lecherers[.]
> To satiate? Nay, to tyer thee with the use
> Of weakning lust. Yee fainers, leave t'abuse
> Our better thoughts with your hipocrisie,
> Or by the ever-living Veritie,
> I'le stryp you nak'd, and whyp you with my rimes,
> Causing your shame to live to after times.
>
> (9:119–30)

There is a sense of exaggeration and posturing in the passage that is characteristic of *The Scourge of Villanie*. And although the stripping recalls a line early in the satire, "Come downe yee Apes, or I will strip you quite" (11), and hence the satire's motto, "Here's a toy to mocke an Ape indeede," there is more to the humor than mockery. The "hissing boyes," the parallel bold threats, "I'le teare thy maske" and "I'le stryp you naked," the mouth-filling, Latinate oath, and the rhyming insistence on stripping and whipping all contribute to a comic undertone that laughs not only at the explicit targets but also at the attitude that would confront them with unrelieved seriousness. For in Marston, the convictions of plainness are subject to doubt, skeptical awareness, and comic perspective.

It is this mixture of the rage and withdrawal of plainness with a comic self-consciousness that suggests that the final couplet of Satire 11 applies to more than just that satire's explicit humorousness: "Here ends my rage, though angry brow was bent, / Yet I have sung in sporting merriment" (239–40). It is this mixture, moreover, that leads to the self-portrait with which Marston begins the "Satyra Nova" that he added to the 1599 edition as Satire 10:

> From out the sadnes of my discontent,
> Hating my wonted jocund merriment,
> (Onely to give dull Time a swifter wing)
> Thus scorning scorne of Ideot fooles, I sing.
> I dread no bending of an angry brow,
> Or rage of fooles that I shall purchase now.
> Who'le scorne to sitte in ranke of foolery
> When I'le be maister of the company?
> For pre-thee *Ned*, I pre-thee gentle lad,
> Is not he frantique, foolish, bedlam mad,
> That wastes his spright, that melts his very braine
> In deepe designes, in wits darke gloomie straine?
> That scourgeth great slaves with a dreadlesse fist,
> Playing the rough part of a Satyrist,
> To be perus'd by all the dung-scum rable
> Of thin-braind Ideots, dull, uncapable?
>
> (1–16)

Though Marston sounds a note of disillusionment here, it is difficult to believe, particularly when savoring the energetic rhythm of the last eight lines, that he regrets his "mad" behavior: he has been consciously playing a part and has enjoyed it, just as he is now enjoying playing the part of the man made wiser by the foolishness of his youth. His "wonted jocund merriment" underlies both postures, enticing us "to sitte in ranke of foolery." It tells us that life is a game, and what matters most is to play it with such skill that others will believe you know the rules.

The Scourge of Villanie in this way reveals Marston's desire to be "maister of the company." He claims a privilege, but not a privilege that serves his conviction in the usual sense. One might say instead that Marston's conviction is that he has a privilege to perform. His performance—as we have seen, largely an angry one—functions like Ralegh's or Wyatt's to persuade us, but because Marston comically undercuts even his own anger, the performance protects his inner self more successfully than Ralegh's pure anger. Much like the author of "I Am as I Am," Marston taunts us with his mystery; he seems to say, "You don't know what I am, but here I am assaulting your senses, forcing myself upon you—or is it me, or just a part I'm playing?" Mystery thus gives way to mastery, a skillful performance that aims to persuade us, not that "trouth" is on the writer's side, but that the writer is so talented and clever that he deserves the freedom to say whatever he likes, even though we are unable to understand or judge him in our own terms. If Marston's satire succeeds, then— and clearly it does not succeed with most twentieth-century readers—it succeeds by persuading us by the virtuosity of its performance that it deserves the privilege to perform freely whatever roles it chooses.

Marston continues to interrogate plainness in the Antonio plays. Probably because it is easier to separate Marston the playwright from his characters than it is to separate Marston the poet from his satirist, W. Kinsayder, and perhaps because the criticism of drama is still generally more aware of the role-playing inherent in rhetorical address than is the criticism of poetry, critical opinion has more easily come to terms with the parodic and metatheatrical aspects of these plays than with the corresponding aspects of the satires. Indeed, some recent critics have moved beyond the study of parody to ask how earnest emotion still manages to sneak into the plays.[38] It is my contention that Marston's

[38] Joel Altman, for example, argues that *Antonio's Revenge* explores "how men tend to assume imaginative postures as a way of dealing with the evil in which they find themselves" (*The Tudor Play of Mind: Rhetorical Inquiry and the De-*

skeptical investigation of withdrawal and anger leads him to discover the potential of improvisational performance to satisfy emotional needs—particularly those of anger—regardless of moral scruples. In *Antonio and Mellida* it seems that this discovery entails a rejection of plainness, but in *Antonio's Revenge* Antonio uses the same discovery to gain partial control of his amoral desire for revenge and to forge a plainness that is less principled but more aware of its own performance than Hieronimo's.

Antonio and Mellida builds a comic denouement on the tragic potential of the revenging rage and stoic withdrawal of plainness. Both Piero and Andrugio are carefully established as would-be revengers, and our knowledge that Andrugio and Antonio are the chief protagonists raises expectations of a bloody death for Piero. But in the end there is no violent revenge; instead, the two parties are reconciled, their vows of revenge forgotten.

This comic deflation of anger is furthered by several overtly comic scenes. At the beginning of the second act, for example, Marston burlesques the anger tradition when Dildo persuades Catzo to share a capon:

> *Dil.* My stomach's up.
> *Cat.* I think thou art hungry.
> *Dil.* The match of fury is lighted, fastened to the linstock of rage, and will presently set fire to the touchhole of intemperance, discharging the double culverin of my incensement in the face of thy opprobrious speech.
> *Cat.* I'll stop the barrel thus [*gives him food*]; good Dildo, set not fire to the touchhole.
> *Dil.* My rage is stopp'd, and I will eat to the health of the fool thy master, Castilio.[39]

---

velopment of Elizabethan Drama* [Berkeley: University of California Press, 1978], 294); Barbara Baines sees the tragic feeling of *Antonio's Revenge* arising from the predicament of the characters who are trapped in conventional roles that permit them only an "emotional and aesthetic" response, rather than a "rational and moral" one ("Antonio's Revenge: Marston's Play on Revenge Plays," *SEL* 23 [1983], 277–94). Foakes's seminal article on the parodic elements of the plays is "John Marston's Fantastical Plays," *Philological Quarterly* 41 (1962), 229–39.

[39] John Marston, *Antonio and Mellida*, ed. G. K. Hunter, Regents Renaissance Drama Series (Lincoln: University of Nebraska Press, 1965), 2.1.13–22. Further references appear in the text.

Elsewhere, Marston turns the tradition of the epileptic Herculean warrior into the occasion for a ribald double entendre arising from Antonio's disguise:

> Anto. O how impatience cramps my cracked veins,
>   And cruddles thick my blood with boiling rage.
>   O eyes, why leap you not like thunderbolts
>   Or cannon bullets in my rivals' face?
>   *Ohime infelice misero, o lamentevol fato.*
>   [*Falls on the ground.*]
> Alber. What means the lady fall upon the ground?
> Ross.   Belike the falling sickness.
>   (2.1.196–202)[40]

Here even Antonio's speech is a parody. A playgoer seeking serious anger with serious consequences would be very disappointed with *Antonio and Mellida*.

So too would the playgoer in search of a consistent example of stoic withdrawal. The most likely example is the plainspeaking Feliche, a sometime satirist who proclaims his devotion to stoic content and his freedom from envy in a soliloquy notable for its invocations of satire and plain truth. But shortly after Feliche declares himself free from envy, Castilio's boasting throws him into an envious rant (3.2.1–89). Very much the same comedy is played out between Andrugio and his servant, Lucio. Andrugio claims in a ringing speech to be content with his new state, but with one word Lucio bursts his delusion:

> Luc. My lord, the Genoese had wont to say—
> And. Name not the Genoese; that very word
>   Unkings me quite, makes me vile passion's slave.
>   (4.1.67–69)

Again, the ideal of self-sufficient content is strongly articulated only to be exposed as a lie.

Marston continues to subject the privileged, stoic self to radical

---

[40] On the epilepsy of the Herculean hero, see Rolf Soellner, "The Madness of Hercules and the Elizabethans," *Comparative Literature* 10 (1958), 309–24.

scrutiny by denying plainness the tragic seriousness it requires
for fulfillment. The pattern of expectation and denial lasts into
the final scene, where Andrugio urges Piero to murder him. But
Piero does not strike. Similarly, the "tragic spectacle" that Piero
then sees is not the "breathless trunk of young Antonio" (5.2.73–
75), but Antonio vivens. This pattern is complemented by references in the play to the comedy that the characters feel they are in
(e.g., 5.1.66; 5.2.50). The general sense of playacting is increased
by the discussion of the actors' roles in the induction, as well as
by the difficulty the characters have taking each other seriously.
Rossaline, for instance, says of her many suitors that "I love all of
them lightly for something, but affect none of them seriously for
anything" (5.2.53–55). Hence, Andrugio's declaration that

> There's nothing left
> Unto Andrugio, but Andrugio;
> And that nor mischief, force, distress, nor hell can take.
> Fortune my fortunes, not my mind shall shake.
>
> (3.1.59–62)

is less convincing than Antonio's skepticism:

> *And.* Art thou Antonio?
> *Ant.* I think I am.
> *And.* Dost thou but think? What, dost not know thyself?
> *Ant.* He is a fool that thinks he knows himself.
>
> (4.1.102–5)

When behavior and identity are so subject to questioning, and
especially when characters so often find their sense of certainty
one moment compromised by their actions the next, the conviction of plainness disappears as a viable alternative.

The challenge to plainness seems to make the play a rejection
of stoic absoluteness in favor of "confusion," of immersion in a
varying, uncertain world. Confusion is mentioned several times
in the play as a horror feared by those seeking content, as, for
example, when Andrugio refers to the "confused din" of the
"multitudes" (4.1.51–52). Feliche appeals to the same fear when
he tells Piero, who has been playing the Herculean warrior, that

"Confusion's train blows up this Babel pride" (1.1.58). Here, however, because Feliche is criticizing the absolute self by equating it
with pride, the suggestion is that confusion, God's punishment,
may act as an agent of good. And Piero's evil purpose *is* thwarted
by a sort of confusion, the linguistic trick Andrugio and Antonio
play with the spirit and letter of Piero's decree by bringing their
own heads before him. But confusion reigns supreme when the
newly reunited Antonio and Mellida break into Italian, leading
the Page to remark: "I think confusion of Babel is fall'n upon
these lovers, that they change their language" (4.1.219–20). It is
an odd moment: throughout the play, one searches in vain for a
moment of pure feeling not comically undercut. The love of the
title characters is the most important emotion to stand the test of
time, and when they finally come to express it, they change languages, as if to show that their virtuosity as performers who can
adjust to the moment proves their love's truth. The scene bears
comparison with Hieronimo's "confusion" in *The Spanish Tragedy*. While Hieronimo's confusion served his anger, Antonio and
Mellida's serves their love; while Hieronimo's confusion was en-
tered unwillingly as a necessary evil by the revenger, Antonio and
Mellida's is embraced without necessity by the lovers; while
Hieronimo's confusion failed to break down the barriers to understanding, Antonio and Mellida's is perhaps the most sincere communication of feeling in the play. Plainness seems a long way off.

Until we realize, that is, that the confusion of Antonio and
Mellida's love both proclaims their mastery and protects their
mystery. It may be love, but it is unfathomable and unanswerable
to the ordinary observer—we may know Italian, but can we know
any more of Antonio and Mellida than their mysterious performance reveals? Hence the lovers' flexibility and improvisational
skill appear to be an alternative to the plain, stoic self only because we are accustomed to thinking of stoic selves as constant.
So they are—in their desire. Antonio and Mellida are as constant
in their love as Ralegh is in his anger. But a constant desire may
prove very flexible in its expression, and it is consequently the
potential of improvisational performance to give mysterious expression to selves, plain or otherwise, that *Antonio and Mellida*
finally suggests.

In doing so, however, *Antonio and Mellida* temporarily abandons anger, so it is left to the sequel to retrieve it. In *Antonio's Revenge*, anger and withdrawal are initially suspect, but by the end of the play anger has come to fruition in Antonio's masterful performance. The play initially offers us two contrasting responses to tragic loss and two very different perspectives on the utility of angry performance. Pandulpho, first of all, accepts the death of his son Feliche with stoic calm, rejecting anger as a false performance issuing from an ignorant madness:

> Wouldst have me cry, run raving up and down
> For my son's loss? Wouldst have me turn rank mad,
> Or wring my face with mimic action,
> Stamp, curse, weep, rage, and then my bosom strike?
> Away, 'tis apish action, play-like.
> If he is guiltless, why should tears be spent?
> Thrice blessed soul that dieth innocent.[41]

However, the triteness of this last couplet foreshadows Pandulpho's eventual realization that his content, too, is an act:

> Man will break out, despite philosophy.
> Why, all this while I ha' but played a part,
> Like to some boy that acts a tragedy,
> Speaks burly words and raves out passion;
> But when he thinks upon his infant weakness,
> He droops his eye. I spake more than a god,
> Yet am less than a man.
> I am the miserablest soul that breathes.
>
> (4.5.46–53)

Pandulpho's experience, then, seems to agree with the suggestion in *Antonio and Mellida* that anger and content are only roles that fail to touch the core of the self.

Yet the possibility remains that it is not plainness itself, but plainness in Pandulpho's hands, that is the problem. For Pandul-

---

[41] John Marston, *Antonio's Revenge*, ed. W. Reavley Gair, The Revels Plays (Baltimore: Johns Hopkins University Press, 1978), 1.5.76–82. Further references appear in the text.

pho, performance entails an insincerity from which he has difficulty escaping. For instance, even after he has proclaimed his woe
and decided to join in league with Antonio to seek Piero's death,
Pandulpho continues to spout Senecan clichés:

> Death, exile, plaints and woe,
> Are but man's lackeys, not his foe.
> No mortal 'scapes from fortune's war
> Without a wound, at least a scar.
> Many have led these to the grave,
> But all shall follow, none shall save.
> Blood of my youth, rot and consume;
> Virtue, in dirt, doth life assume.
> With this old saw close up this dust:
> Thrice blessed man that dieth just.
>
> (4.5.74–83)

Conventional forms of expression seem limited to lifeless old
saws for Pandulpho, and even when he joins wholeheartedly in
the plot for revenge he remains essentially a follower. Performance in his hands seems to hamper the conviction of plainness.

Viewed in this light, Pandulpho offers a very interesting comparison with Antonio, whose initial response to the death of his
father and dishonoring of his fiancée is the opposite of Pandulpho's. He argues that content is an unsatisfying response to such
loss, and he proclaims his woe:

> *Alb.* Sweet prince, be patient.
> *Ant.* 'Slid, sir, I will not, in despite of thee.
> Patience is slave to fools, a chain that's fixed
> Only to posts and senseless log-like dolts.
> *Alb.* 'Tis reason's glory to command affects.
> *Ant.* Lies thy cold father dead, his glossed eyes
> New closed up by thy sad mother's hands?
> Hast thou a love as spotless as the brow
> Of clearest heaven, blurred with false defames?. . .
> *Alb.*   Take comfort.
> *Ant.* Confusion to all comfort! I defy it. . . .
> O, now my fate is more than I could fear,
> My woes more weighty than my soul can bear.
>
> (1.5.34–57)

The core of Antonio's argument is that content's claim to control or "command" one's feeling of well-being is a false one. Instead Antonio finds his happiness subject to his fate, the "comfort" of his internal order lost to the discontent caused by the "Confusion" of the world outside. To be so controlled, he argues later, is a mark of heroic stature: "Pigmy cares / Can shelter under patience' shield, but giant griefs / Will burst all covert" (2.5.4–6). Only a "dank, marish spirit" would not be "fired with impatience" (55–56) at Antonio's misfortunes; "Let none out-woe me," he concludes, "mine's Herculean woe" (133). With this spirited response, so different from Pandulpho's tentative stoicism, Antonio turns the discontent of woe into a Herculean virtue.

When the visit of Andrugio's Ghost turns the discontent of woe into the discontent of anger, Antonio approaches his new role with equal zeal. Before, he said his "pined heart shall eat on naught but woe" (2.3.8); now he vows to "suck red vengeance / Out of Piero's wounds" (3.2.78–79). His mother, already afraid that he was "stark mad" (2.4.10) in his woe, now finds that he seems "distraught," and pleads with him to "appease / [his] mutining affections" (3.2.23–24). But Antonio continues to embrace the confusion of the emotions that control him and of the world that controls his emotions, and is consequently led to the murder of the innocent Julio. Unable to distinguish the good from the bad, the son from the father, Antonio murders both indiscriminately:

> O that I knew which joint, which side, which limb
> Were father all, and had no mother in't,
> That I might rip it vein by vein and carve revenge
> In bleeding rases! But since 'tis mixed together,
> Have at adventure, pell-mell, no reverse.
> (3.3.20–24)

Antonio at this point views his emotion as self-validating: its intensity licenses anything it leads him to. What he fails to see is that by letting his anger control him he is letting Piero, who caused his anger, control him. To be "mixed together" is to be confused, and "pell-mell" is synonymous with confusion: Piero, for instance, exclaims, "Pell mell! Confusion and black murder guides / The organs of my spirit" (2.5.47–48). Uncontrolled confusion, which is to say complete submission to the historical performances surrounding us, is a type of insanity.[42]

While Antonio's uncontrollable anger is thus uncompromised by the conventions of anger, he, too, has a lesson to learn. In contrast to Pandulpho, who comes to see his stoicism as too controlled and theatrical, Antonio eventually realizes that his almost unbearably authentic response to Piero's treachery is self-defeating. In the final speech of act 3, the Ghost tells him to disguise himself, and when Antonio reappears in act 4 he eloquently explains the advantages of dressing one's self as a fool. A fool, he explains, has "a patent of immunities, / Confirmed by custom, sealed by policy, / As large as spacious thought" (4.1.13–15). Antonio also explains that he envies the fool the unshakable content caused by his insensibility to misfortunes such as Antonio's:

> Had heaven been kind,
> Creating me an honest, senseless dolt,
> A good, poor fool, I should not want sense to feel
> The stings of anguish shoot through every vein;
> I should not know what 'twere to lose a father;
> I should be dead of sense to view defame
> Blur my bright love; I could not thus run mad
> As one confounded in a maze of mischief
> Staggered, stark felled with bruising stroke of chance.
>   (48–56)

This reflection on the fool's lot brings Antonio to the realization that his madness and confusion do not assist his revenge, and he

---

[42] Defying the almost unanimous modern condemnation of the murder of Julio, Karen Robertson defends it as being within the Senecan bounds of anger's privilege. This is wrong, I think, because Antonio's confusion at this point in the action entails a surrender to the circumstances that the Senecan revenger aims to conquer. Although Robertson notes the prominence of the word "pell-mell" in the play, she doesn't realize that the mastery of confusion in Antonio's later performance implicitly criticizes his earlier, uncontrolled confusion. See "*Antonio's Revenge*: The Tyrant, the Stoic, and the Passionate Man," *Medieval and Renaissance Drama in England* 4 (1989), 91–106.

therefore resolves to restrain his anger with foolish content (66–68). He is not renouncing the confusion of anger, but, like Hieronimo, claiming control of it, the ability to use it as his plan requires: "Let's think a plot; then pell-mell vengeance!" (4.5.95). The plot demands skilful acting in his fool's costume and in the masque; but the freedom gained by these performances puts Antonio in the position where he can unleash his fury. "Now," he says, "grim fire-eyed rage / Possess us wholly" (5.5.58–60). "Now, pell-mell" (76). Claiming the fool's privilege of free performance has helped him uphold anger's privilege.

Antonio's discovery of the private utility of performance is underscored in the last act by the presence and comments of the Ghost of Andrugio, who becomes a Kydian audience: "Here will I sit, spectator of revenge, / And glad my ghost in anguish of my foe" (5.5.22–23). This reminder of *The Spanish Tragedy* can be misleading, however, for the status of performance in the two plays is very different. Hieronimo uses performance as a way to achieve the revenge that he is convinced is right. His concern throughout is with justice, even after he loses his trust in public justice, and his long speech after the performance is intended to justify his actions to the public. In contrast, Antonio never cries for justice and seems equally disinterested in legal and moral issues. For example, when his decision to disguise himself as a fool is met with opposition from Alberto and Maria, who argue that "such feigning, known, disgraceth much" (4.1.29), Antonio responds in a very un-Hieronimo-like way, paying tribute to Machiavelli and proclaiming his own moral relativism or even nihilism:

> Why, by the genius of that Florentine,
> Deep, deep-observing, sound-brained Machiavel,
> He is not wise that strives not to seem fool. . . .
> Pish! Most things that morally adhere to souls
> Wholly exist in drunk opinion,
> Whose reeling censure, if I value not,
> It values nought.
>
> (23–33)

This is a plainness without the moral concerns of "trouth."

Jonathan Dollimore has argued that *Antonio's Revenge* dramatizes a subculture of revenge that is able to reintegrate the individual revengers into the community damaged by Piero's tyranny, but this strikes me as too optimistic.[43] Antonio's concern at the end of the play is less with restoring a just community than with realizing his self-image through performance. Far from feeling justified when the senators excuse him, Antonio is "amazed" (5.6.28). To the senators and Galeatzo, Antonio is a "poor orphan" (19) and a "Hercules" who has rid the state of "huge pollution" (12–13); but Antonio sees himself as a Hercules in woe and a master revenger who stands "triumphant over Belzebub" (21) because he has fulfilled Atreus's *sententia*, quoted earlier by Adrugio's Ghost—"*Scelera non ulcisceris, nisi vincis*" (3.1.51): "Crimes thou dost not avenge, save as thou dost surpass them."[44] His performance has not been aimed at seeing justice done, but at bringing this self-image to fruition. In the final speech of the play, then, Antonio is able to view his recent history as a singularly woeful revenge tragedy:

> Sound doleful tunes, a solemn hymn advance,
> To close the last act of my vengeance;
> And when the subject of your passion's spent,
> Sing 'Mellida is dead', all hearts will relent
> In sad condolement at that heavy sound;
> Never more woe in lesser plot was found.
>
> (5.6.56–59)

And he can look forward to the day when his story will grace the stage as a "black tragedy" (63). Instead of viewing performance as

---

[43] Jonathan Dollimore, *Radical Tragedy: Religion, Ideology, and Power in the Drama of Shakespeare and His Contemporaries* (Brighton: Harvester Press, 1984). For a criticism of Dollimore's argument on this point, see Harry Keyishian's review of *Radical Tragedy*, in *Journal of Medieval and Renaissance Drama in England* 2 (1985), 314–20. Also, for a strong argument that the individual revengers in *Antonio's Revenge* remain separate from the society that is too corrupt to be redeemed, see Thomas Babula, "The Avenger and the Satirist: John Marston's Malevole," in *The Elizabethan Theatre VI*, ed. G. R. Hibbard (Hamden, Conn.: Archon Books, 1975), pp. 48–50.

[44] Seneca, *Thyestes*, in *Seneca's Tragedies*, trans. Frank Justus Miller, rev. ed., Loeb Classical Library, vol. 2 (New York: Putnam, 1929), ll. 195–96.

a means to an end, then, Antonio sees it as an end in itself, as a choice of ways of being. Whereas Hieronimo's final concern was justice, Antonio's is to write his own part in the performance of discontent.

More consistently than Greville, Marston follows through the logic of a plainness emancipated from the communal concerns of "trouth." Private plainness always walks a line between responsibility to community and freedom from ordinary moral judgment. This is the nature of the privilege of "I Am as I Am," of Greville's peace, and of anger. Kyd shows in Hieronimo the vengeful anger that enforces the penalties determined by private judgment; but because Hieronimo wishes his anger to be publicly justifiable, his anger remains primarily moral. Ralegh strains against the bounds of this moral anger in "The Lie," but remains within them. It is left to Marston to push plainness past the constraints of morality and into an amoral sphere where the privilege earned by performance finally exists only for the sake of private conviction. Conviction is now free from the responsibility to correspond to any order, divine or human; it is a belief only in the primacy of self, a primacy extending to the self's command of forms. Marston not only transforms anger, he transforms the performance of conviction by releasing it from the responsibility of reflecting a prior reality: Antonio's plainness is autotelic, a product of his mysterious mastery. Instead of asking if their convictions are true, then, the heroes of Marston's early work might ask, as Malevole does, "What, play I well the free-breath'd discontent?"[45]

[45] John Marston, *The Malcontent*, Regents Renaissance Drama Series (Lincoln: University of Nebraska Press, 1964), 1.4.31.

5 The Performance of Pride: Desire, Truth, and Power in *Coriolanus* and *Timon of Athens*

The problem of anger highlights the fundamental ethical uncertainty of a conviction that cannot be judged by any shared criteria. Writers like Kyd and Ralegh show the moral struggle this uncertainty can produce in angry people, while Marston shows how the breakdown of rhetorical judgment can lead anger to assume a skeptical pose not just toward the world but toward its own claims to truth, at the same time that those claims are being challenged from without. The trajectory from moral concern to moral relativism that I have followed through these writers thus opens the possibility of seeing plainness as essentially self-interested rather than essentially just—as simply a mystification rather than simply mysterious. If the consequence of this skeptical transformation in Marston's satirist and revengers is a tendency to downplay conviction and to emphasize performance as an end in itself, the title characters of Shakespeare's *Timon of Athens* and *Coriolanus* will tolerate no such skepticism and no such separation of conviction from performance. Nevertheless, Shakespeare depicts a devalued plainness in these plays, showing an anger where the truth of conviction depends upon the power of performance.

In this chapter I explain this confusion of truth and power in terms of the psychological and political dynamic of plainness. I begin with two preliminary observations. First, both *Coriolanus* and *Timon of Athens* show plainness as fundamentally oppositional, a quality that is as evident in the plays' language as in their action and that is shown to be central to the characters of the chief plainspeakers.[1] Second, plainness presents itself in these plays as an alternative to the debased version of rhetorical conversation that flattery represents. Together, then, the plays present a world without trust or consensus in which efforts to negotiate rhetorically have given way to bitter opposition and a splintering of society.

Such a world is consistent with the world of satire and revenge tragedy, as well as with the Reformation world in which religious "disputation" tends toward persecution and martyrdom. But in these plays Shakespeare not only depicts the antirhetorical world with which we are by now familiar, he also presents a dramatic analysis of plainness in terms of desire, truth, and power. As a contrast, rhetorical theory can be understood as a placing of desire (or appetite or will)—as seen through its linguistic expression—

---

[1] The centrality of opposition in these plays has been recognized and explored by critics who have rightly concentrated on the extreme antipathy between the title characters and their worlds and on the lack of a "middle term" that might bring the two together. Such studies include Richard Fly, "Confounding Contraries: The Unmediated World of *Timon of Athens*," in *Shakespeare's Mediated World* (Amherst: University of Massachusetts Press, 1976), pp. 119–42; Lesley W. Brill, "Truth and *Timon of Athens*," *Modern Language Quarterly* 40 (1979), 17–36; Madeleine Doran, "'All's in anger': The Language of Contention in *Coriolanus*," in *Shakespeare's Dramatic Language* (Madison: University of Wisconsin Press, 1976), pp. 182–217; and Kenneth Burke, "*Coriolanus* and the Delights of Faction," in *Language as Symbolic Action* (Berkeley: University of California Press, 1968), pp. 81–97.

Many studies of the late tragedies have attempted to define the special nature of the conflict between the "heroes" and their world. Willard Farnham sees *Timon*, *Coriolanus*, *Antony and Cleopatra*, and *Macbeth* as joined by the "paradoxical nobility" of heroes whose individual greatness elicits sympathy, but whose violation of the social order generates antipathy (*Shakespeare's Tragic Frontier: The World of His Final Tragedies* [Berkeley: University of California Press, 1950]). G. K. Hunter holds that the same four plays "offer alternative absolutes of exclusion and inclusion, of denying the world and of swallowing it" ("Shakespeare's Last Tragic Heroes"; first published 1966; rpt. in Robert B. Heilman, ed., *Shakespeare: The Tragedies, New Perspectives* [Englewood Cliffs, N.J.: Prentice-Hall, 1984]). And R. A. Foakes argues that in *Timon*, *Coriolanus*, and *Antony and Cleopatra* the central characters prove "unable to adapt themselves to a world of relative values which sanctions the flexible man (like Alcibiades) in place of the man of absolutes (like Timon)" (*Shakespeare, The Dark Comedies to the Last Plays: From Satire to Celebration* [London: Routledge & Kegan Paul, 1971]).

at the intersection of knowledge and action, or, as rhetoricians might say to avoid hypostatizing historical process, of knowing and doing.[2] Language and desire are not identical with truth in this model, but they can participate in the construction of knowledge by judging what is probable. They are not identical with action, but their participation in the manufacture of consent helps to create power by determining what is possible. Plainness, on the other hand, omits rhetorical judgment and persuasion and instead identifies its words and desires directly with both truth and power, or rather, it *insists* that its words are true and powerful and denies any importance to desire (the existence of which would indicate a lack of these attributes). Hence, while rhetoric historicizes desire, positioning it within a network of trusting relationships from which it draws what temporary satisfactions it can, plainness in effect desires, as Stanley Cavell has said of Coriolanus, not to desire.[3] Lacking historical consciousness and self-awareness, that is, and unwilling to settle for the partial satisfactions of rhetorical desire, plainness restricts desire to the hostile appetite that remains when trust vanishes, and insists on the rewards of certainty (truth) and immediate gratification (power).[4] It thus asserts the absoluteness of both its conviction and its

---

[2] I have generally avoided the word "will" to prevent confusion between its popular meaning as a synonym for desire and its specialized meaning in faculty psychology as the faculty of deliberate or reasoned action. As my discussion makes clear, I regard the second sense as largely irrelevant to Timon and Coriolanus, who commonly act on impulse without thinking. For a discussion of the role of desire in rhetorical epistemology during the Renaissance, see Joel B. Altman, "'Preposterous Conclusions': Eros, *Enargeia*, and the Composition of *Othello*," *Representations* 18 (1987), 129–57. The locus classicus for such discussions is Plato's *Phaedrus*.

[3] See Stanley Cavell's valuable chapter on the play, "*Coriolanus* and Interpretations of Politics ('Who does the wolf love?')," in *Disowning Knowledge in Six Plays of Shakespeare* (Cambridge: Cambridge University Press, 1987). I have found particularly suggestive for my own line of inquiry Cavell's argument that anger is presented in the play as a lament for something that one lacks but is unable to acknowledge the lack of. More generally, Cavell's work on skepticism and tragedy has informed my thinking about the relation of plainness to skepticism. Especially important is the wonderful essay on *King Lear*, "The Avoidance of Love," in *Must We Mean What We Say?* (1969; rpt. Cambridge: Cambridge University Press, 1976), and included in *Disowning Knowledge*.

[4] The childishness of such an insistence is suggested by Kenneth Burke's remarks about the role of invective in *Timon* and *Coriolanus*. Invective, he writes,

performance in a way that establishes their interdependence: because both are treated as identical with language and desire, the one depends upon the other, and the ethical separation of truth from power ceases to be made.[5]

In *Coriolanus* and *Timon of Athens*, I contend, Shakespeare shows how the title characters confuse truth and power by refusing the functions of rhetorical desire. After showing the rejection of the desiring world by Coriolanus and Timon, I investigate their dual attempts to escape their own desire, first by making it true, then by making it powerful. I conclude by exploring the reasons why their public, political failure is inseparable from their private, psychological failure—why the ethical emptiness of an exclusively antirhetorical plainness is also an inner emptiness.

Unable to trust in a world they regard as full of flattery, Apemantus, Timon, and Coriolanus share a vision of a world of wolfish and cannibalistic appetite. Apemantus connects the flattery of "the common tongue" (1.1.174) to cannibalism in a series of remarks in the first two scenes. The central instance comes when Timon, mildly irritated by Apemantus's "churlish" refusal to participate courteously in Timon's circle of friends, offers him food to silence his dissent:

> *Tim.* I take no heed of thee. Thou'rt an Athenian, therefore welcome. I myself would have no power; prithee let my meat make thee silent.

"is a primary 'freedom of speech,' rooted extralinguistically in the helpless rage of an infant that states its attitude by utterances wholly unbridled. In this sense, no mode of expression could be more 'radical,' unless it be the closely allied motive of sheer *lamentation*, undirected wailing." See "*Timon of Athens* and Misanthropic Gold," in *Language as Symbolic Action*, p. 120.

[5] Something very like the analysis I outline here is put forward by Ulysses in his speech on degree in *Troilus and Cressida*. He traces the degeneration by which justice has become subordinate to power, power to will (in its specialized sense), and will to appetite (1.3.116–24). (This agreement does not mean that Shakespeare and I share Ulysses's optimism about the healing powers of degree.) Ulysses's argument in turn agrees fundamentally with Plato's argument in the *Gorgias* that *rhetoric* confuses truth and power by ignoring the difference between opinion and true knowledge. The surprising similarity between the Platonic critique of the Sophists and my argument here about the extreme antirhetorical position suggests some common ground between these two ends of the rhetorical spectrum. I return to this matter briefly in the Epilogue.

Ape. I scorn thy meat. 'Twould choke me; for I should ne'er
flatter thee. O you gods, what a number of men eats
Timon, and he sees 'em not! It grieves me to see so many
dip their meat in one man's blood. (1.2.33–39)

The structure of the passage, like that of the play as a whole,
explodes Timon's false belief that he is a member of a rhetorical
community. As true friendship generally makes ceremony super-
erogatory, so in this instance the social reality of a shared meal,
with all the attendant psychological and religious suggestions,
quells (Timon believes) dissenting voices in the silence of a promise that is always already performed. But Apemantus points out
the true situation: Timon is surrounded by those for whom Timon's "meat" is a sign not of his love but of his "power," which
Timon incorrectly believes he has kept separate from his love.
These men share his meat not in silent communion but in the
false promise that is flattery, just as they fake the ceremonies of
friendship generally; they participate in a proliferation of false
words that enables them to feed on Timon's bounty by betraying
his trust. Hence, what Timon believes is sharing is in fact the
figurative smothering and consumption of him by those who
"promise" without intending to "perform," those who abuse language in order to grow fat off him (4.3.73–76; 5.1.22–28). When
Timon finally recoils from this abuse, he joins the long tradition
contrasting the verbal integrity of the plainspeaker to the self-
serving deceit of the flatterer—a deceit he and Apemantus see as
the expression of a cannibalistic appetite.

For Coriolanus, too, fickle, flattering voices reveal the voracious
appetite of greedy people. His attitude is revealed when he refers
satirically to the people as "desirers" (2.3.98). In the first scene, for
example, Coriolanus tells the crowd that their "affections are / A
sick man's appetite, who desires most that / Which would increase his evil" (1.1.172–74). If the senate didn't keep them "in
awe," they would "feed on one another" (182–83), as they later feed
like wolves on Coriolanus himself. To Coriolanus, as to Timon and
Apemantus, human nature features a potentially cannibalistic
appetite, a selfish and voracious desire that threatens to consume
society and that finds expression in a cacophony of false voices.

Coriolanus and Timon respond to the collapse of society into competing desires by insisting that they know the truth, particularly about themselves. We might say that they replace desire with desert:

> Cor. You know the cause, sir, of my standing here.
> 3 Cit. We do, sir. Tell us what hath brought you to't.
> Cor. Mine own desert.
> 2 Cit. Your own desert?
> Cor. Ay, not mine own desire.
> 3 Cit. How not your own desire?
> Cor. No, sir, 'twas never my desire yet to trouble the poor
> with begging. (2.3.61–68)

The distinction is crucial: it is the difference between wanting to learn the truth, and insisting that one already knows it, between believing that value resides in the activity of seeking truth—that, as Montaigne writes, "we are born to quest after truth" but that "to possess it belongs to a greater power"—and believing that value lies in the unchanging essence of things in themselves.[6] It is the difference, in short, between rhetorical and antirhetorical outlooks. One seeks; one *knows*.

By implying that truth is not just sought but known, Coriolanus's wish to replace desire with desert raises the question of value in the play. In *Coriolanus* the issue of desert, or merit, is part of a nexus of concerns centering around the nature of fame. As D. J. Gordon has shown, Shakespeare places Coriolanus's conviction of intrinsic (or inherent) merit in a context that forces recognition of how values such as fame and honor are (at least in part) constructed by communities.[7] Hence, the play can be thought of as presenting the legal problem of how to judge—or

---

[6] Michel de Montaigne, "On the Art of Discussion," in *The Complete Essays*, trans. Donald M. Frame (Stanford: Stanford University Press, 1958), p. 708.

[7] D. J. Gordon, "Name and Fame in *Coriolanus*"; first published 1964; rpt. in *The Renaissance Imagination*, ed. Stephen Orgel (Berkeley: University of California Press, 1975), pp. 203–19. See also the related reflections of James L. Calderwood, "Wordless Meanings and Meaningless Words," *SEL* 6 (1966), 211–24, and Norman Rabkin, *Shakespeare and the Common Understanding* (New York: Free Press, 1967), pp. 119–44.

who's to judge—what Coriolanus deserves. The tribunes are sure that death is merited; the people are of two minds, wavering between beliefs that, as the Fourth Citizen says to Coriolanus, "You have deserved nobly of your country, and you have not deserved nobly" (2.3.84–85); and the senators counter the tribunes' confident charges against Coriolanus with equally certain denials that he has "Deserved this dishonored rub, laid falsely / I' th' plain way of his merit" (3.1.60–61).

Like his patrician friends, Coriolanus believes his merit is "plain." When he claims desert, therefore, he means to claim that his private judgment of his worth is true and to substitute the truth of that antirhetorical privilege for the faulty public justice of "desirers" (2.3.98). On the one hand, rhetorical justice searches for truth within history; it is a process, involving desire and the flexible, consensual judgment that takes place in a political dialogue. Coriolanus, on the other hand, wants to be pure product, finished, complete in himself, happy to continue being the man he has already become.[8] As Cominius understands when he tells Coriolanus that any recognition he receives will be "In sign of what you are, not to reward / What you have done" (1.9.26–27), Coriolanus is unwilling, in effect, to *become* a consul at all: in his mind, he *is* a consul already, on the basis of essential merit, and recognition of this fact should be automatic—or better, unnecessary, since public recognition is itself a political process carried out in language. He has thus taken the antirhetorical desire for the perfect being of a self-authorizing truth to its fulfillment in withdrawal from the contingent, desiring world of politics.

The question of worth plays a similar role in *Timon*, but the principal form in which it appears there is more accurately described as economic than as political. From the parallel discussions between the Poet and the Painter and the Merchant and the Jeweller with which the play opens, words such as "worthy," "goodness," "good," "fortune," "value," and even "trust" have an

---

[8] Coriolanus's aversion to "becoming" is explored further by Stanley Fish, "How to Do Things with Austin and Searle: Speech-Act Theory and Literary Criticism," in *Is There a Text in This Class?* (Cambridge: Harvard University Press, 1980).

inescapable financial cast.[9] Economic exchange, particularly in the forms of usury and indiscriminate gift-giving, generally exerts a corrupting influence. For example, the word "use" rarely escapes some hint of its financial sense and stains most human relations; people "use our hearts" (1.2.80), "use the time" (3.1.34), "use Lord Timon" (3.2.49), and finally "use" prostitutes, who epitomize the debasement of love—"They love thee not that use thee" (4.3.84), Timon says to Timandra and Phrynia.[10] When Alcibiades accuses the senators in the play's final scene of "making your wills the scope of justice" (5.4.4–5), it has long since been apparent that the desire for money chiefly determines justice, value, and truth in Athens.

Apemantus and Timon both reject the fluctuating values created by economic desire in favor of the certainty of plain conviction. Just as the senators' insistence on "the plain way" of Coriolanus's merit ties plainness explicitly to a rejection of the political determination of desert and honor, so Apemantus's preference for plain-dealing to jewels offers plainness as an alternative to market forces:

> Tim. How dost thou like this jewel, Apemantus?
> Ape. Not so well as plain-dealing, which will not cost a man a doit.
> Tim. What dost thou think 'tis worth?
> Ape. Not worth my thinking. (1.1.208–12)

[9] Studies of the economic dimensions of *Timon* include Kenneth Muir, "*Timon of Athens* and the Cash-Nexus"; first published 1947; rpt. in *The Singularity of Shakespeare and Other Essays* (Liverpool: Liverpool University Press, 1977), pp. 56–75; W. H. Bizley, "Language and Currency in *Timon of Athens*," *Theoria* 44 (1975), 21–42; John M. Wallace, "*Timon of Athens* and the Three Graces: Shakespeare's Senecan Study," *Modern Philology* 83 (1986), 349–63; and Coppelia Kahn, "'Magic of bounty': *Timon of Athens*, Jacobean Patronage, and Maternal Power," *Shakespeare Quarterly* 38 (1987), 34–57.

[10] This mixing of economic value with love leads to some of the richest language in the play. See Lewis Walker, "Fortune and Friendship in *Timon of Athens*," *Texas Studies in Literature and Language* 18 (1977), 577–600. The frequent metaphoric comparisons of friendship to merchant shipping (e.g., 2.2.173–77; 2.2.226–67; 4.2.19–21) suggest that Shakespeare was thinking of the academic *Timon* (written after 1601), in which Timon, like Antonio in *The Merchant of Venice*, loses all his ships at sea. See *Narrative and Dramatic Sources of Shakespeare*, ed. Geoffrey Bullough, vol. 6 (New York: Columbia University Press, 1966), p. 317.

Timon's plainness initially works in a different way, however. His mistake is to think that money offers perfect "security" (3.1.40), a source of "worth" as "certain" (3.4.47) as essential truth. He is a Midas figure who, like Silas Marner, finds a substitute for love in money, but he does so by giving rather than by hoarding: he believes that if he can give money endlessly and unconditionally, he will guarantee a secure future. He believes that the worth that economic good fortune confers upon him, and of which gift-giving is the sign, is a quality of his essence. He doesn't realize that this economic worth is a kind of corrupt rhetorical currency, fluctuating according to the desires of the society of flatterers over which he presides.

Once outside the cash-nexus, however, Timon seeks to find a new source of worth by replacing desire with stoic content. Like desert, content is seen as unconditional, an intrinsic quality of a person that in no way depends on outside valuations. Content like desert constitutes a self-authenticating value, promising an escape from the dependence of desire to the independence of conviction. Timon attempts to achieve this content by means of a withdrawal that includes a near-rejection of food. Outside the walls of Athens, he discards Athenian consumption and embraces a minimalist primitivism. His decision to eat roots dramatizes at an almost symbolic level his reduction of human needs to less than the "mere necessities" (4.3.373). "Allow not nature more than nature needs, / Man's life is cheap as beast's," cries Lear, who also explores a primitivist impulse (2.4.261–62); but to Timon the point is rather that man's life need not be any more expensive than beast's. To want more than you need is to fall into the trap of cannibalism, as Timon explains to the banditti:

> *Tim.*   Your greatest want is, you want much of meat.
>   Why should you want? Behold, the earth hath roots;
>   Within this mile break forth a hundred springs;
>   The oaks bear mast, the briers scarlet hips;
>   The bounteous housewife Nature on each bush
>   Lays her full mess before you. Want? Why want?
> *1 Bandit.* We cannot live on grass, on berries, water,
>   As beasts and birds and fishes.

> *Tim.* Nor on the beasts themselves, the birds and fishes;
> You must eat men.
>
> (4.3.412–21)

The only way to avoid cannibalism and thievery, in Timon's eyes, is stoic self-sufficiency, the plainness of the uninvolved heart. Its inner content, as Apemantus says, is impervious to the blows of fortune (in either sense) and thus always preferable to a desiring state:

> Willing misery
> Outlives incertain pomp, is crowned before;
> The one is filling still, never complete,
> The other at high wish; best state, contentless,
> Hath a distracted and most wretched being,
> Worse than the worst, content.
> Thou shouldst desire to die, being miserable.
>
> (4.3.242–48)

The desireless content of withdrawal thus remains the goal of plainness.

These attempts to transform desire into various forms of essential worth, and thus to make it true, accompany attempts by Timon and Coriolanus to make desire powerful by converting even its linguistic expression into immediate action. Understood in this way, their plainness reflects a common Renaissance view of linguistic power. As critics like Juliet Fleming and Patricia Parker have shown, improper control of rhetorical *copia* and *dispositio* was sometimes believed to lead to delay, disorder, and indecisiveness. The opposing emphasis fell on hierarchical order and the uncontradicted exercise of power, on deeds rather than words.[11] Of course, so straightforward an opposition of words and

---

[11] Juliet Fleming, "*Différance Féminine*: The Case of Euphuism" (unpublished essay; a later version was delivered at the annual meeting of the Renaissance Society of America, April 1991), and Patricia Parker, *Literary Fat Ladies: Rhetoric, Gender, Property* (London: Methuen, 1987), esp. chaps. 2 and 6. Fleming and Parker both investigate the implications of this understanding for sexual identity. Fleming argues that euphuism (though originating in a circle of disaffected men) was seen as a feminine style partly because it was feared that its balanced clauses

deeds is simplistic. Words are, in a sense, always deeds.[12] What varies is what kind of deeds they are. Some uses of words are more characteristically linguistic—deliberation, questioning, amplification. Some are more like other types of actions—sentencing, commanding. Some *seek* to be like other actions—cursing, railing. Persuasion falls somewhere in the middle, depending on how much coercion it involves. The point is that the closer words are to deeds, and the more their signifying practices reflect and seek to perform or enact convictions, the closer they are to an antirhetorical pole.

Such a pole is theoretical only. In practice, desire for the power of a language that is exclusively active conflicts with language's deliberative qualities. Renaissance plainstylists commonly strive to resolve this conflict by balancing the power of performance and the rhetorical truth of deliberation. Hence, while Jonson seeks the strong, lean, and implicitly active sinews of a "plain" style and Montaigne declares his affection for a mode of speech that is "vehement and brusque," "sinewy, brief and compressed"—"not pedantic, not monkish, not lawyer-like, but rather soldierly"— neither would endorse a statement such as the following:

> Men finde, that action is another thing,
> Then what they in discoursing papers read:
> The worlds affaires require in managing,
> More Artes then those wherein you Clerkes proceede:
> Whilst timorous Knowledge stands considering,
> Audacious Ignorance hath done the deede;
> For who knowes most, the more he knowes to doubt;
> The least discourse is commonly most stout.

---

made skepticism inescapable and action impossible. Parker shows that women were often associated with an uncontrollable garrulity that was seen as a threat to rhetorical and political order alike. In turn, men were associated with deeds and order. Parker examines the sexual anxieties caused by exceptions to the "women are words, men deeds" stereotypes in "On the Tongue: Cross-Gendering, Effeminacy, and the Art of Words," *Style* 23 (1989), 445–65. She continues to investigate the relation of gender to language and style in "Gender Ideology, Gender Change: The Case of Marie Germain," *Critical Inquiry* 19 (1992–93), 337–64.

[12] See especially J. L. Austin, *How to Do Things with Words* (Cambridge: Harvard University Press, 1962).

This extreme position belongs to Philocosmus in Samuel Daniel's "Musophilus," where it leads his attack on the "sweet inchaunting Knowledge" of poetry. Daniel, too, disagrees with so bald a preference for doing to knowing, and his response through Musophilus is to defend a style of discovery that enables action, "To shew true knowledge can both speake and do."[13] But the difficulty of meeting such an ideal increases as the desire for certainty increases and as faith in the possibilities of community decreases. In theory the desire for plain truth tries to simplify existence so that it can be more easily controlled by words that translate belief directly into deeds. But in practice the desire for control always stumbles upon an uncontrollable complexity; the desire for antirhetorical language clashes with language's rhetorical pull. Word and deed will not unite in obedience to the will.

Timon and Coriolanus, however, repeatedly try to establish just such a unity. They seek to simplify knowledge in order to make control and satisfying action easier. Timon's two most common linguistic modes, his curses in the second half of the play and his oaths of friendship in the first half, both match this description.[14] Both are antirhetorical forms of "promise." The world of promises is normally the world in which contracts are made, laws written, understandings set down, expectations established. It should be, in other words, the social world of rhetorical faith. When someone keeps a rhetorical promise, the result is a trust-

[13] Samuel Daniel, "Musophilus," in *The Complete Works in Verse and Prose of Samuel Daniel*, ed. Alexander B. Grosart, vol. 1 (1885; rpt. New York: Russell & Russell, 1963), ll. 486–93, 494, 836. Montaigne's comments are from "Of the education of children," *Complete Essays*, p. 127. In *Discoveries*, Jonson follows classical precedent in comparing a variety of styles to body types, among them the fleshy, the bloody, and the bony. Although he suggests that each of these may be appropriate in certain circumstances, his own preference appears to be for the plain style. On Jonson, plainness, and the body, see Bruce Thomas Boehrer's intriguing "Renaissance Overeating: The Sad Case of Ben Jonson," *PMLA* (1990), 1071–81.

[14] Marianna da Vinci Nichols argues for the continuity in Timon's linguistic performance in "*Timon of Athens* and the Rhetoric of *No*," *Cahiers Elisabethains* 9 (1976), 29–40. Robert C. Elliott suggests that in the eyes of the early Timon there is "exact correspondence . . . between word and concept"; he believes his language is "performing its ancient creative function: what it states, by virtue of being stated, is." See *The Power of Satire: Magic, Ritual, Art* (Princeton: Princeton University Press, 1960), p. 146.

worthy performance, an agreement of word and deed that is what the Painter means by the "deed of saying" (5.1.25). But it is a very different agreement between word and deed that Timon seeks through his curses and oaths of friendship, forms that reject public laws and understandings in favor of the private judgments they seek to perform. The similarity between the two forms is most evident in Timon's refusal to acknowledge the limits of his power. In both cases Timon wants his language to be performative—that is, he wants his words to have the power to make the understanding they express a reality—but in neither case can it be so. His curses are an implicit admission of powerlessness: even as they combine incantation and intimidation in an attempt to destroy Athens and all mankind, they call upon a higher power to effect the destruction. Their main purpose is to enable Timon to retain the delusion that he controls what is happening.

The same self-deception occurs in the first half of the play, when Timon refuses to listen to the financial advice of his steward, Flavius, preferring instead to continue promising gifts he doesn't have. Flavius says:

> He commands us to provide and give great gifts,
> And all out of an empty coffer;
> Nor will he know his purse, or yield me this,
> To show him what a beggar his heart is,
> Being of no power to make his wishes good.
> His promises fly so beyond his state
> That what he speaks is all in debt; he owes
> For every word.
>   (1.2.186–93)

Timon won't "know his purse" because he is convinced that his own power is boundless; he is intoxicated by his own bounty and the "love" it buys him. His promises of love are antirhetorical because they function primarily as attempts to assert conviction and to coerce a loving response rather than to maintain reciprocity and trust in a relationship.[15] Even Timon's mock banquet,

---

[15] Timon's failure to understand reciprocity is a favorite theme of those critics who fault his early behavior. These include Robert B. Heilman, " 'From Mine Own

which marks the transition from his promises of friendship to his curses, can be seen as an attempt to maintain his power. At the banquet, he is the governor who distributes wealth, the judge who pronounces guilt or worth, the physician who knows what is needed to maintain health:

> Live loathed and long,
> Most smiling, smooth, detested parasites,
> Courteous destroyers, affable wolves, meek bears,
> You fools of fortune, trencher-friends, time's flies,
> Cap-and-knee slaves, vapors, and minute-jacks!
> Of man and beast the infinite malady
> Crust you quite o'er! What, dost thou go?
> Soft, take thy physic first; thou too, and thou!
>
> (3.6.90–97)

The stones Timon prescribes are both his last attempt to nourish and his first attempt to destroy Athens, and thus illustrate his character's surprising consistency: throughout the play, he wants language to be both exclusively performative and absolutely true, so he denies it its deliberative and persuasive—its rhetorical—qualities.

Coriolanus, last in a long line of plainspeaking Shakespearean soldiers that includes the Bastard in *King John*, Hotspur, Henry V (when it suits him), Othello, and Enobarbus, also seeks a more powerful alternative to the rhetorical language he scorns. As feminist critics have pointed out, he feels instinctively that linguistic performance is effeminate, that is, an implicit admission of human finitude and dependency.[16] His attitude is illustrated by one

---

Knowledge': A Theme in the Later Tragedies," *Centennial Review* 8 (1964), 17–38; Terence Eagleton, "A Note on *Timon of Athens*," in *Shakespeare and Society: Critical Studies in Shakespearean Drama* (New York: Schocken, 1967), pp. 171–76; Nichols, "*Timon of Athens* and the Rhetoric of *No*"; and Fly, "Confounding Contraries."

[16] See Janet Adelman's seminal essay, "'Anger's My Meat': Feeding, Dependency, and Aggression in *Coriolanus*," in *Shakespeare, Pattern of Excelling Nature*, ed. David Bevington and Jay Halio (Newark, Del.: Associated University Presses, 1978), pp. 108–24; rpt. in *William Shakespeare's Coriolanus*, ed. Harold Bloom, Modern Critical Interpretations (New York: Chelsea House, 1988), pp. 75–89; Phyllis Rackin, "*Coriolanus*: Shakespeare's Anatomy of *Virtus*," *Modern Lan-*

of his many satirical depictions of what asking the people's voices would require of him:

> Away, my disposition, and possess me
> Some harlot's spirit! My throat of war be turned,
> Which quired with my drum, into a pipe
> Small as an eunuch, or the virgin voice
> That babies lulls asleep!
>
> (3.2.111–15)

"Spirit" here seems to carry partly the sense of "breath," and Coriolanus's depiction of what is being asked of him recalls Hamlet's disgust that instead of acting his revenge he should "like a whore unpack my heart with words" (2.2.571).[17] At such moments both characters see action as a man's proper sphere and language as more appropriate for those uncertain of their calling. But unlike Hamlet, Coriolanus has a theory of male speech as an active, aggressive "throat of war." Thus Coriolanus's view of language reflects the ideology of the male-dominated, warrior society of Rome, which prefers aggressive action to affection, sympathy, and nurture, all of which it sees as womanly and weak.

Accordingly, Coriolanus like Timon often seeks linguistic control through the magical power of curses. Curses and satirical railing are among his most characteristic forms of speech, and his most famous speech is no exception:

---

guage Studies 13 (1983), 68–79; Madelon Sprengnether, "Annihilating Intimacy in *Coriolanus*," in *Women in the Middle Ages and the Renaissance*, ed. Mary Beth Rose (Syracuse: Syracuse University Press, 1986), pp. 89–111; and Jane Carducci, "Shakespeare's Coriolanus: 'Could I find out / The woman's part in me'," *Literature and Psychology* 33.2 (1987), 11–20.

Feminist/psychoanalytic readings of *Timon* include Stephen A. Reid, " 'I Am Misanthropos'—A Psychoanalytic Reading of Shakespeare's *Timon of Athens*," *Psychoanalytic Review* 56 (1969), 442–52; Susan Handelman, "*Timon of Athens*: The Rage of Disillusion," *American Imago* 36 (1979), 445–68; and Kahn, "Magic of Bounty." For a brief and cogent discussion of both plays, see C. L. Barber and Richard P. Wheeler, *The Whole Journey: Shakespeare's Power of Development* (Berkeley: University of California Press, 1986), pp. 303–10.

[17] Hamlet contrasts with Coriolanus and Timon, however, in recognizing cursing as a weak alternative to revenge (2.2.572).

> You common cry of curs, whose breath I hate
> As reek o'th'rotten fens, whose loves I prize
> As the dead carcasses of unburied men
> That do corrupt my air, I banish you!
>
> (3.3.121–24)

Like Alcibiades's similar remark when he is banished—

> Banish me?
> Banish your dotage, banish usury,
> That makes the senate ugly!
>
> (3.5.97–99)—

like Celia's when Rosalind is banished—

> Now go we in content
> To liberty, and not to banishment.
>
> (1.3.133–34)—

and like Kent's when *he* is banished—

> Fare thee well, King. Sith thus thou wilt appear,
> Freedom lives hence, and banishment is here.
>
> (1.1.180–81)—

Coriolanus's response to his sentence is to deny its power over him by reversing it. He thus asserts his own control of the situation. But because Coriolanus at this point doesn't have the political power to support his words, they can be seen as attempting to enlist the magical powers of words rooted in the angry speech of curses and satire.[18]

---

[18] As Linda Woodbridge has noted (public lecture, University of Alberta, 19 March 1992), another magical dimension of the speech-act of banishment (and one that Shakespeare's emphasis on the body politic in *Coriolanus* draws attention to) is the ancient belief that words can expel infections from the body. On this belief, see Pedro Lain Entralgo, *The Therapy of the Word in Classical Antiquity*, ed. and trans. L. J. Rather and John M. Sharp, foreword by Walter J. Ong (New Haven: Yale University Press, 1970). For a survey of ideas of language in Shakespeare, including language as a therapeutic purging of the heart, see Jane Donawerth, *Shakespeare and the Sixteenth-Century Study of Language* (Urbana: University of Illinois Press, 1984).

The political consequence of Coriolanus's desire for power is a kind of absolutism. For Coriolanus, political debate is not a possibility; power cannot be shared. He fears that a struggle of all against all will result if the plebeians are allowed to participate in political decision making—if their power, that is, becomes more than ceremonial, "a power," as they say, "that we have no power to do" (2.3.5). Consequently, when he hears Sicinius's "absolute 'shall'," he sees a challenge that would oppose the people's power and "prerogative" (3.3.17) to the senators'. Power must be granted either to the patricians or to the plebeians; there must be one supreme authority to decide questions, or the result is sure to be confusion:

> If he have power,
> Then vail your ignorance; if none, awake
> Your dangerous lenity. If you are learned,
> Be not as common fools; if you are not,
> Let them have cushions by you. You are plebeians
> If they be senators; and they are no less
> When, both your voices blended, the great'st taste
> Most palates theirs. They choose their magistrate;
> And such a one as he, who puts his 'shall,'
> His popular 'shall,' against a graver bench
> Than ever frowned in Greece. By Jove himself,
> It makes the consuls base! and my soul aches
> To know, when two authorities are up,
> Neither supreme, how soon confusion
> May enter 'twixt the gap of both and take
> The one by th'other.
>   (3.1.97–112)[19]

The passage illustrates Coriolanus's characteristically liberal use of antithetical constructions to express the black-and-white dis-

---

[19] "Confusion" again proves to be an important word in defining the anti-rhetorical outlook. The word often appears in descriptions of mobs within discussions of fame and glory (see the examples cited in Gordon, "Name and Fame," 211, 212). This larger context of the voices and breaths that determine fame and glory gives Coriolanus's use of the word suggestiveness reaching beyond the immediate sense of two irreconcilable options.

tinctions and sharp oppositions familiar to us from Wyatt on.[20] Coriolanus's alternative to confusion is the "absolute" linguistic power that he deplores in the tribunes, but seeks for himself. As Coriolanus uses the word, and as it is used of him, it means something that is unconditional and nonnegotiable.[21] It signifies a statement made with the understanding that what it predicates shall be so, or a person unwilling to compromise his conviction of how things should be.

It is a critical commonplace that Coriolanus frequently expresses a contempt for words, preferring the hard certainty of deeds. But his recognition of the force of the tribunes' linguistic challenge and his belief that such power should belong exclusively to the senators show again that he does have a conception of linguistic utility. Coriolanus believes that politically valuable language functions absolutely—it proclaims, it declares, it sentences, it lays down the law. It is normative and performative, a true reflection of what should be and a contributor to what is. Rhetorical functions such as discovery and deliberation play no part in this view of language; hence, forms of government based on debate between various interests are beyond Coriolanus's understanding. His antirhetorical desire to unite words and deeds thus fosters an absolutist political stance.[22]

[20] Coriolanus's use of antitheses is examined at length by Doran in "Language of Contention."

[21] Wesley Trimpi examines the understanding of this absolutism in Greek thought in *Muses of One Mind: The Literary Analysis of Experience and Its Continuity* (Princeton: Princeton University Press, 1983), esp. pp. 117–29 and 132–34.

[22] Leonard Tennenhouse places Coriolanus's failure to acknowledge that the speech of the people may be a legitimate political action in the context of parliamentary history under James in "*Coriolanus*: History and the Crisis of the Semantic Order," in *Drama in the Renaissance*, ed. Clifford Davidson, C. J. Gianakaris, and John H. Stroupe (New York: AMS Press, 1986), pp. 217–35. He concludes that "Coriolanus dies because of this incapacity to be a political man, this inability to use language rhetorically" (228). On the relation of *Coriolanus* to parliamentary history see also W. Gordon Zeeveld, "'Coriolanus' and Jacobean Politics," *Modern Language Review* 57 (1962), 321–34. For the play's relation to the Midlands Rising, see E. C. Pettet, "*Coriolanus* and the Midlands Insurrection of 1607," *Shakespeare Survey* 3 (1950), 34–42. And for recent reflections on both, see Annabel Patterson, *Shakespeare and the Popular Voice* (Cambridge, Mass.: Basil Blackwell, 1989), chap. 6, especially her discussion on the meanings of "power" in the play, pp. 141–43.

In the course of their histories, Timon and Coriolanus change suddenly from being (in their own minds) true citizens of Athens and Rome to being their cities' fierce enemies. Yet because both characters are consistent in the absolute demands they make of their existence, the change they undergo is not from blindness to tragic recognition, but rather from one version of absolutism to another—from a feebly public plainness to an unabashedly private plainness. Because even the public worlds of these plays are atomistic, the chief difference between the two forms of plainness is the degree of power attaching to each. Indeed, Apemantus's best-known evaluation of Timon—"The middle of humanity thou never knewest, but the extremity of both ends" (4.3.299–300)—can be taken to mean that Timon went from powerful to powerless without ever experiencing the middle state of rhetorical conversation and political compromise. Timon begins as a member of an Athenian establishment where friendship is coerced by the monetary power of gifts. After leaving Athens he tries to subvert its social structures with curses and, later, the gold he finds. Coriolanus, too, stands initially for the power of aristocratic Rome, but after his banishment he becomes a revenging rebel. Both men die in solitary opposition, but they are curiously alone even in their public positions, and the anger that dominates their final acts simply clarifies the nature of their initial public roles. They are shown to represent orthodoxies that themselves thrive on conflict, orthodoxies in which truth is a function of power.

The power of plainness thus subsumes its truth in these plays. With rare exceptions, Shakespeare has made clear ethical distinctions impossible by showing that virtually all claims to truth disguise self-interest. The rhetorical worlds of both plays teem with hungry mouths, and the alternatives of desert, true economic worth, and content disguise appetite no more successfully: Timon and Coriolanus seek revenge, as Seneca would say, not because it is just, but because it will bring them pleasure. Because the plays present neither shared criteria of truth nor dramatically justified private convictions, disputation proves a barren struggle of wills often ending in a contest of insults, as in Timon's absurd meeting with Apemantus in the forest. One can only overwhelm one's opponents, not persuade them. Hence power rather than truth forms the oppositional core of the plays, and plainness is more a performance of proud desire than of true conviction.

The general loss of truth and value in these plays extends to the characters' inner selves. It has often been observed that neither Timon nor Coriolanus appears to have much of an inner life, and that neither embodies an inner value that could plausibly be defended as an alternative to the degraded values of the public worlds they detest.[23] The charge that Greenblatt brings unsuccessfully against Wyatt sticks here: Timon and Coriolanus have nothing to express—nothing, that is, except anger. This inner emptiness results, I believe, from two failures of intelligence, one manifest in the attempt to make desire true (which is the form withdrawal takes in *Timon* and *Coriolanus*), the other in the attempt to make desire powerful (which is the form anger takes). First, because Timon and Coriolanus fail to convince us that they are motivated by truths that they can distinguish from their own desires, they appear to lack a center of moral choice (reason). Other plainspeakers entertain ideals (such as Wyatt's "trouth," Greville's Christian stoic peace, or Hieronimo's justice) which transcend the desire whose limits they have recognized, and hence face an inner struggle to choose an ethical course of action. But because Timon and Coriolanus (however unknowingly) collapse the distinction between truth and desire, they appear to be compulsive rather than morally responsible. Like Hotspur, they "cannot choose" (3.1.146). Second, Timon and Coriolanus seem to lack consciousness because they refuse to acknowledge the gap between desire and power, between the reality they seek and the

---

[23] For example, Michael McCanles sees Coriolanus as having no separate existence, but as existing only in a love-hate relation with his world ("The Dialectic of Transcendence in Shakespeare's *Coriolanus*," *PMLA* 82 [1967], 44–53); Richard Fly notes of *Timon* that the "sphere of total free speech and unmediated self-expression . . . is finally hopelessly sterile" ("Confounding Contraries," 137); Janette Dillon sees Coriolanus as representative of "the egotism and pride which defines itself by antagonism to society rather than from within," ("'Too Absolute': *Macbeth, Coriolanus, Timon of Athens*," in *Shakespeare and the Solitary Man* [London: Macmillan, 1981], 147); and Michael Taylor argues that Coriolanus's "authentic self" is inescapably tied up with the public service and display that form the core of Roman patrician values ("Playing the Man He Is: Role-Playing in Shakespeare's 'Coriolanus'," *Ariel* 15 [1984], 19–28).

reality they face, between self and world. Coriolanus comes closest to attaining this knowledge when he concedes that the "true"
differs from the "convenient" (5.3.190–91). But we find no sustained self-awareness here as we do, say, in Wyatt or Greville, in
whose writings the difference between desire and power is always
felt, if sometimes grudgingly acknowledged. Instead, Timon and
Coriolanus seem unself-conscious, unaware of themselves as limited historical agents, unwilling or unable to acknowledge the
limits of their power. In both these ways a loss of value results
from the extreme plainness that makes the self absolute. Timon
and Coriolanus glorify their own desire, confusing it in one direction with truth and in the other direction with power. At the
points furthest away from the rhetorical middle, withdrawal and
anger merge as twin expressions of appetite.

Plainness therefore fails to provide a valuable alternative to the
rhetorical judgment that is itself so degraded in these plays.
Shakespeare shows how, in the context of the epistemological
breakdown that accompanies the title characters' anger, life without rhetorical faith becomes a contest of wills. He shows how
Timon and Coriolanus, disgusted with desire, attempt to turn
their own desire into worth, thus making it true, and into act,
thus making it powerful. Unwilling to accept the imperfections of
human society and unwilling to acknowledge their own, Timon
and Coriolanus reject society and attempt to withdraw from political and economic involvement, Timon by rejecting shared
banquets in favor of the solitary consumption of roots, Coriolanus by refusing the customary showing of wounds, with the
power it grants to others to confirm his identity. They seek to
escape from history to eternity, from becoming to being, from the
world of learning, acting, and changing to a state of pure knowledge, accomplishment, and constancy. Shakespeare also shows,
however, that the plainness that seems to be their means of escape does not offer an independent truth, but rather the continuing dependence of desire; thus it cannot free them from historical
involvement. Timon and Coriolanus cannot preserve their truth
without convincing themselves that they have also preserved
their power. Instead of turning desire to desert and action through
the language of private justice, then, Coriolanus and Timon are

caught between contradictory attempts to erase their desire and to satisfy it; instead of creating a worthwhile inwardness through a withdrawal that separates value from power, their opposition has the effect of destroying their inner selves through an angry pride that refuses to acknowledge the difference between the two. Shakespeare thus shows how plainness at both the political and psychological levels may express a self-regarding desire whose performance attempts only to satisfy itself, a desire that renders plainness—even in a repugnant public world—little more than a performance of pride.

6 "Without the form of justice": Plainness and the Performance of Love in *King Lear*

Justice, Thomas Elyot wrote, "is a will perpetual and constant, which giveth to every man his right. In that it is named constant, it importeth fortitude; in discerning what is right or wrong, prudence is required; and to proportion the sentence or judgment in an equality, it belongeth to temperance."[1] This is a handy definition, disposing of a difficult concept neatly in terms of the traditional scheme of the cardinal virtues (themselves difficult concepts), and doing so in nicely balanced prose. Such neatness and balance could hardly be further away from the world of *King Lear*. Here justice is anything but constant, and fortitude, prudence, and temperance are called into question. In *Lear*, justice is inseparable from conflicts of will and power, the forms and structures of law are subservient to individual desires, and the vagaries of human justice eventually raise doubts even about divine justice. The inability to judge justly in matters of the highest importance might justly be judged the play's tragedy.

It is therefore unsurprising that over the last thirty years critics have found one of the play's chief themes to be the inadequacy of human judgment—and especially of traditional formulations like Elyot's—to the task of interpreting human experience. The play's

---

[1] Sir Thomas Elyot, *The Book Named The Governor*, Everyman's Library (London: Dent, 1962), p. 159.

many sententiae and commonplaces, once culled confidently as
evidence that the play affirmed universal human truths, are now
most often seen as faulty generalizations exposed as such by the
process of the play. For example, Nicholas Brooke, one of the most
influential of "new *Lear*" critics, writes that fatalistic and Christian ideas can be found in the play, "but stronger than either is the
sense of nature, internal and external, as immediate experience
on which any superstructure of interpretation may be mere delusion."[2] In recent years New Critical readings like Brooke's have
been supplemented by studies placing the play in the context of
Renaissance skepticism. Two of the best of these are James
Siemon's investigation of Renaissance iconoclasm and Jonathan
Dollimore's identification of a "radical tragedy" that challenges
the assumptions of the conservative "world picture" of the Elizabethans. With the new-historical support such critics add to the
many older strands of *Lear* criticism that stress the play's skepticism, it is now difficult to take seriously the idea that truths of
any importance in *King Lear* might be, in any important sense,
plain.[3]

[2] Nicholas Brooke, *Shakespeare: King Lear*, Studies in English Literature, no.
15 (London: Arnold, 1963), p. 36. Brooke's influence was extended by his essay
"The Ending of *King Lear*," which appeared in *Shakespeare, 1564–1964*, ed. Edward A. Bloom (Providence: Brown University Press, 1964), pp. 71–87. If Brooke is
the father of the new orthodoxy in Lear criticism, the mother is Barbara Everett,
whose article "The New *King Lear*" first appeared in *Critical Quarterly* 2 (1960),
325–39 and was reprinted in *Shakespeare: King Lear: A Casebook*, ed. Frank
Kermode (London: Macmillan, 1969), pp. 184–202. Criticizing the Romantic tendency to view poetic drama as "plot-less—Being, so to speak, rather than Becoming" (187), Everett praises the play for bringing together extremes of nothingness
and life, instead of separating them into good and evil in the fashion of a morality
play.

[3] James Siemon in *Shakespearean Iconoclasm* (Berkeley: University of California Press, 1985) and Jonathan Dollimore in *Radical Tragedy: Religion, Ideology,
and Power in the Drama of Shakespeare and His Contemporaries* (Brighton: Harvester Press, 1984) illustrate the continuance of this line of criticism in critics of
quite different persuasions. Siemon traces "a conflict between action and emblem
apparent throughout the play" (251) and argues that the play shows the inadequacy of "artful means of imposing order on dramatic action" (250). Dollimore
argues that *King Lear* lays bare "social process and its forms of ideological mis-
recognition" (72), that is, "a way of thinking which represents the contingent as
the necessary" (78). Prominent among the many other critical works belonging
to this tradition are Jan Kott, *Shakespeare Our Contemporary*, trans. Boleslaw

Nevertheless, I propose to do exactly this, with the expectation that the role of plainness in *King Lear* will prove more complicated than either side in the debate between skeptical and affirmative readings allows.[4] In *King Lear*, I argue, Shakespeare subjects plainness to the full force of a skeptical challenge, yet shows it withstanding that challenge in a somewhat altered form. Consequently the play is, to adapt something Stanley Cavell has said of the Romantics, both a skeptical response to plainness and a plain response to skepticism.[5] With some degree of explicitness, *King Lear* asks the value of private plainness as a form of justice, asks, in other words, whether its conviction is a reliable criterion of judgment. Less explicitly, it asks the value of public plainness, which the play tends to reduce to the self-interest of the powerful. In response, Shakespeare shows how conviction that seems abso-

---

Taborski (London: Methuen, 1964); William R. Elton, *King Lear and the Gods* (San Marino: Huntington Library, 1966); A. L. French, *Shakespeare and the Critics* (Cambridge: Cambridge University Press, 1972); and Stephen Booth, *King Lear, Macbeth, Indefinition, and Tragedy* (New Haven: Yale University Press, 1983).

The influence of this tradition extends, moreover, to a good many different strands of Lear criticism. So, for example, elements of ritual, morality play, and fairy tale (including such staples of the plain truth as sententiae and proverbs) are seen to give way before the onslaught of political realism. The old order of "medieval" moral hierarchy is seen to be unable to respond to the challenge of flexible, amoral Machiavellianism. And a concentration on dramatic technique, the play as performance, replaces the old emphasis on the play as dramatic poem, as a text that might be said to yield "statements." Marvin Rosenberg's exhaustive study in *The Masks of King Lear* (Berkeley: University of California Press, 1972) of the play as it has been performed best illustrates the possibilities of such a concentration.

[4] There is, of course, some middle ground in this debate. A number of critics focus attention on contradiction, uncertainty, and the violation of expectations in *King Lear* while seeking a more balanced view of the play overall. I include among these Rosalie L. Colie, *Paradoxia Epidemica* (Princeton: Princeton University Press, 1966), chap. 15; John Reibetanz, "Theatrical Emblems in *King Lear*," in *Some Facets of "King Lear": Essays in Prismatic Criticism*, ed. Rosalie L. Colie and F. T. Flahiff (Toronto: University of Toronto Press, 1974), pp. 39–57; and Martha Andresen, "'Ripeness is All': Sententiae and Commonplaces in *King Lear*," in Colie and Flahiff, eds., *Some Facets of "King Lear*," pp. 145–68. One of the best of these efforts remains that of Colie, whose study of paradoxes shows how they can point to a confusing reality and an ideal morality at once.

[5] I am thinking of Stanley Cavell's comment to a Berkeley seminar in February 1983 that it was his intention to study Romanticism as both a response to skepticism and a response to responses to skepticism.

lutely true and powerful when silent can be diminished when compelled to speak and act. Yet he also shows that the necessity of performance can make conviction most real if the plainspeaker acknowledges that knowledge and actions are rhetorically mediated.

Moreover, Shakespeare probes the distinction between public and private by dramatizing the resistance to public authority of a community of private plainspeakers. Although the ability of such plainspeakers to perform what they believe to be true is limited by their powerlessness in a tragically unjust world, the resistance they offer to that injustice maintains the presence of justice and truth to the extent that it can be maintained in such a world. To make its resistance matter, plainness must therefore cease to be simply private or simply public; it must cease to insist that it is absolutely powerful and absolutely true; and it must instead find new ways to perform. It must forego self-preservation and sincerity in favor of the calculated risks and subterfuge that help to prove the legitimacy of its virtue, which is that of a love stronger than self-interest. It must become part of tragic process, responding to particular occasions rather than to generalized ideas of right and wrong. *King Lear*, then, makes the positive case for plainness, as *Coriolanus* and *Timon* do the negative case. Understanding the more rhetorical performance of conviction that emerges from *Lear* is essential to understanding the play's look at the problem of justice in a situation where the usual forms of justice have broken down, lost with the trust and good faith that maintained them and enabled them to function.

The first scene of *King Lear* presents, among other things, a problem of justice. Lear, proclaiming his "constant will" (1.1.43), presents himself as a prudent and temperate judge about to decide a question of distributive justice. His daughters are to be given their "right," the proportion of the kingdom to which their love entitles them. Lear's question—"Which of you shall we say doth love us most?"—asks for the evidence on which his judgment will be based. That the ritual should be a mere formality, effecting Lear's intention to divide his kingdom equally among his three daughters, doesn't affect its legal status: Lear's identification with the role of absolute monarch, hence of supreme justice, is so

complete that it is difficult to imagine him performing his last
royal act without the form of justice. For the Lear who presides so
majestically over his court, formality is reality. This may be his
last royal act, but his word is still law.

It is important to bear this legal context in mind when considering Cordelia's response. She faces the task of declaring her love
to the court, and she expresses her discomfort with this situation
in terms that emphasize the inability of verbal forms to reveal the
inner truth of the heart. She is unhappy that she cannot heave her
heart into her mouth (1.1.92), yet fortunate that her heart is more
substantial than the tongue that fails to represent it truly (78). In
this paradox lies the mixed blessing of her legal predicament: by
failing to speak as Lear commands, she offends the law, yet she
implies (without appearing to understand fully her own implications) that an exception should be made in her case because her
silent conviction possesses a degree of truth greater than any that
the spoken forms of the present law can reach.[6]

As the scene unfolds, first Cordelia and then Kent develop the
idea that this special truth makes Cordelia's an exceptional case,
one that should be judged by criteria different from those Lear is
applying. Cordelia does so clumsily, her attempt at the Elyot-like
balance exemplified by Goneril quickly yielding to the more agi-
tated rhythms in which she contrasts her sisters' falseness to her
own sincerity:

> Good my lord,
> You have begot me, bred me, loved me. I
> Return those duties back as are right fit,
> Obey you, love you, and most honor you.
> Why have my sisters husbands if they say
> They love you all? Haply, when I shall wed,

---

[6] Paolo Valesio gives an unusual twist to skeptical readings of the play by con-
tending that Cordelia's words are, from first to last, part of a rhetorical strategy
calculated to win control of the entire kingdom. This is, to my mind, an extreme
example of the inability to deal intelligently with conviction that has plagued the
study of plainness and the issues it raises. See "The Rhetoric of Antirhetoric," in
Novantiqua: Rhetorics as a Contemporary Theory (Bloomington: Indiana University Press, 1980), pp. 41–60.

> That lord whose hand must take my plight shall carry
> Half my love with him, half my care and duty.
> Sure I shall never marry like my sisters,
> [To love my father all].
>
> (95–104)[7]

She wants to be judged by her deeds rather than by her words, since, as she says later in the scene, she lacks "that glib and oily art / To speak and purpose not" (224–25). But Cordelia's anger and indignation lead her slightly astray; the more immediate problem is that she cannot *artfully* speak even what she purposes. She can only speak plainly, and it is Kent who points out that judgment in her case depends on a true apprehension of the significance of that plainness:

> Answer my life my judgment,
> Thy youngest daughter does not love thee least,
> Nor are those empty-hearted whose low sounds
> Reverb no hollowness.
>
> (151–54)

The implied contrast of the hollow forms dear to those with no true feeling with the plain and simple expressions of those who refuse to falsify their deep and genuine emotion is central to the antirhetorical feeling of plainness and would be understood as such by Shakespeare's contemporaries. An observation of Brutus's in *Julius Caesar* is apposite here:

> When love begins to sicken and decay
> It useth an enforced ceremony.
> There are no tricks in plain and simple faith;
> But hollow men, like horses hot at hand,
> Make gallant show and promise of their mettle.
>
> (4.2.20–24)

---

[7] I have followed the Pelican editors' lead in enclosing quarto additions in square brackets. My reading, however, is not significantly affected by the choice of texts.

Or as Timon says:

> ceremony was but devised at first
> To set a gloss on faint deeds, hollow welcomes,
> Recanting goodness, sorry ere 'tis shown;
> But where there is true friendship, there needs none.
>   (1.2.15–18)

True love and friendship obliterate the distinction between form (seen as contrived, conscious, artful) and essence (spontaneous, genuine, natural) because they are artless or formless, an essential reality unaltered by time and the changing forms of history and human justice—or so the theory of plainness holds. Hence they also render meaningless the distinction between word and deed, since such a distinction assumes the greater authenticity of actions: Cordelia shouldn't need to be judged by her deeds, because her speech and her actions are both part of the same core of being, the same heart. Kent points out that Cordelia's refusal to split word and deed is a refusal to allow the imperfect forms of justice and language to compromise inner reality in any way. She should therefore be judged by the reality revealed in her own, apparently "formless," forms of speech.

Kent speaks a commonplace. Everyone should understand Cordelia's plain reaction to the love test. And everyone does— except Lear, who refuses at this point in the play to acknowledge either that good might exist outside the ceremonial forms over which he presides or that evil might exist within them. After Cordelia ineptly contrasts her love with her sisters' implied insincerity, Lear asks, as if he didn't hear her say that she couldn't heave her heart into her mouth: "But goes thy heart with this?" (1.1.105)—a question meant to determine whether she is to be condemned on the basis of what she has said. Here, perhaps, Cordelia might restate her discomfort with the performance demanded by the ritual, her sense of the inadequacy of her words to represent her love. But she has tried to be true to her self, if not the occasion, and her father should understand. She says simply, plainly, yes:

> *Cord.*   Ay, my good lord.
> *Lear.*   So young, and so untender?
> *Cord.*   So young, my lord, and true.
>
> (105–7)

Lear's questioning response gives her one more opportunity to invoke the language of private plainness. By calling herself "true," she is summoning to plead on her behalf the entire tradition of sincere resistance to public forms, a tradition that depends on the assumption of an essential selfhood that precedes and survives particular times and places, and is asking that an exception be made in her case. But Lear responds unsympathetically.

Although he now shows that he understands, at least formally, the tradition in which Cordelia stands, Lear does so only to attack its truthfulness. From "thy truth then be thy dower" (108), he advances to "Let pride, which she calls plainness, marry her" (129)—the first mention of plainness in the play, and one that joins his criticism of Cordelia to criticism of Timon, Apemantus, and especially Coriolanus: people who reject public forms, Lear implies, are saying such forms aren't good enough for them, and thus implying that they are too good for such forms.[8] Others may be content with the semblance of truth offered by conventional forms, but the plain man or woman knows better—or so he or she thinks. So, satirically, Lear calls his youngest daughter "that little seeming substance" (198), whose essence refuses to fit itself to the forms that are Lear's reality, yet whose own forms somehow are her substance. The claim to sincerity, to a uniquely outward inwardness, Lear suggests, is a fraud, indicating nothing other than the deadliest sin, pride.

---

[8] Kenneth Burke suggests several grounds for comparison between *Coriolanus* and *Lear*. "Though Shakespeare's theater is," he writes, "from start to finish, a masterful enterprise in the arts of persuasion, high among his resources is the building of characters who are weak in such devices. Indeed, considered from this point of view, Coriolanus' bluntness is in the same class with Cordelia's fatal inability to flatter Lear." And he notes that "Lear is sick old age that falls into infantile tantrums, a Coriolanus without the physical power." See "*Coriolanus* and the Delights of Faction," in *Language as Symbolic Action* (Berkeley: University of California Press, 1968), pp. 84 and 96.

This criticism is expanded and clarified in Lear's clash with Kent and Kent's later argument with Cornwall about his tussle with Oswald. "To plainness honor's bound / When majesty falls to folly" (148), Kent says to justify his blunt criticism of Lear's actions; and, in the encounter that leads to his being stocked, Kent, disguised as the plainspeaking Caius, claims that it is his "occupation to be plain" (2.2.87). Lear accuses Kent of "strained pride" (1.1.169); Cornwall, now a judge himself, develops the accusation further:

> This is some fellow
> Who, having been praised for bluntness, doth affect
> A saucy roughness, and constrains the garb
> Quite from his nature. He cannot flatter, he;
> An honest mind and plain—he must speak truth.
> An they will take it, so; if not, he's plain.
> These kind of knaves I know which in this plainness
> Harbor more craft and more corrupter ends
> Than twenty silly-ducking observants
> That stretch their duties nicely.
>
> (2.2.90–99)

In both cases the same fundamental problem surfaces: how is private plainness to justify itself? More precisely, that is, to what criterion or criteria can a private or inwardly determined truth appeal to defend itself in a public forum?

Kent's answer is that "anger hath a privilege" (2.2.65). He thus claims the special legal status of private plainness, its right of private judgment and redress. But Kent's claim works against him because Lear and Cornwall are suspicious of the motives, the possible self-consuming pride, behind it. Kent's plainness proves powerless with Lear (in 1.1) and Cornwall (in 2.2)—in fact, it looks ridiculous when Cornwall, suggesting that Kent's anger is madness (2.2.80), presses him for his reasons for assaulting Oswald, and Kent can only reply: "His countenance likes me not" (85). The assumption that conviction offers a reliable criterion for judgment is thoroughly discredited here, as Kent, who earlier praised Lear for having "authority" in his "countenance," seems to expect a true judge to be able to see the mind's construction in the face and to hear it in the tongue. "He that beguiled you in a plain accent," he tells Cornwall, "was a plain knave, which, for my part, I will not be" (105–7). A plain knave would say no different. The "unmannerly" violation of public forms cannot justify itself publicly because it is based on a publicly inaccessible source of truth, the heart. If Cordelia and Kent wish to have an effect on the uncertain and unjust world of *King Lear*, they will have to find ways to perform their convictions that do not depend on the support of public authority.

Cordelia and Kent are only two of the many characters who face this challenge to realize true convictions in a world where public justice is not to be counted on. Lear, too, is thrown into this process when he divides his kingdom. But for him it is a special shock because, as king, he had been the embodiment of the anti-rhetorical wish to wed form and essence, power and truth, performance and conviction. By virtue of his position, his word had been law. Lear encapsulates this relation when he accuses Kent of trying to "come betwixt our sentence and our power" (1.1.170). "Sentence" in Shakespeare almost always has its legal sense of pronouncing a judgment, and as such it signifies a performative use of language: by saying a sentence, one makes it so (e.g., "I banish you"). Sentence and political power are one, for one only has power so long as one can pronounce sentences and have them be so. Consequently, in *Richard II* it is a sure sign of Richard's demise when he must revoke his banishment of Bolingbroke ("After our sentence plaining comes too late," he had said earlier [1.3.175]):

> O God, O God! that e'er this tongue of mine
> That laid the sentence of dread banishment
> On yon proud man, should take it off again
> With words of sooth!
>
> (3.3.133–36)

Such a unity of sentence and power realizes the desire of Coriolanus and Timon to eliminate the gap between language and reality, to say what is true and have it be so. It universalizes Cordelia's desire to unite her own words and deeds, so that *all deeds* will agree with one's words. It is, then, the desire for the absolute point at which knowledge and power are one, at which one's conviction of the timeless essence of things becomes the same as performance in the historical world of forms.

Lear loses the power to pronounce sentences, but he emphatically retains the desire. Consequently, when Goneril and Regan challenge his hundred-knight retinue and decline any longer to accept his word as law, King Lear, private citizen, responds in the familiar forms of private plainness. Like Kent, Lear becomes angry and finds himself unable to reason persuasively. Unlike Kent, however, who explains while in the stocks that he had "more man than wit" (2.4.41) about him when he drew on Oswald, Lear finds the manhood of which anger is a vital part slipping away. Goneril and Regan refer repeatedly to his "dotage" (1.4.284, 317; 2.4.192), responding to his charge that they have treated him unjustly by asserting his inability to see what is in his own best interests:

> *Regan.*   O, sir, you are old;
> Nature in you stands on the very verge
> Of his confine. You should be ruled, and led
> By some discretion that discerns your state
> Better than you yourself. Therefore I pray you
> That to our sister you do make return;
> Say you have wronged her.
>
>   (2.4.141–47)

Throughout the scenes of confrontation, Lear, who, according to the Fool, has become a "shadow" (1.4.221), and who has vowed to regain his former "shape" (300), teeters helplessly between "reasonableness," the "patience" that suffers and waits in silence, and "passion," the "noble anger" (2.4.271) that seeks justice through revenge.

What Shakespeare shows here is a Lear torn between the two aspects of private plainness. His patience is the stoic endurance that guards self-sufficiency, and his silence—"I will be the pattern of all patience; / I will say nothing" (3.2.37–38)—attempts to preserve the absoluteness of the conviction that, like Cordelia's, would risk imperfection if it ventured into the contingent forms of speech. His anger takes a different approach, asserting his will in outward domination, but the end is the same: to guard the self's inner sense of justice and to maintain it as absolute, free from contradiction. For Lear, no longer guaranteed the right of kings, patience and anger are initially his desperate means of preserving a conviction that is both certain and powerful.

Lear's desire to wed sentence and power also seeks satisfaction through curses, a form that shows the futility of private plainness in the corrupt public world of *King Lear*. Having few or no means to make his word law, Lear becomes more and more frustrated. His wits fail as his madness grows. A "poor, infirm, weak, and despised old man" (3.2.20), he doesn't have the physical strength that makes threatening the anger of Kent, or even of the combative Edgar, whose warning in dialect to Oswald—"Chill be plain with you" (4.6.237), meaning, roughly, "I'll cudgel you"—proves to be less laughable than it might seem. Nor does he have the stoic patience to conquer by submission. But even if he did, he wouldn't likely prevail against characters as remorseless as Goneril, Regan, and Cornwall. He is left with curses, which, like Kent's railing, attempt to intimidate with their sheer assertive force, but which also attempt to enlist the magical power of words to make things so. As I suggested in the previous chapter, cursing is a form of angry assertion for the powerless and as such is an appropriate vehicle for Lear's last-ditch attempt to perform his conviction. But it is also a form that discredits Lear, exposing the petulance and willfulness of a man who, like King Richard, sees pride everywhere but in himself.

Despite Lear's rejection of Cordelia's plainness, then, his character is the most compelling instance in the play of an unreliable and unsuccessful private plainness. But because he begins the play as a reigning monarch, he is also the chief demonstration of the unreliability of public plainness. If private plainness is figured ideally in *King Lear* as an undeniable inner truth that justifies the privilege of an "unmannerly" violation of forms, public plainness is ideally a setting aside of personal feelings and interests in favor of a balanced consideration of the situation in terms of public wisdom—an ideal Lear violates in the first scene. It is "wit," rather than "man"; "reason," rather than "need." It lives, in other words, in the domain of rhetoric. But in distinguishing public plainness from rhetorical plainness throughout this study, I have been concerned with the tendency of public forms of knowledge to become hypostatized in a way that identifies them with certain established interests. Such a hardening carries with it unavoidable legal consequences. In a society governed according to rhetorical principles, the judgments of law are ideally those of public consensus; but when the powerful would rather inculcate right judgment in doctrine than cooperate with a consensus whose conclusions are disagreeable to them, laws can become an instrument that stamps the decisions of the powerful as plain truth. Public plainness, as the truth understood by those in power, as *doctrine*, can consequently become associated with a particular understanding of justice. "Truly in every covenant, bargain, or promise," Thomas Elyot writes, "ought to be a simplicity, that is to say, one plain understanding or meaning between the parties. And that simplicity is properly justice."[9] Since this plain understanding "giveth to every man his right," as we saw earlier, it can easily be used to preserve the existing distribution of rights and property. Small wonder, then, that the same terms are used by James I when he writes that a king should

> Reward the just, be steadfast, true, and plaine,
> Represse the proud, maintayning aye the right,
> Walke always so, as ever in his sight,
> Who guardes the godly, plaguing the prophane.[10]

In this way public plainness can become the justice of the established political order.

The corruption of the public realm is abundantly illustrated in *King Lear*. Considering the harm that results from Cordelia's, Kent's, and especially Lear's private plainness, the public forms of reason and wit might seem attractive commodities; in fact, how-

9 Elyot, *The Book Named The Governor*, p. 170.
10 James I of England, *Basilikon Doron*, prefatory sonnet, in *The Political Works of James I*, ed. Charles Howard McIlwain, Harvard Political Classics (1918; rpt. New York: Russell & Russell, 1965), p. 3. James also stresses the importance of judicial plainness in the *Basilikon Doron* proper, pp. 39–40, while stating, like Elyot, that "Justice . . . giveth every man his owne."

ever, the play shows that such forms are no more reliable criteria
of judgment than anger and the truth of withdrawal. "Reason"
becomes the lackey of Regan and Goneril, a means of deriving
justice from the premises of the powerful. "Wit" (1.2.176) is the
tool Edmund uses to deceive Gloucester when, Iago-like, he "in-
vents" characters and motives that exploit the expectations of his
audience.[11] Edmund himself is a classic case of a powerful rhetorical imagination unfettered by the faith in public good that ideally accompanies it. Public forms of justice also suffer in the play.
For example, Cornwall (although it is not always clear how consciously) abuses the language of public virtue and justice, at
times appearing confident that his power will protect his distor-
tions. "For you, Edmund," he says to his "son" ("thou shalt find a
dearer father in my love" [3.5.23–24]),

> Whose virtue and obedience doth this instant
> So much commend itself, you shall be ours.
> Natures of such deep trust we shall much need.
>   (2.1.112–15)

Lear, of course, destroys public plainness in a different way than
the Gonerils and the Edmunds do: they are evil, he is foolish.
Nevertheless, Lear *is* public justice at the beginning of the play,
and the sentence he pronounces with such certainty is wrong

---

[11] In a fine chapter of *Shakespeare's Dramatic Language* (Madison: University
of Wisconsin Press, 1976) entitled " 'Give me the map there!' Command, Question, and Assertion in *King Lear*," Madeleine Doran notes that the difference
between Lear's world and Othello's world is betrayed by the different uses of
conditional tenses in the two plays: "Conditional sentences, which in *Othello*
accompany every significant move in the action, are relatively sparse in *King Lear*.
The very core of Othello's tragedy is his betrayal by false conditions, which he is
made to believe are true; the conditional sentences in his part and in Iago's occur
in nearly every possible grammatical variation in the indicative and subjunctive
moods. In *King Lear* conditional sentences occur largely in the parts of the Fool
and of the plotting characters, i.e., Edmund, Goneril, and Regan. . . . In the 'prac-
tisers' ' parts they remind us merely of the possibilities recognized and exploited
by the opportunist. . . . The world the King inhabits at the beginning of the play is
a world of certainties and absolutes, not a world of uncertainties or contingencies.
. . . He never says: 'If this were so, I should do such and such,' but always, 'Let this
be so' " (101). Doran's chapter on *Othello*, "Conditional and Subjunctive in
Othello," expands suggestively on this view of *Othello*.

precisely because his own desires have superseded true justice. Cornwall's treatment of Gloucester only makes conscious and explicit the principle behind Lear's actions earlier:

> Though well we may not pass upon his life
> Without the form of justice, yet our power
> Shall do a court'sy to our wrath, which men
> May blame, but not control.
>
> (3.7.23–26)

The forms of justice and the language of virtue have been reduced to a cover for the sins of kings, who use law to make might right: as Goneril says, "the laws are mine, not thine" (5.3.159). Public plainness is thus destroyed from within, its forms rendered empty and meaningless by the actions of those very public figures who pay them lip service.

Public plainness fails, to put it another way, because law in a monarchy is susceptible to distortion by the desire of the monarch. Law, as a public extension of the king's will and words, should mediate between his private desires and the public good. Ideally, the two are one. But the play provides plenty of examples of ruling will becoming mere willfulness—a quality characteristic of private plainness. In this way public plainness proves to be unreliable for very much the same reason as private plainness. Lear, for example, is the same person before and after he abdicates his throne and divides his kingdom; his willfulness remains, although it begins to weaken almost immediately. Before, his will is law; after, it is the powerless desire of a private citizen. But the same proud willfulness taints Lear's public and private worlds. Cornwall and Lear's elder daughters also show a Lear-like willfulness in ruling, and their confrontation with Lear, ostensibly a debate of their official public truth with his private one, is in fact a battle of wills like those in *Timon* and *Coriolanus*. Neither side in the dispute is about to consider the other's point of view. Their judgment is closed, fixed, final. Thus plainness of both kinds shows the potential for precisely the error of premature and inflexible judgment that critics have found to be exposed in the play. And this error results from pride and self-interest.

In both the power of his public plainness and the powerlessness of his private plainness, Lear's pride ties him to Timon and Coriolanus. The three share a common desire, albeit one they articulate in different terms. Lear wants to wed sentence and power. Timon wants to join promise and performance. Coriolanus wants to unite words and deeds. All three, that is, want their words to indicate precisely what is happening (Lear—"I make thee lady"), or precisely what is going to happen (Timon—"I'll pay the debt and free him"), or precisely what has happened (Coriolanus—"Alone I did it"): they want their words to be a perfect, transhistorical mirror of reality. More exactly, they want their words to *make* reality, to control what happens, to be the instrument that turns their desire into action. None truly loves, because none admits any mutuality or reciprocity into his relationships. What they desire is absolute control, both in giving out and in taking in. Hence, Timon indulges in absolute expenditure—until he attempts to achieve absolute frugality; Coriolanus engages in absolute warfare on behalf of Rome—until he seeks absolute revenge against Rome; and Lear begins as the absolute distributor of lands—until he becomes the absolute distributor of curses. Almost everything the three do attempts to retain the ability to make the fantasy of absolute power into reality. But all three fail absolutely.

Clearly, there is much to be said against both the private and public modes of plainness as they appear in all three plays. But unlike *Coriolanus* and *Timon*, *Lear* presents a response to the skeptical perspective that views plainness exclusively as the performance of pride.[12] If the private aspect of public plainness can reduce it to self-interest, Shakespeare suggests in *Lear*, the public dimension of private plainness can expand its reach beyond the self. Private conviction can seek the public good, and the performance of conviction can serve others as well as the self. For characters such as Cordelia, Kent, Edgar, and the Fool, plainness to a considerable degree comprises the conviction and performance of

[12] There is no inconsistency in arguing that the earlier play goes further in its treatment of plainness. Plainness is not the whole play, and, even if it were, a sequence of works need not unfold wholly in accordance with some internal logic, as if a writer's life were free from the influence of a changing world.

love, and their plain love enables them to escape from the self-justifying prison of a purely antirhetorical plainness to the contingent relations of a rhetorical engagement with the world. At the same time, the rhetorical intelligence that informs their love allows them to leave behind the insistence of Lear, Timon, and Coriolanus that their words are absolutely true and powerful. Instead of relying on the failing forms of justice or on the doomed assertiveness of anger, Cordelia, Kent, Edgar, and the Fool struggle with will *and* wit to find ways to perform their love, ways that will retain their effectiveness despite the challenges of tragic process. They thus forge a more resilient and resourceful plainness to preserve the truth that is so vulnerable to injustice.

We can begin to see the qualities of this new plainness by studying the progress of Edgar, whose character, although admittedly puzzling in many particulars, shows an overall movement from scared self-preservation to courageous service to others. When he first disguises himself as Tom o' Bedlam, he says simply: "I will preserve myself" (2.3.6). The statement is borne out by his long and troublesome continuance in disguise, of course, but in addition his speeches as Tom reveal a self-pity and sense of injustice that ring true to Edgar's stated motivation at this point. Edgar's concern with justice is expressed most memorably in Tom's list of commandments:

> Take heed o' th' foul fiend; obey thy parents; keep thy words' justice; swear not; commit not with man's sworn spouse; set not thy sweet heart on proud array. Tom's acold. (3.5.76–79)

Coming from a man bent on self-preservation, such a position of moral and legal wisdom fails to convince: it is too abstract, too far from the ethical activity, the performance, that must support it. It is, in fact, the type of thing that skeptical critics of the play point to when they talk about its empty commonplaces. As Tom o'Bedlam, then, Edgar displays characteristics of a plainness too trapped within its own concerns to engage in the activities demanded by its sworn convictions.

Almost immediately, however, Edgar begins to change in response to the greater sufferings of others. His exclamation ("Bless thy five wits!") to Lear in the hovel scene and his subsequent

aside—"My tears begin to take his part so much / They mar my
counterfeiting" (3.6.56, 59–60)—cue the audience to his awaken-
ing sympathy. The soliloquy with which he ends this scene in the
quarto continues this development:

> [When we our betters see bearing our woes,
> We scarcely think our miseries our foes.
> Who alone suffers suffers most i'th'mind,
> Leaving free things and happy shows behind;
> But then the mind much sufferance doth o'erskip
> When grief hath mates, and bearing fellowship.
> How light and portable my pain seems now,
> When that which makes me bend makes the King bow.
> He childed as I fathered. Tom, away.
> Mark the high noises, and thyself bewray
> When false opinion, whose wrong thoughts defile thee,
> In thy just proof repeals and reconciles thee.
> What will hap more to-night, safe 'scape the King!
> Lurk, lurk.]
>
>   (3.6.100–113)

In defense of this speech's contested authenticity, one can say
that it expands on the important pity Edgar voiced earlier in the
scene, that it accurately states his continuing intention to do
nothing yet, and that its sententiousness is consistent with
Edgar's moral pose throughout the early acts. Against it, one can
note not only that it is unnecessary but also that it develops
Edgar's sympathies beyond the point at which we find them when
he speaks next, at the beginning of act 4:

> Yet better thus, and known to be contemned,
> Than still contemned and flattered. To be worst,
> The lowest and most dejected thing of fortune,
> Stands still in esperance, lives not in fear.
> The lamentable change is from the best;
> The worst returns to laughter. Welcome then,
> Thou unsubstantial air that I embrace:
> The wretch that thou hast blown unto the worst
> Owes nothing to thy blasts.
>
>   (4.1.1–9)

Edgar's preoccupation with his own "worst" condition is inconsistent with his previous soliloquy; it proves that he still has a long way to travel in an education that resumes immediately upon the appearance of Gloucester.

Why Edgar behaves as he does with his father is a conundrum I cannot solve to my own satisfaction, although I am inclined to agree with Cavell that Edgar is still avoiding love, that his sympathies and desire to perform the conviction of his love are still deficient. But while Edgar perhaps never reaches the goodness of Cordelia and Kent, he moves toward it through the "services" he performs for Gloucester. He makes his most important progress, though, when Gloucester and Lear are reunited, a scene that he says breaks his heart (4.6.139–40). After this, he describes himself to Gloucester as

> A most poor man, made tame to fortune's blows,
> Who, by the art of known and feeling sorrows,
> Am pregnant to good pity.
>
> (217–19)

This appears to be a much more heartfelt statement than the commonplaces he spouted earlier, and strong evidence that he has undergone a genuine change follows immediately. Although he still does not tell Gloucester who he is, he begins to use disguise to achieve definite public ends, goals that serve others rather than just preserving himself. First he is "plain" with Oswald, and then he claims the "privilege" of judicial combat with Edmund (5.3.126–31). He has moved, in short, to quite a different type of plainness.

This new plainness is best described not in terms of public or private but of the ideal of loving service that motivates it.[13] Edgar

---

[13] In a valuable essay on service in *King Lear,* Jonas Barish and Marshall Waingrow describe the code of service that operates in the play. Fundamental to this code, they note, is the idea that one should be devoted above all to the truth. Personal desires as well as prudence must on occasion be set aside in favor of this primary devotion. See " 'Service' in *King Lear,*" *Shakespeare Quarterly* 9 (1958), 347–55. Richard Strier pursues the idea of service in *King Lear* in an excellent essay that anticipates many of the points I make here. Strier argues "that Shake-

seems to learn that to prevent the unjust actions of pride and self-interest from overcoming his own virtuous convictions he must counter them not with sententiae or angry withdrawal but with actions—performance—of his own. And it is precisely a *performance* of love that the ideal of loving *service* demands. From the first scene on, loving service is the response (at first imperfectly realized) of plainness to self-interest; or, to put it more precisely, plainness is the response of love and sympathy to the tragic violation of justice by self-interest. At the beginning of the play, Lear, who makes the accusations of pride, is confused about the nature of love, seeing it, as Madeleine Doran has shown, as the one contingency in a world of absolutes.[14] His confusion opens the door to a situation in which love is nearly lost in a barrage of shifting and self-serving forms. But being part of a world of historical process need not destroy love; rather, the process of service preserves and restores love, giving it new life and continuing meaning in time. The plainness that Edgar discovers during the play is therefore a continuing effort to create a performance of love, which can turn the threat posed by the contingency of performance—namely, that process will enable pride to obscure true justice—into a virtue that actually assists in the preservation of love's absoluteness.

Cordelia and Kent also learn to modify their private plainness in response to unfavorable public conditions. At the start of the play, as we have seen, they accept unquestioningly the paradox that the formlessness of sincerity is a form of public truth. They believe that the identity of word and deed is necessary for love to function. They soon find, however, that antirhetorical plainness can obstruct love. Cordelia allows her feelings to overwhelm her

---

speare sets up . . . special circumstances in *King Lear*, and that the play can be seen, in part, as an extended meditation on the kinds of situation in which resistance to legally constituted authority becomes a moral necessity, and in which neutrality is not a viable possibility." See "Faithful Servants: Shakespeare's Praise of Disobedience," in *The Historical Renaissance: New Essays on Tudor and Stuart Literature and Culture*, ed. Heather Dubrow and Richard Strier (Chicago: University of Chicago Press, 1988), p. 104.

[14] Doran, "Command, Question, and Assertion in *King Lear*," p. 102.

sense of rhetorical occasion, and therefore fails to serve Lear as she wishes. It is a small fault and one excused by her youth, the impossible situation Lear has placed her in, and her reasonable expectation that Lear will honor the conventions of private plainness; nevertheless, once she sees that public authority can no longer be trusted, she undertakes persistent political efforts to save Lear that are much more successful at realizing her conviction than were her words in the first scene. These efforts, which are at first secret, are paralleled by Kent's renewed service as Caius. Although Kent's behavior in the first scene is arguably more artful in its bluntness than is Cordelia's, he nevertheless becomes a more conscious performer by adopting his disguise. It is again arguable that he is art*less* as Caius, but even so his remains an artful artlessness, supplemented by his work behind the scenes and, in the storm and hovel scenes, by his direct service (though still disguised) to Lear. Cordelia and Kent, then, have by the end of the play become much better at performing their convictions; they have learned to combine the private, inward reality—ahistorical, incommunicable—that is the essence of private plainness with the public, outer realm of historical dialogue.

Cordelia and Kent have made such progress because they have realized that public power has ceased to represent the public interest. As we have seen, everyone except Lear understands the justice of Cordelia's case, and afterward almost everyone understands the justice of Lear's. The exceptions, of course, are those with political authority: first Lear, then Goneril, Cornwall, and Regan. Consequently, if the apparently private plainness of Cordelia, Kent, and Lear is public as well, it is still private in the sense that it is powerless, unable to change the decisions of the official justice it struggles to resist. This resistance is the defining feature of the new plainness of which Cordelia, Kent, Edgar, and the Fool are the principal representatives. It is the resistance of a consensual moral law that has been driven underground; it is the survival of remote public criteria of judgment in evil times.[15]

---

[15] I take the phrase "remote criteria" from Frederick G. Lawrence, translator's introduction, in Hans-Georg Gadamer, *Reason in the Age of Science* (Cambridge:

It depends on heroic representatives of a sort of Renaissance community of virtue who break that group's silence to perform its convictions—specifically, love, or, one might say in light of the implied medieval background, charity—thus challenging the corrupt morality of the powerful. This plainness is therefore aware of the skeptical threat posed by the self-interest of the powerful, and acts accordingly. Its performance is designed to protect a conviction that is private but public, and public but powerless.

To do so, it does not simply substitute love for anger and withdrawal. These characteristics of private plainness remain important in a corrupt public world. The play is a tragedy, and love must take steps to protect itself. Consider France's speech:

> My Lord of Burgundy,
> What say you to the lady? Love's not love
> When it is mingled with regards that stands
> Aloof from th' entire point. Will you have her?
> She is herself a dowry.
>
> (1.1.237–41)

As often as this passage is praised for its sonnetlike sentiment, it is more often blamed, with the rest of France's part, for its flowery, romantic expression and its easy generalizations. Yet both responses mistake France's relation to the action of the play. France is regal in the best sense, but his magnificence belongs to a happier kingdom.[16] Although his justice and military might will eventually play a vital role, the power of his royal speech is limited in a kingdom where true sentiment is mistaken for flattery or pride. His place is on the periphery of the *Lear* world. Within Lear's kingdom, love must be performed instead by those who

---

MIT Press, 1981), p. xxvi. More generally, my thinking about the significance of plainness has been influenced by Gadamer's writings on hermeneutics, social reason, and the prejudice against prejudice.

16 For a reading of France's part that sees his use of the closed couplet as a sign of his nobility, see John Baxter, *Shakespeare's Poetic Styles: Verse into Drama* (London: Routledge & Kegan Paul, 1980), pp. 165–66.

realize that honor is bound to plainness when majesty falls to folly. Virtue in *Lear* belongs mainly to those who, like Kent, are not only sympathetic and kind but also made angry by the ascendancy of flattery:

> Corn. Why art thou angry?
> Kent. That such a slave as this should wear a sword,
>   Who wears no honesty. Such smiling rogues as these
>   Like rats oft bite the holy cords atwain
>   Which are too intrinse t'unloose; smooth every passion
>   That in the natures of their lords rebel,
>   Being oil to fire, snow to the colder moods;
>   Renege, affirm, and turn their halcyon beaks
>   With every gale and vary of their masters,
>   Knowing naught, like dogs, but following.
>
> (2.2.66–75)

Evil in this play takes as its standard of judgment the belief, in Edmund's words, that "men / Are as the time is" (5.3.30–31). Kent attacks Oswald's willingness to seek personal gain by saying ay and no to the passing whims of the powerful on the grounds that it fails the test of a truer criterion. One must not follow cynically, selfishly, or blindly: one must *know* (that is, have a firm and unchanging conviction of the truth) and must serve that truth above all (always remembering that service implies action and the changing forms of performance). Conviction, in other words, must guide historical performance. One must therefore be willing, when circumstances warrant, to withdraw from discussion and to state a firm and angry ay to his master's no, as Kent does soon after in a passage that is almost a parody of the plain style of debate:

> Lear. What's he that hath so much thy place mistook
>   To set thee here?
> Kent.   It is both he and she,
>   Your son and daughter.
> Lear. No.
> Kent. Yes.
> Lear. No, I say.

> *Kent.* I say yea.
> [*Lear.* No, no, they would not.
> *Kent.* Yes, they have.]
> *Lear.* By Jupiter, I swear no!
> *Kent.* By Juno, I swear ay!
>   (2.4.11–21)[17]

True service in *King Lear* is inconsistent with France's initial courtliness because the court of justice has itself capitulated to time-servers like Oswald.

The attempt to combine the withdrawal and especially the anger of private plainness with the service of love is exemplified by Shakespeare's most brilliant variation on the plainness of Cordelia, Kent, and Edgar—namely, the Fool. There is never any doubt that the Fool is in the tradition of native plainness. His first act is to offer his coxcomb to Kent, who has just won Lear's favor by proclaiming and demonstrating his plainness as Caius; thus, right away plainness and foolishness are associated. The Fool quickly establishes an identity as a truthteller, positioning himself between those who prefer flattery and those who prefer the plain truth:

> I marvel what kin thou and thy daughters are. They'll have me
> whipped for speaking true; thou'lt have me whipped for lying; and
> sometimes I am whipped for holding my peace. (1.4.173–76)

He has been onstage scarcely one hundred lines when Goneril refers to him as "all-licensed" (191), thereby suggesting the similarity of the free speech permitted to court jesters to the privilege Kent is shortly to claim. Finally, the Fool's fondness for the popular poetic forms of the native plain style—proverbs, riddles, satire, balanced opposites, short, frequently rhymed lines—is quickly established.

---

[17] If Shakespeare did eliminate lines 18–19 in revision, it is likely that he did so to decrease the likelihood that the exchange would become too comical. The frequent references to saying "ay" and "no" in the play are in fact a serious indication of the failure of dialogue that has made plainness so important. Significantly, the final such reference is in Edgar's challenge to Edmund—"Say thou 'no'" (5.3.139)—when Edgar comes closest to performing his conviction.

However, the Fool is just as quick to distinguish himself from the plainness of Kent. He offers Kent his coxcomb, he says, as a reward

> For taking one's part that's out of favor. Nay, an thou canst not smile as the wind sits, thou'lt catch cold shortly. (1.4.94–96)

Characteristically, the Fool is bitterly ironic, and this irony is the most important part of his plainness. It is his way of acknowledging the corruption that surrounds him without giving in to it. The function of this irony is misunderstood by Brooke, who sees only "the negation of any real sense of value" in the Fool.[18] On the contrary the Fool's irony is, Sheldon Zitner explains, "a way of being at once angry and kind," angry at the bitter fact and kind in remaining true to the sweetness of the ideal.[19] It allows him to admit that reality has debased the ideal of service, yet it also guards against that debasement and permits him to continue loving the ideal. The Fool can achieve the bittersweetness of irony because, unlike Cordelia and Kent, he is willing to divorce his

---

[18] Brooke, *Shakespeare: King Lear*, p. 24.

[19] Sheldon P. Zitner, "*King Lear* and Its Language," in Colie and Flahiff, eds., p. 12. Zitner's excellent essay is one of four studies of the play's language that I have found especially helpful. The others are Wolfgang H. Clemen, *The Development of Shakespeare's Imagery*, 2d ed. (London: Methuen, 1977), chap. 14; Doran's "Command, Question, and Assertion in *King Lear*"; and Lawrence Danson, *Tragic Alphabet* (New Haven: Yale University Press, 1974), chap. 8. All these critics see the emptiness and unresponsiveness of an overly formal language at the start of the play leading to a search for a stripped-down, genuine language; all, in addition, point to the central role of the Fool in this search. Clemen argues that because the "usual manner of speech can . . . no longer move" Lear, the Fool speaks to him in "simile, proverb and image and in rhymed adages and sayings" (141). "Between Lear and the Fool," he continues, "a new form of dialogue develops which is no longer based upon rational communication . . . but which is a finer and more subtle interplay of shifting meanings and hints" (142). Zitner makes the similar argument that the play provides a more authentic alternative to courtly style "in the obscurity or 'impertinency' of the heath scenes, in the uncouthness of Edgar's dialect and in Kent's 'plainness', . . . [which] together . . . form a counter-system of language, subversive of the inadequate system of decorum and reasonable discourse" (5). For Danson "the language of the play 'imitates' one of the play's dominant actions, the breaking down and stripping away of old social forms until they are as naked as 'the thing itself'" (178). Finally, Doran's emphasis on a movement from absoluteness to contingency in Lear's speech leads to very similar conclusions.

words from his intentions. He knows that speaking cynically doesn't make one a cynic any more than speaking loyally makes one loyal. What matters most in the end is what one does, not what form one follows:

> That sir which serves and seeks for gain,
>   And follows but for form,
> Will pack when it begins to rain
>   And leave thee in the storm.
> But I will tarry; the fool will stay,
>   And let the wise man fly.
> The knave turns fool that runs away;
>   The fool no knave, perdy.
>
>   (2.4.72–81)

Although the Fool drops his irony in speaking to the stocked Kent here, he quickly regains it in the brief exchange that follows:

> *Kent.* Where learned you this, fool?
> *Fool.* Not i'th'stocks, fool.
>
>   (82–83)

Loyalty is foolish in this fallen world, and the lack of prudence that landed Kent in the stocks is especially foolish. While Kent and the Fool are both true, then, the blunt truth of one has landed him in the stocks, while the ironic truth of the other has left him at liberty. The Fool's irony, combining anger and love behind a protective shield, proves a particularly effective medium for the performance of conviction.

This is not to suggest that the Fool's irony is better or more defensible than Kent's bluntness. Each is to some extent a type of performance appropriate to its speaker. The determining factor is the different amount of power that each man has. Although both are relatively powerless, the Fool is as truly powerless as anyone in the play. He can take no direct action against Goneril and Regan; he can only follow Lear and, protected by his ironic posture, try to needle the consciences of those around him with the indirect suggestion of lost virtue. Kent, on the other hand, has physical strength, the political power of Caius, and, behind the scenes, his own continuing influence with Cordelia and France. This may or may not justify the risk of quarreling with Oswald, but it does explain the differences between his strategies and the Fool's without violating their essential kinship.

I am arguing that, whatever our historical judgment of plainness may be, Shakespeare has created in *King Lear* the conditions that plainness needs to flourish. For plainness to appear most positively, in a play or elsewhere, the powerful must truly be corrupt and the integrity and honor of the plainspeakers must guarantee their moral superiority. Both of these conditions are met in *King Lear*. Within the world of the play, true justice is absolute, love serves justice absolutely, and injustice must be stopped by love. To this extent the play is *plain*. This is not to deny that the play violates dramatic conventions and surprises many of the expectations we have of fiction. Nor is it to deny the questioning of commonplaces in the play, or the impression, common to many of the best students of the play's language, that familiar forms of language are being stripped away in a search for some new and primal form of expression. These two sets of observations are, I believe, reconcilable, and it is through the role of plainness as the performance of love in a tragic world that the reconciliation is effected.

The clearest illustration of this process is the scene in which Lear recognizes Cordelia. As much as any scene in the play, this recognition scene has moved critics to testify to the power of its language, and the quality almost universally recognized in that language is simplicity or plainness. Lear, waking up slowly, sees himself as if for the first time:

> Where have I been? Where am I? Fair daylight?
> I am mightily abused. I should e'en die with pity
> To see another thus. I know not what to say.
> I will not swear these are my hands. Let's see—
> I feel this pin prick. Would I were reassured
> Of my condition.
>
> (4.7.52–57)

Lear, who no longer feels the absoluteness that he had felt as a king whose sentences were powerful, feels instead a need for reas-

surance. But in the immediate absence of the certainty he felt at
the beginning of the play, he kneels in humility and, with a view
of plainness much altered from his early confrontations with Cordelia and Kent, identifies himself only by his weakness and in
relation to those he loves:

> Pray, do not mock me.
> I am a very foolish fond old man,
> Fourscore and upward, not an hour more nor less;
> And, to deal plainly,
> I fear I am not in my perfect mind.
> Methinks I should know you, and know this man;
> Yet I am doubtful, for I am mainly ignorant
> What place this is; and all the skill I have
> Remembers not these garments; nor I know not
> Where I did lodge last night. Do not laugh at me;
> For, as I am a man, I think this lady
> To be my child Cordelia.
>
> (59–69)

Lear appears to sense that plainness is necessary for his new perception: only by letting go of the layers of ceremony to which he
clung earlier can his mind free itself from the residue that still
clogs it. We realize now, if we had not before, that Cordelia was
not the only member of the family who had difficulty performing
her love amid the elaborate formality of the opening scene: Lear,
too, was unable to realize his love so long as he clung to the ves-
tiges of his royal authority. It has taken this much to propel him
into the plainness that Cordelia sought then, the plainness that
creates love anew at each unique moment of performance, and
that he still grasps only dimly. But it is not a misnomer that the
scene is sometimes called the recognition scene rather than the
cognition scene, because the same plainness is revealing familiar
territory to Lear, allowing him to remember, if just for a moment,
what he had almost forgotten. In *King Lear*, only plainness can
achieve this simultaneous discovery of new truth and memory of
old truth, this performance of conviction, and it can achieve it
only, as in the recognition scene, in the absence of pride and the
presence of love. Only plainness can be the performance of love.

I don't mean to push a redemptivist reading of the play by concluding with the recognition scene. The tendency of some critics to do just this is as deplorable as the tendency of skeptical critics to concentrate almost exclusively on the cliff scene and the ending.[20] The play ends tragically, and even the positives in the play are conditioned by their existence in a tragic world. My argument is that it is to the tragic failure of most forms of public truth and justice, and to the search for a truth that will remain active in such conditions, that plainness owes its prominence in *King Lear*. In the play the private and public forms of plainness most common in the early English Renaissance both suffer because the powerful have found it in their interests to manipulate and undermine the public criteria of judgment. These powerful few attempt to usurp the language of plain truth and virtue to justify their own ends. But they are outnumbered by those who maintain the plain truth by finding new ways to perform the conviction of love. Love in *King Lear* does not "sicken and decay" behind the walls of "an enforced ceremony": rather, informed by rhetorical intelligence, it maintains a vibrant relationship to the world in which public and private are neither entirely the same nor entirely different, and from which moral values emerge as the property of all. The new plainness this love embodies retains the anger and withdrawal of private plainness, but concerns itself less with sincerity and with absolute power and truth, and more with performing services it is convinced are in the public interest. Plainness is thus the principle that permits the rediscovery of "commonplace" truths in corrupt and skeptical surroundings. Truth is on the defensive, and conviction is required to resist evil

[20] The ending of the play has always been the focus of attention for those who argue that the play resists closure. "In *King Lear*," Frank Kermode writes, "everything tends towards a conclusion that does not occur" (*The Sense of an Ending: Studies in the Theory of Fiction* [Oxford: Oxford University Press, 1966], p. 82). Perhaps the most ingenious formulation of this idea is Booth's remark that *"King Lear* ends but does not stop" (*King Lear, Macbeth, Indefinition, and Tragedy*, 11). It is worth noting that Brooke has nowhere been more vigorously attacked than for his remark that the play's ending provides its "one fixed and final image," "an emblem that sums up all" ("Ending," 78). Dollimore and Siemon make almost identical observations on the limitations of Brooke's reading at this point. See Dollimore, *Radical Tragedy*, p. 82, and Siemon, *Shakespearean Iconoclasm*, p. 247.

and to maintain—to remember, to recognize, to keep alive through performance—virtue. Despite efforts to turn it into the performance of pride, then, plainness emerges from *King Lear* as the performance of love. But the play shows just how costly such a performance can be.

Epilogue:
A Precious Jewel?

When we know a thing, and have decided about it, there is no further use in speaking about it.
 —Aristotle, *Rhetoric* 1391b8–10

The purpose of this dissociation of certain irrefutable elements from the sum total of our opinions . . . , and of making them independent of the conditions of perception and linguistic expression, is to withdraw them beyond the realm of discussion and argumentation.
 —Chaim Perelman and Lucie Olbrechts-Tyteca, *The New Rhetoric*

At least since Plato attacked the Sophists, rhetoric and philosophy have quarreled about the relationship between language and truth and about the possibilities of human knowledge. In my view, rhetoric is most accurately understood within this quarrel as the province of opinion rather than knowledge, of question rather than statement, and of persuasion rather than conviction. Hence, the old and new rhetorics of Aristotle and Perelman both exclude certain knowledge from the realm of useful discussion. The purpose of rhetoric, for them, is to reach decisions about matters that "present us with alternative possibilities."[1]

This book, in contrast, investigates the purposes of speaking when we do know a thing—or believe we do—and have decided about it. Focusing on the claim to speak the plain truth in the early English Renaissance, it describes the forms of literary perfor-

---

[1] Aristotle, *Rhetoric*, trans. W. Rhys Roberts, in *The Basic Works of Aristotle*, ed. Richard McKeon (New York: Random House, 1941), 1357a5, 26.

mance typical of this epistemological plainness, relates its forms to its aims, describes its characteristic emotional dynamic, shows its operation in both radical and conservative contexts, and charts its interaction with the opposing claims of rhetorical persuasion. It takes, in short, a rhetorical approach to antirhetorical plainness. By doing so, it understands plainness as a phenomenon reaching, like rhetoric itself, across broad stretches of early modern culture, and as participating in the conflicts of authority by which a society in transition was attempting to revise its conceptions of truth, justice, government, self, society, and love. It thus offers plainness as a historical force whose importance matches that of the rhetorical anthropology it opposes.

I have concentrated on two problems raised by the phenomenon of plainness. The first, the focus of the first three chapters, is the relation of private to public in which plainness participates— that is, which it reveals and to which it perhaps contributes (ultimate historical causality being beyond the scope of this study). I have argued that plainness may be private or public or both at once; and I have argued that when both private and public authorities are plain, the personal voice and hence the self may become indistinguishable from its public commitments, and the distinction between private and public may in effect disappear. The second problem, which occupies the remainder of the book, is the ethical status of an unverifiable conviction. Here I have argued that the epistemological stalemate in which plainness participates may lead to a contest of wills. In this contest, language loses its rhetorical dimension as a realm in which truth is discovered (or perhaps manufactured) and decisions are made, leading to action; instead, the performance of conviction, insofar as it is truly antirhetorical, confuses language both with truth and with power. Truth and power consequently collapse into each other, and ethical value disappears both from the individual and from the public world.

Both these arguments imply that rhetoric provides a vital element in a meaningful and distinctive human existence. The verdict of literary history supports this implication. When Greville inveighed against rhetoric's feigned truth and attempted to erase it from his life, he condemned his writings to centuries of relative neglect. When, on the other hand, Shakespeare gave the plainness of Cordelia, Kent, and the Fool the ethical value of a truth separated from political power but connected to a flexible tradition of shared moral values, he guaranteed *King Lear* a place in the literary canon far surpassing that of *Coriolanus* and *Timon of Athens*, in which the characters' plainness is more unrelentingly antirhetorical. In view of my arguments, rhetoric may be seen, first, as a midpoint between public and private, as a place where they meet in conversation or dialogue, and hence as permitting the distinction between them even as it draws them together. Second, in its emphasis on deliberation and discussion, rhetoric may be seen as the precondition for distinguishing desire and language from truth and power, and hence for the ethical separation of truth from power. Rhetoric, understood as historically variable dialogue, therefore appears to solve both the public-private problem and the ethical problem of plainness.

However, to conclude that rhetoric by itself is the solution to these problems would be wrong. Although I have examined the problems of a conviction that lacks rhetorical awareness, I have not done the same for a rhetoric that lacks conviction—except, implicitly, in my consideration of Marston, which discovers a different set of difficulties. If rhetoric for the most part emerges from this study as an ideal, it may be because my identification of it with a kind of faith qualifies its skepticism. Rhetorical faith, I suggested in my introduction, is itself a kind of mystery, and so is not entirely different from conviction, the mystery of angry plainness. Hence my definition of rhetoric distinguishes it from the radical skepticism that Plato faced in the Sophists, and that our own age finds in deconstruction. It may be more accurate, therefore, to conclude that a combination of rhetoric and plainness such as the one I locate in *King Lear* responds most successfully to the problems I have raised. If there is only conviction, there is nothing we would recognize as consciousness; but if there is no conviction, a human subject may be no less invisible.

As a final note, then, I wish to forestall a possible misreading of this book. Though I have used different terms than are currently in vogue—terms that seem to me less tendentious and more historical—much that I have written about plainness is consonant with the critical community's underlying antiessentialism. Insofar as the revalorization of rhetoric as an alternative to philosophy parallels other recent critiques of the Western philosophical tradition, my opposition of plainness to rhetoric will work to the detriment of plainness. But this is only half the story. My argument also implies that critiques of essentialism and efforts to decenter the self may go too far (as I think they often have in the case of *Lear* criticism) if they fail to grant some value to conviction. In the present situation, I believe, this book's greatest contribution is its attempt to determine the values of different shades of conviction in different situations—an attempt that culminates in the opposition between the pathological plainness of *Coriolanus* and *Timon* and the "blessed hierarchy of English plain speakers" in *King Lear*.[2] This book's challenge is its suggestion that centeredness may be as important as flexibility, that conviction may be as important as sophistication, that plainness, if often fraudulent, may sometimes be a precious jewel.

[2] Lionel Trilling, *Sincerity and Authenticity* (Cambridge: Harvard University Press, 1972), p. 23.

Index